TEACHING AND LEARNING WITH MICROSOFT® OFFICE AND FRONTPAGE
BASIC BUILDING BLOCKS FOR COMPUTER INTEGRATION

Timothy J. Newby
Purdue University

PEARSON

Merrill
Prentice Hall

Upper Saddle River, New Jersey
Columbus, Ohio

Library of Congress Cataloging-in-Publication Data
Newby, Timothy J.
    Teaching and learning with Microsoft Office and FrontPage : basic
building blocks for computer integration / T.J. Newby.
        p. cm.
Includes bibliographical references and index.
    ISBN 0-13-029287-7
    1. Application software.   2. Microsoft software—Study and teaching.
I. Title.
    QA76.76.A65N45 2004
    005.36—dc21

2003013918

Vice President and Executive Publisher: Jeffery W. Johnston
Executive Editor: Debra Stollenwerk
Editorial Assistant: Mary Morrill
Production Editor: JoEllen Gohr
Production Coordination: *The GTS Companies*/York, PA Campus
Design Coordinator: Diane C. Lorenzo
Cover Designer: Ali Mohrman
Cover Image: Getty One
Production Manager: Laura Messerly
Director of Marketing: Ann Castel Davis
Marketing Manager: Darcy Betts Prybella
Marketing Coordinator: Tyra Poole

This book was set in Palatino by *The GTS Companies*/York, PA Campus. It was printed and
bound by Courier Kendallville, Inc. The cover was printed by Phoenix Color Corp.

Microsoft®, Microsoft® Word, Microsoft® PowerPoint®, and Microsoft® Excel are either
trademarks or registered trademarks of the Microsoft Corporation in the United States and/or
other countries.

Pearson Education Ltd.   Pearson Education Australia Pty. Limited
Pearson Education Singapore Pte. Ltd.   Pearson Education North Asia Ltd.
Pearson Education Canada, Ltd.   Pearson Educación de Mexico, S.A. de C.V.
Pearson Education—Japan   Pearson Education Malaysia Pte. Ltd.

10 9 8 7 6 5 4 3 2 1
ISBN: 0-13-029287-7

PREFACE

Vision of the text

Teaching and Learning with Microsoft Office and Frontpage has been designed to give busy (and often overwhelmed) teachers and students a quick way to understand the basics of key software applications. Our vision is threefold:

- to give a foundation of the basics of common application software;
- to provide a vision and a path of how to integrate and utilize the software within classroom settings (*Note:* Our goal is for you to frequently say, "Yes, I can use this!");
- to create a learning environment that is engaging, interesting, and effective.

Why so basic?

Three points we want you to remember:

1. Teachers and students have more demands put on them than ever before.
2. *Application software* (e.g., word processors) are more powerful (i.e., have more features) and can offer more help to the teacher and students than in the past.
3. More than 90 percent of the time that teachers and students use computers they are working on the *basic* features of the most common software programs.

An understanding of the *basic* features will help you use the computer in the classroom. Once you have that foundation, you will know what information to request and how to find it as additional, more advanced features are needed. Without the basic foundation, you won't know when, why, or how to use those advanced features. That would only lead to frustration—and we don't want you to experience more of that than necessary.

Who is this?

The subtitle for this text is "Basic Building Blocks for Computer Integration." This is our "Basic Block" who will guide you through the text.

Why was this text written?

As for most projects of this nature, this text came about because of specific needs. In teaching our pre-service and in-service teacher courses, we needed a text that would

a. quickly get students and teachers up and running with the basic Office software suite of programs;
b. provide examples and projects relevant to individuals who were or wanted to be teachers;
c. help preservice and inservice teachers develop the skill, as well as the desire, to integrate these powerful tools into their own classrooms in a manner that would significantly enhance the learning experiences of their present and future students.

How does this text address those needs?	There were several basic philosophies used throughout the development of this text.

- **Don't overkill.** Select and use basic key features of the software, but don't try to teach everything. Have learners understand the potential of the software, but let them be aware that they don't have to know it all in order to use the software effectively. As experience and confidence grow, more features can be added to their repertoires.
- **Help individuals quickly gain independence.** Although some step-by-step "hand-holding" procedures may be needed in the beginning, quickly show learners how to find features and resolve problems on their own. Help them recognize when and how to obtain answers to questions they will have as they use the software.
- **Support their efforts, but have students grow their own ideas and applications.** Students should quickly come to feel this information is relevant now and in their futures. Provide them with examples they can relate to, and support their use of the software to address their own projects and needs. Using the software on their own projects quickly ensures the investment of effort that sustains the long-term use of these tools.
- **Envision the impact of integration.** The impact of such tools on personal productivity should be immediately apparent; however, an extended goal is to demonstrate how software can be integrated in the classroom to enhance the educational experiences they develop and experience with their own students in the future.

What's the target content?	The text focuses on teaching Microsoft (MS) Windows XP, *Office XP*, and *FrontPage XP*. However, MS Office for Macintosh (Mac) users is also highlighted throughout.

Why use Microsoft Office and FrontPage?	Basically, two reasons drove this decision. First, this software is prevalent in the majority of homes and schools. Second, because they are from the same "family" of software, they work in an integrated manner with many common toolbars, menus, and so on. For the novice, a feeling of familiarity when going from one program to the next is important in building confidence as well as in increasing speed and skill.

Why use a three-level approach?	A three-level approach is utilized within this text to help those who enter the course at various levels of expertise.

- Level 1 is for the true beginner or novice. It is designed to give step-by-step "hand holding" help on accomplishing basic tasks with the software. It also offers a good review of main features for the more experienced user.
- Level 2 requires the use of additional and often more advanced features of the software—without the step-by-step instruction. In this level, the software's *Help feature* is used to find solutions to questions and problems encountered. Key words and questions are given as support to assist with the use of Help. The goal is for both students and teachers to gain independence and confidence by answering their own questions with the assistance of Help.
- Level 3 addresses integration of the software. Examples are given and students and teachers practice designing and developing technology-integrated learning experiences. Moreover, the relationship of the use of the software with the National Educational Technology Standards (NETS) is emphasized.

How are the chapters outlined?	All chapters are structured in a similar fashion. However, each is independent and thus the chapter sequence can be modified to fit the schedules and desires of the course instructor.

I.   **Introduction**
This section explains the goals of the chapters, the purpose of the software, reasons for learning, and some basic ideas of how it can be used by teachers and students.

II.   **Orientation**
This section allows one to view and work with the main workspace of the target software. Menus are examined, and key words, organizational concepts, and tools are highlighted and explained.

III. **Level 1**

A short scenario or case is given that incorporates some type of project previously completed using the targeted software. Major steps in the process of constructing the project are highlighted, and users are guided through a step-by-step procedure to create a similar project.

IV. **Level 2**

The scenario from Level 1 generally continues within this lesson and an additional, more complex project is outlined and completed. Users are then directed to alter the program and construct their own version. In this case, users are encouraged to use the program's Help to determine how to complete specific processes. Key words and phrases relevant to completing the task are listed for the individual to use with Help if it is needed. The focus is on using Help to acquire the desired results.

V. **Level 3**

Integration is the focus of this level. Beginning with a presented lesson plan, users are shown how integration of the software can occur. Moreover, they are given opportunities to attempt to develop technology-enhanced lesson plans given specific situations. They are taught to use the Integration Assessment Questionnaire, and they explore and reflect on the relevant NETS Standards and how their work pertains to those standards.

VI. **Resources and references**

The final section of each chapter highlights Web sites that the student can visit to either learn how teachers are using the target software in the classroom or complete tutorials to develop additional skills with the software. In addition, **Quick References** are included to help students recall, identify, and find specific features of the software.

Why is there a CD?

Throughout the text this icon indicates that practice exercises can be found on the text's accompanying CD. These exercises help to develop effective and efficient skills of working with the software. In addition, the contents of the CD will provide needed examples and templates for use on practical teaching and learning tasks.

What are the text's key features?

Lists: The text attempts to present most information in a concise fashion utilizing frequent bulleted and numbered lists.

Workouts: Workouts are regular exercises and projects that the student is directed to work through. These are designed to get the student actively involved early and often with the software. Many of these exercises are augmented by materials found on the accompanying CD.

Modeling: Example products and exercises are used to help students understand what is desired and how it can be achieved.

Reflective/guiding questions: These are used to encourage students to go beyond the immediate application of the software to envision how it could be integrated and transferred to other situations and settings.

Examples: Hundreds of examples of the utilization of the software are given across all age groups and content areas.

Emphasis on Help to gain independence: The use of the softwares' Help programs are highlighted, practiced, and implemented within this training in order to encourage independence and confidence in solving problems encountered when using the software.

Writing style: Concise—get to the point—and move on.

Quick references: At the conclusion of most chapters, there are short synopses or tables identifying basic tasks, formatting, and additional features of the specific software. This tool allows the individual to identify quickly how to access the feature within *the menu* or *toolbars* of the software.

Crib notes: At the end of the text, short concise procedures are given for different tasks that individuals will need to know and will come to use repeatedly when working with this software. These procedures are created for quick reference until the procedure is learned by the user.

How are the technology standards addressed?

Both teacher (NETS*T) and student (NETS*S) Standards from the National Educational Technology Standards are listed in appendix B of this text. Within Level 3 of each chapter the utilization of the standards is discussed, and students demonstrate how they are used and assessed as the software is integrated within self-generated lesson plans.

How can the author be contacted?

The easiest and fastest way is generally through e-mail, but here is all of the needed information.

> Tim Newby
> Purdue University
> Room 3138, BRNG
> 100 N. University St.
> West. Lafayette, IN 47907-2098
>
> Phone: 765-494-5672
> Fax: 765-496-1622
> e-mail: newby@purdue.edu

How is the text currently being used?

We use this text for both undergraduate and graduate students. The undergrad course has over four hundred students each semester. We will be happy to share our ideas on how we structure the course with this text, to give you the benefits and the challenges, as well as to share our syllabi and Web site activities. We also enjoy (when time allows) visiting classes via phone or Internet video links and discussing issues with students and faculty. Just let us know what we can do to help.

Dedication

We are dedicating this book to Deedra, Thea, and Quintan.

- To Deedra, because we have watched you struggle to learn the basics and we think there's a better way than screaming at the machine.
- To Thea, because if we ever run into another student like you, we want to be prepared. We knew you were frustrated; we knew some of your questions weren't answered, and we know that we should have done better.
- And finally, to Quintan—because we like that name and it represents all of the students, teachers, and administrators who know that they need the computer, but the needed "learning time" is always too elusive. We know you Quintans are out there, and we hope this book will supply the needed motivation and answers.

Acknowledgments

No book can be completed without the help of numerous individuals. In particular, we wish to acknowledge Judy Lewandowski, Vicki Hooker, Kathy Steele, and Timbre Newby for their inspiration, input, critiques, practical advice, examples, and editing capabilities. In addition, our in-service and pre-service teachers have presented hundreds of questions to ponder, consider, and respond to within this text. Through the years, their questions have heavily influenced the vision, design, and development of this work.

I would like to thank the following individuals for their constructive suggestions on the manuscript: Ronald J. Anderson, Texas A&M International University; Michael Jackson, Southern Illinois University—Carbondale; David VanEsselstyn, Columbia University; J. B. Browning, Brunswick Community College; Virginia R. Jewell, Columbus State; Mary Juliano, SSJ, Caldwell College; Farah Fisher, California State University, Dominguez Hills; and Judith L. Cope, California State University, Los Angeles.

Educator Learning Center: An Invaluable Online Resource

Merrill Education and the Association for Supervision and Curriculum Development (ASCD) invite you to take advantage of a new online resource, one that provides access to the top research and proven strategies associated with ASCD and Merrill—the Educator Learning Center. At **www.EducatorLearningCenter.com** you will find resources that will enhance your students' understanding of course topics and of current educational issues, in addition to being invaluable for further research.

How the Educator Learning Center will help your students become better teachers

With the combined resources of Merrill Education and ASCD, you and your students will find a wealth of tools and materials to better prepare them for the classroom.

Research

- More than 600 articles from the ASCD journal *Educational Leadership* discuss everyday issues faced by practicing teachers.
- A direct link on the site to Research Navigator™ gives students access to many of the leading education journals, as well as extensive content detailing the research process.
- Excerpts from Merrill Education texts give your students insights on important topics of instructional methods, diverse populations, assessment, classroom management, technology, and refining classroom practice.

Classroom Practice

- Hundreds of lesson plans and teaching strategies are categorized by content area and age range.
- Case studies and classroom video footage provide virtual field experience for student reflection.
- Computer simulations and other electronic tools keep your students abreast of today's classrooms and current technologies.

Look into the value of Educator Learning Center yourself

Preview the value of this educational environment by visiting **www.EducatorLearningCenter.com** and clicking on "Demo." For a free 4-month subscription to the Educator Learning Center in conjunction with this text, simply contact your Merrill/Prentice Hall sales representative.

CONTENTS

INTRODUCTION
What's This All About?

> **READ ME FIRST!**
>
> In many cases, as you open a new purchase that requires a little assembly (e.g., computer, bicycle, shelf unit for your office), there is a set of directions that indicates you should **READ ME FIRST.** You may not have to assemble this book, but it's wise to take a look at this introductory section. It sets the tone, gives insights, and helps you get ready for the learning about to begin. It helps you to know what is expected, and what you can expect from exploring and working on these pages. Things just go smoother when you begin here.

What are we trying to do?

We want you to be able to use computer software such as word processors, databases, spreadsheets, and software associated with the Internet. More importantly, we want you to use the software in ways that enhance your teaching, your curriculum, and your impact on your students (or future students). That is our goal, plain and simple.

Is this only "teacher software"?

We wrote this book as if we had on the eyeglasses of a teacher. That means our examples and projects are focused on the teacher and his or her environment. These basic applications, however, can be used readily by individuals in all walks of life and in all times of their lives.

Don't shy away just because you are going to cooking school, are in the military, or want to become a fireman, dancer, or magician. We have all been in the classroom before—these examples and projects should make sense from all different perspectives.

How does this relate?

This is the big question that we want you to ask over and over as you go through this material. Think to yourself, "How does this relate to my teaching?" "How does this relate to the work that I have to do?" "How does this relate to a positive impact on my curriculum and ultimately on my students?"

We are going to give you some examples and some ideas of how these topics tie together and how they work. Always be mindful of ways to find relevance for your personal classroom or learning situation. Constantly look for ways to make these tools work for you. It is then that you will come to view them as something worthwhile and not just another thing to learn this week and never use again.

We want you to reflect back on these tools and think, "How did I ever get along without them?"

Why should you learn this?

- Saves time
- Saves energy
- Improves quality

There isn't a job in this world that doesn't require these three objectives—and this is especially true for those of us in the teaching profession.

It would be great if we could just hand you those benefits. However (here's the catch), in order for you to reap them, you have to invest a bit of time and energy.

Our goal is to make your investment as efficient and painless as possible. We figure that if we can have fun along the way and help you get some of your work done as you learn this stuff, you'll stick with us.

Why use Microsoft Office and FrontPage?

Two reasons:

1. This software is very prevalent on home and school computers.
2. Many of the same toolbars, menus, and so on, are used from one application program to the next (this speeds the learning process and the feelings of familiarity).

Note: We realize there are *different versions of this software* and that there are other publishers of software with which you may be more familiar. We focus on important skills that can be learned with whatever software you have available—it may not be done in exactly the same way as the Microsoft products—but it is close, and you will soon learn how to figure out the small differences.

Where are we going?

The key topics and tools we explore include the following:

- Navigating the system (Windows)
- Word processing (MS Word)
- Spreadsheet (MS Excel)
- Data management (MS Excel)
- Presentation software (MS PowerPoint)
- Web editor (MS FrontPage)

Each of these topics receives attention. We suggest that you first peruse chapter 1, "Navigating the System" (just to lay the needed foundation); however, after that, go with what you need. If you are in a class, your freedom might be limited (professors like to do that), but if you are working on this independently, look over what you need to get done and where the emphasis in your life is—then go in that direction.

Note: Start thinking now about current or future projects that you might be able to work into the projects for each of these applications. Remember, we want you to use your own projects. From the very beginning we want you to see the importance of this software for helping you and your students achieve.

How are we going to get there?

Basically, the format of each of the chapters is similar.

You will explore some basic background (short and sweet) about the software and complete some quick exercises. This will familiarize you with the software (what it looks like and how it works) and understand the basics of what, when, and why it is important.

LEVEL 1 APPLICATION:

This is directed at the novice. We'll give you examples of something produced with the software. We also supply step-by-step guidance so you can produce something similar that can be altered for use in your own classroom.

LEVEL 2 APPLICATION:

To achieve increased independence, a second set of examples are given at this level. Key features of the products are highlighted and you will learn how to find critical "how-to" information as you create your own set of products using the software. That is, less step-by-step guidance but more general suggestions are provided. Remember, our goal here is *not* to "hold your hand" and give you step-by-step instructions, but to help you become more self-sufficient. We want to show you how to find the answers to your questions. Then when you're on your own, you should be better prepared to find your own solutions to the unique problems you confront.

LEVEL 3 APPLICATION:

With the basics learned, this level gives opportunities to explain, to teach, and to integrate the software within classroom settings. It is a time to solidify your understanding of the basics, but most important, to ponder on the possibilities of the software's use and application for yourself as well as your learners. Here we want you to envision how this could be used, and we provide additional ideas on how to integrate and apply your new skills.

CRIB NOTES:

Within appendix A we have a number of short notes that you may find helpful. These are fairly common procedures that will help as you work with various pieces of software (e.g., saving a document, selecting a file, searching the Internet). We have learned through experience that these procedures help support the novice computer user until they become automatic.

Do you really need to learn about these software programs?

Maybe . . . maybe not. There are a few ways of finding out—but because most of you are associated with teaching and/or learning, we felt that a short assessment (nice word for *test*) would be in order. So take a crack at this, then ponder your answers (no, this is not highly scientific—and it won't be graded).

Circle the number on the scale about how closely the statement resembles something you could or should have said about yourself.

	That's Me				Not Me
1. I have been told that the computer will reduce my workload, but every time I try to use it, it costs more time, energy, and effort than it's worth.	5	4	3	2	1
2. I feel comfortable using the computer for some things—but I'm frustrated because I know I should be using it to do a lot more.	5	4	3	2	1
3. When asked to "cut and paste," my thoughts wander to grade school, blunt-nosed scissors, and Elmer's glue.	5	4	3	2	1
4. I think I have lost things in my computer and I have a feeling I'm not going to get them back.	5	4	3	2	1
5. When I hear the word *spreadsheet*, I think back to the last time I attempted to make my bed.	5	4	3	2	1
6. Everyone else seems to know a lot more about how to use the computer than I do.	5	4	3	2	1
7. In the past, I have usually found someone else to use the computer when I needed something done.	5	4	3	2	1
8. Computers and feelings of inadequacy, for me, seem closely related.	5	4	3	2	1

Now add up your total score and divide by 8 to calculate your average response. Check the scale below for our suggestions on using this book and learning the software.

3.0 +	You've got the right book and there are lots of good things in store.
2.0 to 3.0	Buzz through the Level 1 exercises, and quickly get to the Level 2 assignments.
1.0 to 2.0	Review the Level 1 and Level 2 material, see if there are examples that you haven't experienced or thought about, then look closely at the integration and examples found in Level 3.

How much knowledge of Web/Internet use is required?

We are assuming that most people nowadays have at least a minimum level of knowledge of accessing and using the Web. Throughout this text, you are given resources to examine that are "on the Web." For those who have limited experience, we have developed Crib Note 10 (Simple Web Search Procedures), found in appendix A, that can assist you in accessing specific information. This Crib Note (and the others) was designed to give you support with a new skill until you gain greater comfort in using it.

Is there a connection between information in this text and the NETS standards?

Just as standards are being developed, examined, and utilized throughout all aspects of education, so too they are being generated and applied for computers and other technologies within the realm of education. Appendix B lists the National Educational Technology Standards (NETS) for both teachers and students. Within each chapter devoted to word processing, spreadsheets, databases, presentations, or Web page development, we highlight and emphasize those standards addressed by the various learning activities and Workouts. Look for these as a part of the Level 3 Workouts. Within those Workouts we highlight sections that apply to specific standards and insert reflective questions that should help you contemplate and visualize the relationship of a standard to the learning activity you are completing and/or designing.

What are some philosophies guiding this book?

1. **We aren't going to teach you everything.** There's no need for that. The programs we work with can be wonderful for the right job—they can also be overwhelming if you get involved in unnecessary applications. Our goal is to focus on what you need—and we show you how to find solutions to specific problems you come across.
2. **We believe in application.** If you use it, you won't as easily lose it. Quickly we have you working with this book right alongside your computer. Actual participation (you working the keyboard) is much better than watching someone else do it—we want and need you to be an "active participant."
3. **Kill two birds with one stone.** We want you to develop skills with the computer programs that will help you in *your* work. Make this information as relevant as possible. Look around and find what needs to be accomplished at work, home, or school. As we show you different programs, think of ways that you could get an assignment done by finishing something that you have to do anyway.
4. **Let's keep it short and sweet.** You have limited time and we know that. We use all kinds of job aids, numbered and bulleted lists, and other means to help shorten the amount of reading that you need to do, and to help you find what needs to be found.
5. **Having fun is NOT a crime.** We think that we can have some fun going through this assignment. We attempt to add some smiles along the way—which you can either enjoy or ignore. We have had a lot of classroom experience, and some of these experiences are hilarious and can be used to illustrate different points in this text—so we have chosen to include them to some degree.

6. **We are not the final word.** You are going to find out (if you don't already know) there are several ways to get the job done. That is the way that most things work, and it is definitely the way most well-designed software works. We will show you how we do it, but in some cases you may know of other ways. If it works for you, use it.

7. **Keep frustration under control.** Listen, you are working with computers—computers are one facet of technology—and technology means that funny things will happen, and usually when you least expect it and least need it to happen. So be prepared and the problems will be only molehills, not huge mountains, to overcome.

How should you use this book?

A few points to note here:

- We don't think most of you should read this text like a novel. Use the margin headings to get to the information that you need in as efficient a manner as possible.
- After reading this introduction, jump to the chapter that will service your current needs. That is, if you have a need for upgrading your skills with spreadsheets, go to that chapter and work there. You don't have to work through the other chapters first. A salient way to figure out what you should do next is to look at the "hot" projects that you need to get done as soon as possible. If there's a project that could be enhanced with the development of a Web site—then perhaps you should look to the chapter on that application. But if you have a pressing project on an upcoming presentation—then by all means go to the section on PowerPoint. You'll learn this much quicker and in greater detail IF you are working on a project that has relevance to you.
- We have included **Crib Notes** (see appendix A) and **Quick References** (at the conclusion of the software chapters) to help you reference and quickly recall some of the basics. Once you get through the chapters, use these features to help you retain and continue to use the key features of the software.

A special note to Macintosh users

As you can probably guess, a PC (IBM compatible personal computer) was used during the initial development of this text. However, on the desk next to the PC was a Mac. Once a chapter was completed, the Mac was then used to review what was written and suggested. Although most of the figures are taken from the PC version, any major differences are noted and described for the Mac users. Generally, an icon is used to let you know about those differences. It is important to note, however, there is a remarkable amount of similarity between the MS Office 2001 for Mac and the MS Office 2002/XP for PCs. One main difference is the lack of task panes found in the Mac version. However, this causes only minor differences in the work outlined within this text.

Some "rules to live by"

1. **SAVE, SAVE, SAVE, and then SAVE your work again.** Get in the habit of frequently saving your work. It's as easy as taking out the garbage, and you can do it in a matter of one to two seconds. If you don't you WILL get burned—it is only a matter of time. Don't depend on the software to do this for you—sometimes that may rescue you, but in many cases it won't.

2. **Think CONTENT first, PRETTY later.** In most cases it is better to enter and edit the content of your work first—worry about the formatting (making it look good) later. If you get sidetracked working on the "pretty" (which is frequently done today), your message may never be developed.

3. **SIMPLE IS BETTER.** With so many bells and whistles found in these programs, it is very easy to get into the "throw in the kitchen sink" syndrome. Just because you have hundreds of type fonts, pictures, hyperlinks, and audio or video clips available, it doesn't mean that you should try to include them all.

4. **KEEP YOUR EYES OPEN.** Look for examples of different ways to design and present your information. Sometimes other teachers, texts, magazines, Web-based documents, or even your students may offer some answers to problems and predicaments that you find yourself in. Pay attention and the solution may present itself.

5. **Store and use EXAMPLES and TEMPLATES.** Once you have either developed or located a good example, store it for use later. For example, if you develop a spreadsheet grade book, a newsletter, a seating chart, a Web page—save copies so the next time you need to do something similar you can begin with that original as a template. The second time around you can speed up the process and make higher-quality products. Templates launch you forward into your next project—use them.

Chapter 1
SYSTEM SOFTWARE
MS Windows: The Basics of Navigating the System

Introduction

What should you know about system software?

If you don't know the rules, it's very difficult to succeed. With the computer there are some general features and tips you need to know (in most cases, these will turn into automatic skills) so that your interaction with the computer is simplified. If you don't understand how these features work, you are going to be fighting an uphill battle—forever. When it comes to understanding the "ground rules" of the computer, you need to know some basics about the operating system software. Here are some procedures that you should be familiar with:

- How to communicate and interact with the computer
- How things are reliably created, organized, stored, and then retrieved
- What tools are available and how they are accessed
- How to get **Help**

Terms to know

desktop	windows	*mouse*	*point, click, hold, drag*
Help	*folder*	*file*	menu
toolbar	*task bar*	*icon*	

What is the system software and what does it do?

System software tells the computer how to perform its fundamental, basic operating functions (e.g., turn on, save files, run application programs). In other words, it is the master control program. When the system software is functioning properly, life is good—when it isn't, life can be miserable.

What are some commonly known system software?

Two types of system software (sometimes called "platforms") dominate the school and home market at the present time:

 Microsoft's *Windows*

 Apple's *Macintosh*

What becomes a little confusing is that improved versions of these systems are continually being introduced. For example, you might be working on Windows 95, 98,

2000, ME, NT, or XP; however, you might also have experience working with the Mac OS 7, 8, 9, or even X.

Although there are some basic differences between the main systems (and even within the different versions of a system), their purpose is very similar—to control how the computer functions.

Why bother learning how to use and navigate the system software?

From the time the computer is turned on until it is shut down, the system software is involved and actively participating. Its role is similar to that of the director of a play. The audience may not see the director, but the director controls what transpires on the stage.

Understanding the system software allows you to control the following:

1. starting up and shutting down the computer;
2. storing, moving, and retrieving your work;
3. installing and uninstalling other software on your computer;
4. finding folders, files, and so forth, in your computer storage areas;
5. controlling how peripherals (e.g., *keyboard, mouse, monitors, scanners*) interact with the computer;
6. using application software (e.g., word processors, spreadsheets).

Workout

Here are three tasks that you can perform to see the impact of the system software and its role as "director":

1. Turn on your computer and time how long it takes to "boot up" (get ready) for you to actually use it. (*Note:* While you are waiting, watch the pictures in your monitor to see if it tells you which type and version of system software your computer is using.) It will probably take a minute or more. Have you ever wondered what it does during that time? It's the system software getting all of its ducks in a row so that the computer can work correctly.
2. If possible, start up three different computers with three different types of system software. First, look at the Windows machine and then look over a Macintosh. Finally, if one is available, look over a DOS (disk operating system) based machine. Note the similarities and the differences between how they appear on the monitor. You will probably note the biggest difference is between the DOS and the other two systems. It may surprise you how similar the Macintosh and the Windows systems actually "see and feel" once you become familiar with them.
3. Many individuals complain that they "don't want to work on a Mac," or vice versa with a Windows-based machine. Similar complaints have been made about different brands of cars, stereos, shoes, and so on. In many cases, once you learn how to use one brand, adapting to the others is relatively painless. If you have access to a machine that you don't have much familiarity with (e.g., a Mac when you are a typical Windows-type person), play with it for a short time. Make a list of the key similarities and differences you find. You may find that it isn't all that mysterious and that the commonalities soon become apparent.

Orientation

What's the workspace look like?

When you walk into a new school building for the first time, it's often easy to get lost. We have often found that it helps if you can find out where you are (perhaps the main office), and then see a picture of the building and how it is all laid out. Key landmarks (e.g., the main hallway, the faculty lounge, the numbering system of the rooms) then can be noted and the logic of the building discovered.

Similarly, this is how we need to handle the computer and its various applications. We begin each explanation section with an overview "map" of what the workspace looks like so that you can get a feel for how it's laid out and what the major tools are.

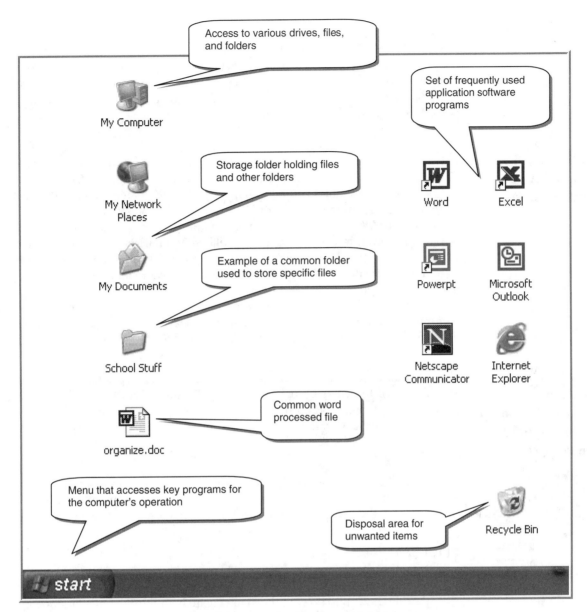

Figure 1.1 View of a Windows XP desktop

Review Figure 1.1. This is a view of a Windows-type computer "desktop." After you start the computer and allow it to boot up, the desktop appears. This is a key land-mark and a place where you will find yourself frequently visiting and working.

(MAC USERS) Don't worry—you also have a desktop with similar items on it—e.g., an easy-to-access main menu, a trash can, a hard drive icon to access items on the hard drive.

What's the "desktop"?

In a normal working office, the top of the desk is where most of the work is completed. There are tools (e.g., pencils, paper clips, writing paper) on the desktop so when needed they are easily available. This is very similar to the computer's desktop. It's here that you have ready access to the needed tools and files so that real work can be accomplished.

> **Note:** Don't be concerned if your desktop looks a bit different than the one in Figure 1.1. The top of the desk in your home or office probably looks different from that of any other person's desk. You can customize the desktop to fit your needs—just like you have done on your personal desk. Generally, there are some basics that you will find (e.g., *Recycle Bin*, key menus, some folders) in and around the desktop. Look for those key landmarks.

Getting it to do what you want

The centerpiece of a good relationship is the ability to communicate. Teachers have to be good at this—you have to handle a variety of students, parents, administrators, and so forth, all of whom may require different communication skills.

Guess what? When working with the computer, communication is also essential. Yes, it can be even more frustrating than telling little Billy not to bring his pet lizard to school for the eighth time. Early on, your biggest problem will be in finding the way to communicate effectively to the computer what you want done. Sounds like the give and take within any relationship, doesn't it?

For most computer systems, **the mouse and keyboard are the critical means of communication.** So look them over, tap them, play with the keys, and note what the different buttons do. You will be using them before long.

The "power of the mouse": *pointing, clicking, selecting, and dragging*

The "Power of the Mouse" (or any mouse substitute—like the *trackball*, *touchpad*, pencil eraser) is that it allows you to tell the computer what to pay attention to, and in many cases, exactly what to do.

Here are the main skills:

POINT:
Move the mouse and watch how the pointer or cursor on the screen moves with it. You need to be able to tell the computer which items to work with—the power of the mouse is that it allows you to point to exactly what you want the computer to attend to.

CLICK:
Note that the mouse has a *button* or two (maybe more) on it. When you depress a button once quickly, it is called a "click." A *click* gives the computer information about what to do with the item you are pointing at. Generally, for a PC the majority of clicks are on the left button. At times you will need to expand your clicking repertoire into a

- double- (or even a triple-) click, or perhaps a
- right click, or even a
- click and hold.

If you do not have access to a mouse (perhaps you are working on a laptop), note that there is still some kind of point and click mechanisms provided. Don't worry—they all are designed to accomplish basically the same task.

Macs have only a single button on the mouse. Thus "right" clicking isn't possible. There are drop-down menus (similar to those on the PC) that are available to access any needed item. The rest of the clicking is very similar.

SELECT OR HIGHLIGHT:
Often you need to identify a specific item (e.g., a picture, word, number) that you want the computer to work on. To do this, you typically put the mouse pointer on top of the item and click. In some cases, you will need to click and

hold in front of the item, and then drag over the item until it is fully selected. When it is "selected," it will change colors (typically becoming darker). If you want it to be "deselected," you just click anywhere else on the screen. Here is an example of a selected word:

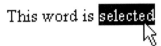

Here are examples of selected and nonselected folders:

My Documents   My Documents

Nonselected   Selected

DRAG:

This is where you point at some object, click and hold (don't release the button), and then move the mouse. The item you have clicked on will then move (drag) or be highlighted in some way. For example, this is one way that you can move a file from one place on the screen to another. Point at the file, click and hold, and drag it to the new location. For more information about dragging, check out Crib Note 3, Dragging a File, in appendix A.

The "power of the keys"

For the computer to be really helpful, there are times when you need to spell out what needs to be done. That's when the keyboard comes in handy. Yes, there will be times ahead in which the keyboard may become obsolete—however, for the near future you will continue to type in the words and commands that are needed via the keyboard.

Workout

On the desktop of your computer, do the following:

1. Move the mouse pointer around. Get a feel for what it's like to move around and point at objects on the screen.
2. Point at an item on the desktop (e.g., Recycle Bin). Select it by clicking it once. Note how it changes color. Click anywhere else on the desktop and note that the selected item is no longer selected.
3. Click and hold on the Recycle Bin, then drag it to a new location. Rearrange some of the items on your desktop by dragging them to different locations. You should start to get the idea of how you can arrange your own desktop to fit your needs.

(MAC USERS)

Do this to the trash can—it works in the same fashion.

Help

Right after receiving a good orientation of the computer layout, it is important for you to know where you can get help if needed.

The main operating systems today have **Help** sections built into their programs. In this text, we continually suggest that you turn to Help to find answers to your questions. In most situations, Help will give you the answer you are looking for.

To find the Help section, look in the **Start** menu (see Figure 1.2).

Figure 1.2 Windows Start menu with Help highlighted

MAC USERS

On the desktop's Main Menu, look for the Help menu (**Help >>> Help Center**). The >>> symbol indicates the selection to be made once the drop-down menu has been revealed.

Remember: Help is like your best friend. When in need—that is where you go.

The three BIG metaphors

The following three metaphors will help you learn the basics about the computer:

1. **Office filing systems metaphor.** Any well-run office (whether at home or at a business) has a means of storing important information. Today, most offices still have file cabinets with drawers full of folders. Each folder contains valuable documents about all kinds of topics. Similarly, for the computer to be used efficiently, a filing system devoted to storing significant documents and files within folders is used.

2. **Restaurant metaphor.** Each time you go to a restaurant to eat you have a selection of food and drink from which to choose. This is most readily accomplished by looking over the menu. Likewise, the computer has menus from which to make a selection of what you want to achieve.

3. **Construction worker metaphor.** Just as a builder has a toolbox and a number of tools he accesses and uses when building a new home or business, the computer user

has access to many tools available within the computer software. Some tools are used more frequently by the builder, but knowledge of many of the others allows great things to be accomplished. The same philosophy applies to using the computer.

Often throughout this text, we refer to these metaphors in order to help you quickly grasp the new information. Get used to them—you will be using them yourself before long.

Why do I need to organize and clean my room?

With the large storage capacity of a computer (one of its greatest assets), you need to have an organizational plan. This will allow you to store and retrieve files and data easily. Organization plays a major role. If you don't attend to how your stuff is organized, you will quickly find that working on the computer can be more frustrating than it needs to be.

In the next few sections, we make suggestions on what you can do to organize your computer so it is efficient and effective.

Important organizers

Files and Folders. To organize what's on the desktop and what's stored within the computer, we use a simple visual metaphor. Just like a filing cabinet in the office contains labeled folders and documents placed inside the folders, so too are objects organized in the Windows platform. The filing system is critical to organizing your workplace (the computer) so you can get the most from it.

An example of files and folders:

Organize.doc

School Stuff

1. Whenever you create something using one of the software applications (e.g., word processing), we will call it a *file*. That file can then be stored by putting it on top of your desktop OR by filing it away within a folder. On the picture of the desktop (Figure 1.1) look for a file that is called "Organize." This is a word-processed document that has been created, named, and stored on the desktop.
2. Look at the desktop in Figure 1.1 again. Note that there is a picture, or "icon," of a folder called "School Stuff." This folder is a place where files and other folders related to school can be put and organized.

> **Note 1:** Both files and folders have names associated with them. This is a great convenience! You can name them so that you can remember what they contain.

> **Note 2:** You have an endless supply of folders, and the size of each can be expanded to hold a huge amount of files, other folders, programs, etc. You never have to go to the store and buy another package of folders.

> **Note 3:** If you want to name them a specific way, you can do so easily. Likewise, if tomorrow you discover a new way to name your folders and files, you can rename them with ease.

Recycle Bin

Recycle bins. An important part of organizing is *getting rid of the stuff you no longer need.* This is done easily by dragging the item to the Recycle Bin (Trash) that's located on the desktop. Once there, it is possible to take out the recycles or trash and "empty" it from your system. *Note:* Discarding trash or recycles on the computer is generally a lot easier (and less smelly) than taking out the kitchen garbage.

The Trash serves this purpose.

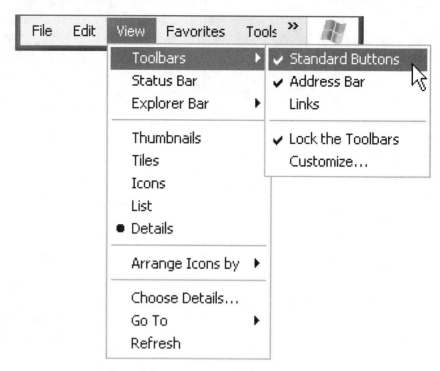

Figure 1.3 Example of an expanded menu

Menus and toolbars

Why menus?   Why not? Restaurants have found them effective. A menu allows you to see lots of choices of food to eat or (as in the case of the computer) activities to perform.

Menus on the computer are often pulled down (or up), and are there until you have made your selection. Once used, they (similar to the restaurant variety) disappear until called on for other selections.

In all programs that we discuss, there are menus and toolbars that you can access and select from. It really is an efficient way to access different tools and other important things (see Figure 1.3 for a common Windows menu that has been expanded).

Tool bars and taskbars.   The computer is capable of many jobs. Subsequently, there is a multitude of tools that can be used to accomplish these jobs. To help with this process, many of these tools have been placed on convenient toolbars that can be shown (or hidden) as you determine their need.

As you become more familiar with an application, you will find certain tools are used frequently, others much less frequently. What is nice is that you can have those you use most often readily available on a visible toolbar (see Figure 1.4), and those that you don't need as often can be neatly tucked away until you ask for them.

Figure 1.4 Common standard and formatting word processing toolbars

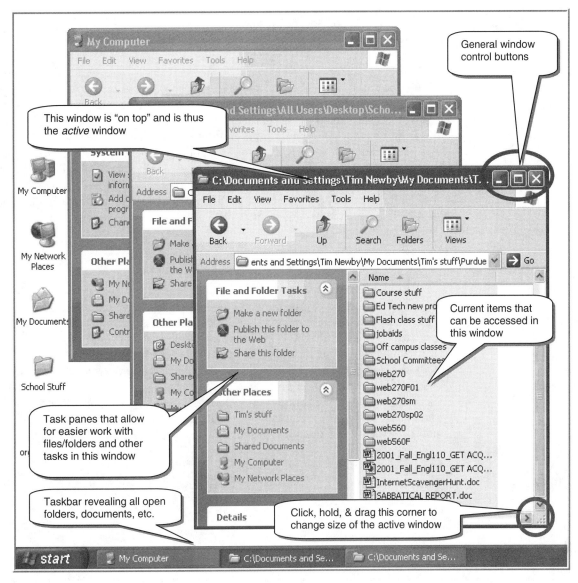

Figure 1.5 View of multiple open windows

Windows, windows, everywhere

Take a look at Figure 1.5. This is an example of several windows being open on one computer screen. Windows allow you to peer into different programs and different parts of the program.

Note how the windows can be made of various sizes and can be made to overlap each other. As you begin to work with the computer, you will find that navigating through these windows, and being able to have multiple windows exposed at a single time, can be very helpful. The *window* you are currently working on (the one on "top") is known as the *active window*. When you have a number of windows on the screen at one time, you can make a specific one active by pointing your mouse directly within the space of that window and clicking once. It will highlight and come to the top.

Look more closely at Figure 1.5. Note the highlighted section in the upper corner of the active window. These buttons allow you to control them (i.e., hide the window temporarily so you can see what else is on the screen, change its size, or close it altogether).

Although the controls look a bit different, they work basically the same way. The idea is that you can open multiple windows and you can readily alter their size.

Think about the application advantage of these multiple windows. For example, you could be grading an assignment that one of your students has submitted and at the same time have the grading rubric in another window that appears on the screen at the same time. Or you might find it fun to have a word processed document up in one window, and you can copy a section of it and paste it into another program (such as a graphics program) without having to do much at all other than select, copy, and then go to the other window and paste.

The **Help** menu has a good section all about windows. Go to the **Help** index and type in "windows"—see what you discover.

Workout: Explore the territory

On the desktop of your computer, do the following:

1. Click on the *Start menu* and see how it reveals its major parts. Become accustomed to highlighting certain parts of the menu and seeing how it can be expanded.
2. Practice opening, changing size, and closing various windows. Check out the menus available within the various windows you open.
3. Try manually changing the size of a window by clicking and holding the lower right corner of a window and dragging it slowly. Try changing the size of a window by placing the mouse pointer on the edge anywhere along the sides of the window.
4. Get used to moving the windows from one location on the desktop to another. Point, click, and hold the mouse pointer on the bar along the top of the active window—now drag the mouse and see if the window follows where you direct it to go.

Open items on the Main Menu bar and explore the Apple menu, as well as the File, Edit, Special menus, etc.

Level 1: Designing, Building, and Using a Good Filing System

What should you be able to do?

At this level, your focus is on creating, naming, renaming, and organizing files and folders. The emphasis here is on organization—putting things in places where you can find and retrieve them later. If you don't have some grasp of this, it won't be long before you become frustrated trying to find stuff you seem to have misplaced.

The situation . . .

To set the stage, let's imagine that your school has just received a new grant where all of the teachers at your grade level have been given laptop computers to use (for some of you this may require *a lot* of imagination). Two weeks before the start of fall classes, you receive your computer, but no training (other than how to turn it on) will be available until after the first day the students return. You know how hectic the start of school can be and you would really like to be comfortable using the computer before the doors open and the kids show up.

When the computer coordinator drops in to see how things are going with the new computer, you ask for her advice. Here are several of her suggestions:

1. Explore on your own.
2. Plan how you would like to use the computer.
3. Walk through (with her guidance) some basic implementation activities.

This Level 1 activity pretty much follows her advice.

The plan

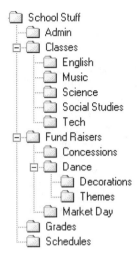

Figure 1.6 Example folder structure

Your technology coordinator suggests that you plan how you will set up the storage system. That is, how you will know where you will put things you create, where to look for them when you need them at a later date, and so on. This requires the use of folders. Here are some simple steps to follow:

a. With a paper and pencil, outline the structure of an efficient filing cabinet. For example, if you have an organized filing system at work, look through it and see what works and what could be improved. You may want to replicate this on your computer.
b. Determine how to label the folders in your filing system and which folders will be "nested" or put within other folders. For example, look at the filing system showing in Figure 1.6.

> **Note:** Don't get too complex or fancy. There is nothing worse than trying to locate a file that is stored in a folder, in a folder, in a folder, that is in a folder (you get the idea). Keep it simple. Also, you can always change folders, rename them, put new things in, and take other things out. Over time, you will find that you need to change and alter how your files and folders are structured.

Workout: by the numbers . . .

Turn on the computer, look around, and try the following:

a. Examine the desktop and see what is there already. Is it pretty clean (nothing much displayed) or does it have lots of icons showing?
b. Identify the Start menu, click it, and examine the names of the different programs that are loaded on your computer; click the Help menu to see what it looks like.
c. Try launching (starting) one or more of the programs to see what they do. To stop the program, look under the File menu and select Exit. If you need assistance, read Crib Note 5 on launching an application program, in appendix A.
d. Review the following "To Do" list. Look at what needs to be done and see if the corresponding "How to Get It Done" explanation helps you accomplish it.

To Do	How to Get It Done
1. Create a new folder on the desktop	Point the mouse at a blank spot on the desktop, *right* click, and a menu will appear; go to New and then select Folder. Mac Users: **File>>>New Folder.**
2. Name a new folder	Once a new folder has been created (and before you do anything else), type in the name that you have selected for your folder. It will appear below the folder icon. Once you have typed it in, press Enter.
3. Rename a folder	Point the mouse pointer on the current name of the folder and click twice (slowly). The name should become selected (highlighted). Type in the new name and it will replace the old one. When you are finished, press Enter.
4. Open a folder to see what is inside	Put the pointer on top of the folder and double-click. A window will open and you will now be able to see the contents of the folder.

continued

To Do	How to Get It Done
5. Create (or place) one folder inside another folder	Open the existing folder. With the existing folder open, follow the instructions for creating a new folder. The new folder will automatically be placed within the open folder. **Note:** You can also create a new folder on the desktop and then click on the new folder, hold and drag it over the top of the folder you want it to go inside of. When the destination folder becomes selected (changes color or shade), then you can release the mouse button. The folder you were dragging will now be dropped into the target folder. To see if it worked, open the target folder and see if the new folder is there.
6. Delete a folder	Put the mouse pointer on the folder to be deleted. Click, hold, and drag the folder to the Recycle Bin. Once the Recycle Bin is highlighted, let go of the mouse button. The folder should now be within the bin. Double-click on the Recycle Bin and a window will open; you can see if your folder really is in there. Additionally, you can delete a folder by putting the cursor on the folder, *right* click, and select the Delete option from the pop-up menu. The folder will automatically be placed in the recycle bin. Drag the folder to the trash.
7. Take out the recycles	When you are sure you want to delete something that has been put in the Recycle Bin, you may want to get rid of it for good. Point the mouse pointer at the Recycle Bin and right click. Choose the option for emptying the bin. **Special>>>Empty Trash . . .**

MAC USERS

MAC USERS

More To Do

Look over and repeat each of these procedures. After a short period of time, they will become second nature.

Once you have reviewed these, create a set of folders as outlined in your plan. Name each of the folders (use names that are relevant to you and your work) and then practice putting some inside of others, renaming some of the folders, and even removing some and putting them in the Trash/Recycle Bin.

As additional practice, go to the CD and review its contents. Do the following:

CD ACTIVITY

- Drag the chp1_Nav folder from the CD to the desktop of your machine. If you need help in navigating to the CD, use Crib Note 7, Accessing Programs, Folders, and Files in appendix A.
- Open the chp1_Nav folder on your desktop. You will see a number of different folders (all empty) nested within the chp1_Nav folder. Play with these. Practice naming, renaming, deleting, putting one inside of another. The idea is just to get used to doing it.
- Develop some type of logical structure for the folders. Create additional folders as needed.

Review what you have just done. It may not look like much, but actually it is quite important. Don't think that you have only explored folders. You have also worked on pointing, left and right clicks, click and holds, dragging, and so forth. You have also explored the Start menu and have seen the locations of various programs to be used later.

> **Note:** If you understand how to create, label, and move these types of folders, this little skill will transfer easily when you name files, place them within folders, and recall them from folders. This is a major function of the computer, and now you know something about how to store and retrieve. Good job.
>
> More information about folders, desktops, and creating, storing, and deleting can be found in Windows **Help.**

Level 2: Help, I Need Some Info

What should you be able to do?

Here, the focus is on getting efficient, effective, and reliable help when it is needed. This is a skill that will be needed and used over and over as you work with the computer.

> **Note:** There is too much information within each of these programs for any sensible person to learn and retain totally. Knowing where and how to access that information is a skill that is well worth the effort to learn.

Introduction

At this level of performance, we want you to become more independent. That is, we want you to begin to answer questions that you have a need to answer—not something we have conjured up for you. This will allow you to get things done, to solve problems, to overcome difficulties, and so on—even when it is just you and the machine.

Don't worry—there will always be questions. You will encounter endless novel situations that will require the use of extra resources. Specifically, the computer's built-in **Help** should become a natural place for you to turn to.

> **Note:** Help doesn't have all the answers—but it does answer many of the common problems individuals run into. You are much further ahead by using **Help** as your personal knowledgeable computer assistant.

> **Another note:** Guess what? There are **Helps** within almost all of the major software application programs available today. That is, if you are working in a word processing program—there will be a word processing **Help** that you can refer to. Likewise, if you are working with a spreadsheet—there is a specific **Help** for spreadsheets. Isn't it nice to know that these people were thinking about you when they were developing their products?

Getting Help

Have you ever bought a new car and then proceeded to *memorize* the owner's manual? Why not? Don't you want to know about everything in your new purchase?

For most of us, that type of memorization task would be too time-consuming, would take too much energy, and would be too boring with little return. We all know that when specific information is needed about the car (e.g., Where is the jack located? What is the procedure for changing a tire?), we can turn to the owner's manual and find the needed information.

Guess what—this is also true for the computer. The nice thing about the computer, however, is that it has a section you can go to and electronically look up answers to your questions and solutions for your problems. This is known as the Help program.

Using Help

Basically, **Help** works like an electronic encyclopedia. It is arranged by topics. If you need something, you tell **Help** the key word or phrase, and it will look up the word or phrase for you and report back the related topics found. You can then select the specific items you feel may have the answer that you seek, and the computer will highlight all of the information that it has on the topic.

Sounds simple, doesn't it? There are a few points to remember:

- You need to know what the key word or phrase is. If you don't specify something at least close to your topic, the computer won't know what to look for. We have given you a bunch of jargon words for this section of the text as examples of key words that can be looked up in Help.
- Sometimes your selected key word gets you close—but not exactly in the right place (this happens sometimes when you are looking for a book in the library). Don't be afraid to look around to see if some of the topics are related and how they relate to your topic. These may help you find exactly what you are looking for.
- There are times when **Help** may cause you frustration. Perhaps there isn't the needed information, the information provided is confusing in some way, or you know the information is in there—but you can't seem to find it. Skills in using **Help** are like anything else—they get better as you use them. Throughout this text we emphasize using **Help** because it is a skill you should develop to gain greater independence with your use of the computer. Your other choice is to memorize everything about this machine and all programs you use with it—and that doesn't seem like a very logical alternative.

Workout: stretching with a little Help . . .

Here are a couple of exercises to help you become comfortable using **Help**.

1. Open Windows **Help**. (Hint: check the Start menu and look for **Help and Support**—see Figure 1.2.) Examine the various topics in the Help and Support window and the area to insert potential search terms or key words. Click on the *Windows basics* link and investigate the following topics (see Figure 1.7):

   - *Core Windows Tasks* (look at the information provided for *Managing windows* and *Working with files and folders*)
   - *Tips for using Help*

   Don't spend a huge amount of time playing with this, but do get a feel for what this has to offer and what can be accessed if needed. There are some great bits of information readily available to you within **Help**.

Help>>>Help Center>>>Mac Help

2. Insert key words or terms in the *Search* area and practice looking up bits of information that may be useful. For example, find out the definitions for "Plug and Play," "HTML," or even "Web searches." Try out several of your own terms and see what types of results are produced.

Why do you *really* need to know how to use Help?

This is a similar question to "Why do I need to know how to use an encyclopedia?" which some of your students may have asked. Those of us who have worked on this book—and any book out there that has to do with the computer—cannot foresee all of the situations that you will find yourself in need. In one way or another, you will find questions that we haven't thought of and definitely haven't attempted to answer.

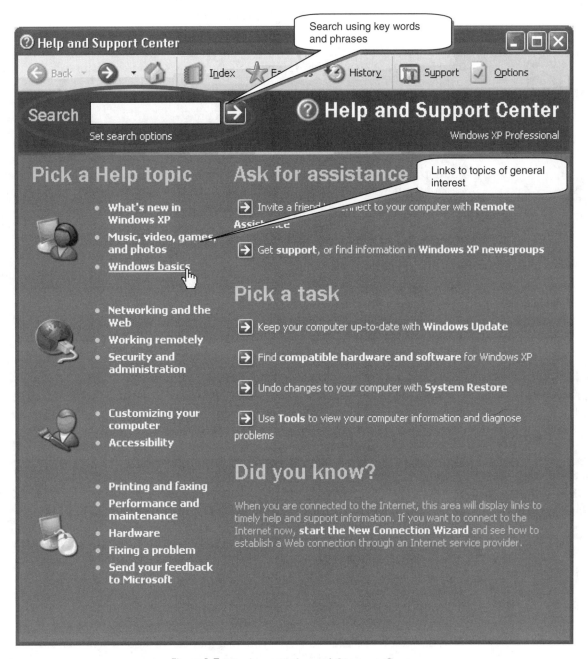

Figure 1.7 Windows **Help** and Support Center

The goal, then, is to help you find the way to get your own answer. For the long haul, this is a much better approach than writing a huge text with "all of the answers" that we would want you to memorize. That is unrealistic and unwanted.

Help is very efficient, and in most cases, for the novice user it will have more than enough information to get you what you need.

Workout: exploring help

Here are a few tasks that you can do to exercise your new knowledge about using **Help**. We aren't going to give you the step-by-step instructions. The idea is for you to go to **Help** and ask it to answer the listed questions.

- What is **Windows Explorer?**
- Is it possible to change the background on your desktop? If so, how?

- Can you protect access to your computer with a password?
- How do you check on things like the monitor or display setting, the amount of computer memory available, or the settings of the computer's clock?
- How do you create and use "shortcuts" and why should you want to know about them?
- Can you adapt the Start menu?
- Can you change the computer's date and time?
- Is it possible to change languages?
- What is speech recognition?

Stump your friends by exploring several of the topics in **Help**. Create some questions about the new things you have found and check with friends, neighbors, colleagues, and so on, to see if anyone else knows what you now know.

Level 3: Integration and Application

What should you be able to do?

The focus at this point is for you to begin to think of ways that this information can be applied. Using these examples, generate ideas on how to use the features of the system software to facilitate your students' learning and the work that you do.

Introduction

Now it's time to stretch. You need to understand how to use this information on your own, and teach it effectively to your students or future students.

Ideas on using the system software as a learning tool

There are a number of ways that the system software can be used to increase the learning of others. Here are some examples to start you thinking about possible ways to use various features of the operating software:

1. Develop a mindset of finding the answers for yourself by focusing on how to find answers to problems or questions that haven't yet been encountered. An example of this is setting up a computer scavenger hunt that involves the use of the system software's **Help** feature. Have students find information that deals with things such as *optimizing performance*, *print queues*, or even *updating drivers*.
2. Develop skills at planning and creating effective organizational filing systems. Have students design a filing system that they can defend as being effective for the storage of their essential documents and files. After they have designed it, have them review what others have planned, make revisions, and then create and use the actual folders and nested folders on their computers.
3. Use the system software **Find** feature to locate specific documents, folders, and so forth, on the computer. Have students locate specific files on the hard drive and explain the path to the file's location.
4. Learn to adapt the computer settings to best fit the user's preferred style. For example, using the Control Panel, change the settings on the monitor to enhance (or diminish) the size of the screen display, adapt the speed with which the cursor blinks, change the size and shape of the mouse pointer, or even alter the size and looks of the icons displayed on the desktop. Also have the students learn how to change these back to their original setting.
5. Develop the ability to open several folders in separate windows at a single time and transfer documents or subfolders between the different folders. In addition, develop the ability to copy folders and documents, and put them on different disks for storage.

Ideas on using the system software as an assistant

1. Use the computer's system software features to help maintain the computer. System software features such as *Disk Defragmenter* and *Scan Disk* can be used to improve the performance of the computer by keeping it in efficient working order.
2. Use Windows Explorer as a means to view where saved items are located and how they can be rearranged or manipulated.
3. Determine the size of a specific file and/or the size of disk space.
4. Use the control panels to alter how the computer functions and looks.
5. Create and use shortcuts to facilitate the effectiveness of accessing salient programs and files.
6. Use the system software to format a diskette.
7. Add and/or remove programs from the Start menu for easy access.
8. Use the system to enhance the access of physically challenged students.

System References

Tutorials and other resources

Here are some resources on the Web that may help you with additional tutorials and provide interesting tips about using the operating system software. If you need more help with how to effectively search the Web, check out Crib Note 10 on simple Web search procedures (appendix A).

> **Note:** Web pages are constantly changing, so it is important to understand that those listed below may not be available when you search for them. That's just part of dealing with the Web. We have included terms that you should find helpful when using a search engine on the Internet (e.g., www.google.com).
> For this topic, a relevant search term/phrase would be
>
> **Windows XP tutorials**

One suggestion is to go to the Microsoft home page (www.microsoft.com) and *search* for the link to "Instructional Resources" and the "Microsoft Classroom Teacher Network." There are several associated links that can prove very beneficial to the classroom teacher.

Here are some links that deal specifically with learning the Windows operating system:

www.microsoft.com/education

This site provides select tutorials and other instructional materials for all of Microsoft products across various grade levels and subject areas.

www.microsoft.com/enable/training

This Microsoft site offers many different tutorials on how to use various accessibility features of the system software (e.g., setting options for people who have visual and aural impairments, use of the magnifier, the narrator, the on-screen keyboard, StickyKeys, etc.)

www.jegsworks.com/Lessons/win/index.html

Simple lessons on Windows operating systems (Win 95 and Win 98) can be found here. These were created by a teacher to help you with the basics of Windows operating systems. Many of these features are still common within Windows XP.

Chapter 2
WORD PROCESSING
MS Word: The Basics of a Writing Assistant

Introduction

What should you know about word processors?

Word processing is *a* (if not *the*) major software tool used by teachers and students. You need to know a few basics to use it effectively. In this opening section, we want you to know

- what a word processor is, what it can do, and how it can help in teaching and learning;
- how to justify the use of the word processor as an effective tool—by knowing when and why it should or should not be used.

Terms to know

font	*graphic*	*style*
table	*format*	*toolbar*
margins	*ruler*	*columns*
headers	*footers*	*alignment*
task panes	*page setup*	

What is a word processor and what does it do?

A word processor is a computer application that allows you to enter, edit, revise, format, store, retrieve, and print text. When you work with text the way that teachers and students do, word processors quickly become a valuable tool. For just a moment, review that list of verbs once again, in relation to the teaching profession. You need this tool!

What are some commonly used word processors?

- Microsoft's Word
- Corel's WordPerfect
- Sun Microsystems' StarOffice Writer
- The word processor within Microsoft's Works
- The word processor inside of AppleWorks (some of you may know it as Clarisworks)

> **Note:** We focus on Microsoft's Word in this text. However, **what we present can be done in any of the other word processors listed.** So if you don't have access to Word, don't be alarmed—you can still complete the projects and learn the basic skills.

Why bother learning how to use a word processor?

- We haven't found anything yet to replace reading and writing. As long as those two skills are needed, there is a need for the processing of words.
- Most of us don't have perfect memories. Word processors are a good way to record ideas, thoughts, and research, and then be able to recall them later.
- We live in a world of repetition. From the written standpoint, word processors help so you don't start needlessly from scratch when confronted with a project that may be the same or similar to one encountered previously. Thus the second time around, you spend your time on improvements instead of reinventing the same thing.
- It just looks better. If this text were handwritten (by me), you would gag. Word processing allows others to be able to quickly decipher what is written. As much as we would like to say that we judge things based on their content, how something looks also matters. Good word processing helps with how information is perceived and processed by the reader.
- It isn't just words anymore. Today's word processors not only handle words, they also incorporate the use of graphics and pictures. These can lead to more proficient and better communication (and possible learning).
- No longer is word processing a lone wolf. That is, what is produced with a good word processor can be coupled with other programs and made even more powerful. Hooking up your words with powerful graphics programs, databases, spreadsheets, and even the Internet can open all kinds of possibilities for classroom projects, fun explorations, and increased efficiency.

How can word processors be used at school? A brief list of ideas

By the teacher:

- Newsletters
- Classroom handouts
- Student assignments and tests
- Calendars
- Lesson plans

By the student:

- Essays (expository, narrative, persuasive)
- Book reports
- Answers to comprehension questions
- Creative writing
- Written science reports

Workout

Word processing is all around us. Take a moment and look for the different ways that you interact with word-processed documents each day. After you have thought about it for a moment, do one of the following:

1. Go to the Web and use a search engine to find classroom uses of word processors. A good set of key words would be *word processing* and *classroom integration.* If you need some assistance on your Web search, review Crib Note 10, on simple Web search procedures (appendix A).
2. List the last three to four items that you have personally word processed. Were they completed perfectly? Why not? What else could or should have been done to the documents?
3. Open up the closest textbook that you have access to. Study a random page. Could you reproduce that page if given access to a word processor and digital graphics (if there are any) that are shown? Why or why not?

Orientation

What's the workspace look like?

Figure 2.1 is an example of the workspace of a common word processor (MS Word). Note where you can enter in your information and some of the common toolbars, buttons, and menus placed around the *workspace.*

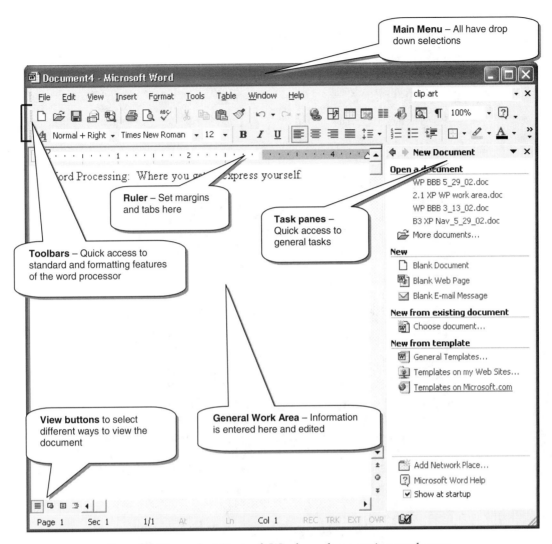

Figure 2.1 View of a Microsoft Word word processing work area

---

Workout: Explore the territory

Turn on the computer and launch your word processing program. Once it's up and running, try the following:

1. Examine the Main Menu. Click on each Menu title (e.g., File, Edit) and note the various selections available under each. You won't need all, but it's a good idea to know where to find them. Pay special attention to where the Help menu is located.

2. Under the View menu (see Figure 2.2), drop down to the Toolbar selection and make sure the Standard and Formatting toolbars are checked. These are the common toolbars that you are to use (also note that there are several others available and later we access and use those). Also make sure that the Ruler is checked.

3. Note that the tools on the toolbars show icons representing the tool's use. If you lay the mouse pointer over any specific tool (don't click), the name of the tool appears. Use of the toolbars is a fast way of accessing commonly used tools.

4. Enter a word or two on the workspace of the word processor. Highlight some or all of the words you enter and then click various tool icons on the Formatting toolbar. Note how your selected words change based on the tool that you have selected to use. (See Crib Note 2a in appendix A, on Selecting More Stuff: Words, Sentences, Paragraphs, and Full Documents, if you need help selecting words.)

5. Play with the toolbar for a few minutes to get a feel for what can be done and how easy it is to use.

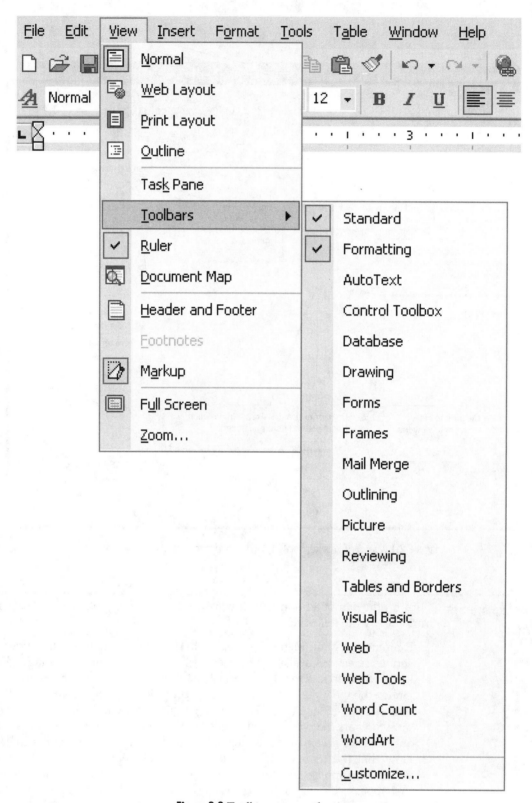

Figure 2.2 Toolbar menu selection

Level 1: Designing, Creating, and Producing Written Documents

What should you be able to do?

At Level 1, the emphasis is on using various tools and techniques of an electronic word processor to format a document given specific guidelines and step-by-step procedures.

A little story . . .

Sally sat staring at a stubby, chewed pencil on her desk. Her second graders had just wiggled on home for the day, and she was too tired to move. She smiled as she thought about the 2.5 million silly second-grade questions she had answered that day, how much chalk was on her dress, and how many times she had to tell Jenni Hatcher to quit acting like a bird—although the bird was actually easier to control than the spotted dinosaur that Jenni had been the day before.

From the hallway behind her, Sally heard Brinna Washington's voice. Brinna was laughing as she looked in at Sally and said, "Don't worry, girl, it does get better." During these first two weeks of the school year, Brinna already had shown herself to be a needed friend and mentor. She had great timing for giving support and providing tidbits of advice.

Brinna continued, "During my prep time this afternoon I was thinking about how overwhelmed you must be feeling right now. Two years ago, I was in your exact position, and it wasn't that much fun. So I made you a little helper gift." She then handed Sally an envelope that obviously contained a computer diskette and a short note. "It's nothing special," continued Brinna, "but it's something I wish I would have had when I first started teaching."

"Thanks . . . but you know that I don't do much on the computer," replied Sally.

"Oh, I know that—but you will," Brinna responded as she disappeared into the hallway.

Sally unfolded the note and looked over what was written:

Sally—

This diskette contains three files. They should be easy to open on your machine in your classroom or on the one you have at home. The first file contains a short newsletter that I sent to my kids last week. You'll see that it's real simple, but it might give you an idea of what could be sent home and what you can build on. The second file is a simple science lesson plan that I was working on for next week. See if you want to use it, or adapt it in some way. We might even want to join our classes together to work on it. And the last file is just something that helps me keep things in perspective. I keep a copy inside my day planner and try to read it every once in awhile.

Hope this helps—

Brinna

P.S.: Did you do a bird unit today? I kept hearing bird sounds coming from your room—aren't second graders great!!

A few minutes later, Sally was packed up and heading out to her car for the trip home. In her new "My School Bag" tote, she carried the diskette. She'd take a look at it over the weekend to discover what treasures her friend had given.

The plan

Let's look at the first item that Brinna offered Sally. It's a newsletter that Brinna wrote to send home with her students (see the accompanying copy of the letter). This newsletter can be used as a template for other letters that may use a similar format. Several key word processing formatting features are used within the letter.

- Take a close look at Figures 2.3a and 2.3b. These figures represent "before" and "after" examples, respectively, of Brinna's "The Happenings" newsletter. Figure 2.4 highlights the unique features that have been added to the newsletter so it looks like a finished product.
- Follow the step-by-step procedures and reproduce the letter with all salient features. It doesn't have to be an exact replica—just demonstrate that you can carry out the highlighted functions.

The Happenings...
Mrs. Washington's Second Grade, Room 8

Week of August 26–30

Hello everyone,

This is the second in our weekly series of newsletters. Things have started to settle down into a regular weekly routine. Hopefully you have all had the chance to look over some of the work that is being done in our class.

Highlights of this week:
We've started our group science project on "Whales". The kids were fascinated by the stories we read from our library books. I think some of them were surprised at the size of a blue whale when we attempted to draw one the right size with chalk in the school parking lot! We are now monitoring the "Whale Search" Web site. If you have access to the Internet at home, try it out and let the kids show you what they have discovered.

In math, we are working with manipulables. We are trying to count about everything possible in our room. If your child counts things at home, that is why.

We have spent a lot of time in the "reading lounge" this week. After a long summer vacation, it is time to get into the habit of regular reading. Encourage this at home. Pick something fun and have your child read to you out loud.

Things to look forward to:
More whale work is coming. We will soon be creating a world globe that highlights many of the key areas that whales can be found in today's world. We will also create one that represents where the whales were 100 years ago. It should make for an interesting comparison.

We will be doing some classroom reading and math assessments next week. These are to help identify any areas that need special attention and encouragement. I will send home individual reports to each of you about your child's performance and my thoughts.

A little help from parents:
Extra boxes of tissues are needed. Could you send an extra box in the next week or two? Thanks.
The school fundraiser is upon us. We will need help in the organization and distribution departments. I will be sending home a sign-up sheet next week. Be looking for it.
Weekly spelling tests will be starting next week on Fridays.

Thanks for all of your support and help. This should be the best year ever!!!!
Mrs. Washington

Figure 2.3a Letter from Mrs. Washington *before* formatting

The Happenings...
Mrs. Washington's Second Grade, Room 8

Week of August 26-30

Hello everyone,

This is the second in our weekly series of newsletters. Things have started to settle down into a regular weekly routine. Hopefully you have all had the chance to look over some of the work that is being done in our class.

Highlights of this week:

- We've started our group science project on "Whales." The kids were fascinated by the stories we read from our library books. I think some of them were surprised at the size of a blue whale when we attempted to draw one the right size with chalk in the school parking lot! We are now monitoring the "Whale Search" Web site. If you have access to the Internet at home, try it out and let the kids show you what they have discovered.

- In math, we are working with manipulables. We are trying to count about everything possible in our room. If your child counts things at home, that is why.

- We have spent a lot of time in the "reading lounge" this week. After a long summer vacation, it is time to get into the habit of regular reading. Encourage this at home. Pick something fun and have your child read to you out loud.

Things to look forward to:

More whale work is coming. We will soon be creating a world globe that highlights many of the key areas that whales can be found in today's world. We will also create one that represents where the whales were 100 years ago. It should make for an interesting comparison.

We will be doing some classroom reading and math assessments next week. These are to help identify any areas that need special attention and encouragement. I will send home individual reports to each of you about your child's performance and my thoughts.

A little help from parents:

1. Extra boxes of tissues are needed. Could you send an extra box in the next week or two? Thanks.
2. The school fund raiser is upon us. We will need help in the organization and distribution departments. I will be sending home a sign-up sheet next week. Be looking for it.
3. Weekly spelling tests will be starting next week on Fridays.

Thanks for all of your support and help. This should be the best year ever!!!!
Mrs. Washington

Figure 2.3b Letter from Mrs. Washington *after* formatting

The Happenings...

Mrs. Washington's Second Grade, Room 8

1. Get it in there

2. Font type, size, and style change

3. Alignment

Week of August 26-30

Hello everyone,

This is the second in our weekly series of newsletters. Things have started to settle down into a regular weekly routine. Hopefully you have all had the chance to look over some of the work that is being done in our class.

5. Paragraph Indent

Highlights of this week:

- We've started our group science project on "Whales." The kids were fascinated by the stories we read from our library books. I think some of them were surprised at the size of a blue whale when we attempted to draw one the right size with chalk in the school parking lot! We are now monitoring the "Whale Search" Web site. If you have access to the Internet at home, try it out and let the kids show you what they

4. Bulleted (& numbered) lists

- In math, we are working with manipulables. We are trying to count about everything possible in our room. If your child counts things at home, that is why.

- We have spent a lot of time in the "reading lounge" this week. After a long summer vacation, it is time to get into the habit of regular reading. Encourage this at home. Pick something fun and have your child read to you out loud.

Things to look forward to:

More whale work is coming. We will soon be creating a world globe that highlights many of the key areas that whales can be found in today's world. We will also create one that represents where the whales were 100 years ago. It should make for an interesting comparison.

We will be doing some classroom reading and math assessments next week. These are to help identify any areas that need special attention and encouragement. I will send home individual reports to each of you about your child's performance and my thoughts.

A little help from parents:

1. Extra boxes of tissues are needed. Could you send an extra box in the next week or two? Thanks.
2. The school fund raiser is upon us. We will need help in the organization and distribution departments. I will be sending home a sign-up sheet next week. Be looking for it.
3. Weekly spelling tests will be starting next week on Fridays.

Thanks for all of your support and help. This should be the best year ever!!!!
Mrs. Washington

7. Page border

6. Insert and size clipart

8. Spell check

Figure 2.4 "The Happenings . . ."newsletter with formatting steps highlighted

Workout: By the numbers . . .

CD ACTIVITY

1. Launch your word processor application program. (See Crib Note 5 on Launching an Application Program, in appendix A, if you need help.)
2. Open the existing unformatted version of "The Happenings" document on the CD [**File>>>Open . . .** and then navigate to the CD, view the CD contents, open the chp2_WP folder, launch (double-click) the "Happen1" file], or if you like, you can open a new document and type in the document yourself. (See Crib Note 7 Accessing Programs, Folders, and Files," in appendix A, if you need help.) Once opened (or once you have typed it in), your document should look something like the "before" portion (Figure 2.3a).
3. Now look over Figure 2.4. This is the finished version of the newsletter, but several features have been highlighted. The numbers correspond to the following table and what you will be doing to alter your version.
4. For simplicity, we are going to word process by the numbers (similar to the old paint by numbers—but that's another story).

No.	To Do	How to Get It Done
1.	**Get it in there**	**Goal:** Get something to work on. **Steps:** 1. Remember one of the key rules—"think content first, pretty later." That applies here. You first enter the newsletter into the computer (either by opening the version on the CD or by entering it in by hand). 2. Generally, don't worry about how the document looks at this point. You just need content to be accurate. Making it look fancy will be part of the formatting to follow. **Note:** Check out Crib Note 4 on Copying, Cutting, and Pasting in appendix A for insights into different ways to enter information.
2.	**Font type, size, style change**	**Goal:** Change the font type, size, and style to selected words or phrases. **Steps:** 1. Select (highlight) the title of the newsletter "The Happenings . . .". 2. Go to the Format menu on the menu bar, click, and select "**Font . . .**" (**Format>>>Font. . .**). 3. A window will open that looks similar to what is pictured in Figure 2.5. 4. Under the subheading of Font: scroll down and select one of the many fonts. You can preview what will occur in your document by looking at the small Preview frame at the bottom of the Font window. Try different fonts and notice what happens. Explore and enjoy. 5. Under the subheading of Size: scroll to a size of 20 or more and click it (or just type in the number you desire). Review what you have done in the Preview frame at the bottom of this window. Try several sizes and select one that you're happy with. 6. Click OK and your changes will now take place. **Note:** There is plenty that you can control within this one set of menus. Different effects, sizes, types of fonts, and styles can be changed here. Common font styles include **bold**, *italics*, <u>underline</u>, SMALL CAPS, and ~~strikethroughs~~. Play around to learn different ways to change the format of the words on your page. 7. Select and change the other headings, words, and phrases that need to stand out in some way.

continued

No.	To Do	How to Get It Done

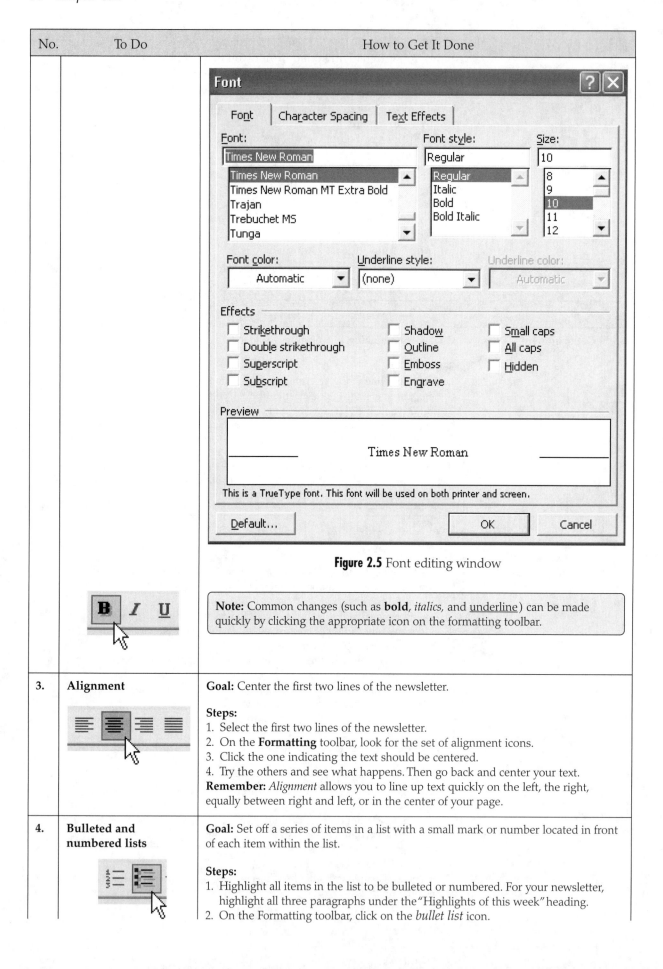

Figure 2.5 Font editing window

Note: Common changes (such as **bold**, *italics*, and <u>underline</u>) can be made quickly by clicking the appropriate icon on the formatting toolbar.

3.	**Alignment**	**Goal:** Center the first two lines of the newsletter.
		Steps: 1. Select the first two lines of the newsletter. 2. On the **Formatting** toolbar, look for the set of alignment icons. 3. Click the one indicating the text should be centered. 4. Try the others and see what happens. Then go back and center your text. **Remember:** *Alignment* allows you to line up text quickly on the left, the right, equally between right and left, or in the center of your page.
4.	**Bulleted and numbered lists**	**Goal:** Set off a series of items in a list with a small mark or number located in front of each item within the list.
		Steps: 1. Highlight all items in the list to be bulleted or numbered. For your newsletter, highlight all three paragraphs under the "Highlights of this week" heading. 2. On the Formatting toolbar, click on the *bullet list* icon.

No.	To Do	How to Get It Done
		3. Review what has been done to your document. Bullets should now appear in front of each paragraph selected. The items are indented, and there's an extra bit of white space between each bulleted item. 4. On the newsletter, highlight the three paragraphs under the subheading "A little help from parents." 5. On the Formatting toolbar, click the number list icon. **Note:** If you don't like the regular bullets or numbers that are normally inserted, you can change them. Go to the **Format Menu>>>Bullets and Numbering.** Explore what you can do to alter the way lists are created. Additionally, go to the Help menu and search for "bullet lists." Select the alternative pertaining to "picture bullets" for another interesting idea.
5.	**Paragraph**	**Goal:** Control the width of the outside edges of selected sections of the document and control paragraph indentation. **Steps:** 1. Locate the ruler at the top of the document (if it's not showing, go to **View Menu>>>Ruler**). Note that sliders for paragraph indents sit on both sides of the ruler. The left one pertains to the left text margin and the right one to the right text margin. Ruler with paragraph indents 2. Select the text where you want to alter the paragraph indents (select the text under the heading "Things to look forward to:"). 3. On the bottom square (left indent) icon, left mouse click, hold, and drag the mouse cursor slowly to the right. A vertical dashed line will appear and it will move the margin of the selected text to the right. Adjust it in and out to sense how this works. This adjusted margin only pertains to the highlighted paragraphs of text. If nothing is highlighted, it pertains to the paragraph where the cursor is currently located. 4. See what happens if you point only at the top triangle and move it to the right or left. The first line will change on your selected text. If you wish to indent the first line of the selected paragraphs, then you would use this tool. Note what happens when you move only the bottom triangle. This is known as the "hanging indent." This leaves the first line where it is and moves the rest of the paragraph. Try each of these to see how they can be used to set and reset any text that is selected. 5. Use the right margin (triangle on the right of the document on the ruler) to set the right margin of the selected text. **Note:** If you begin your document by setting the first line indent, the left indent, and the right indent–all paragraphs that follow will use this same margin setting. Although later you can come back and change any and all of the settings as is needed. If you have already entered the text, then highlight those sections that need to have similar margins and set it one time.
6.	**Insert and size clip art**	**Goal:** Place a picture or graphic within a document and make it the appropriate size. **Steps:** 1. On your document, place the cursor where you want the clip art to be inserted. 2. On the Main Menu bar, click on the Insert menu.

continued

No.	To Do	How to Get It Done

Figure 2.6 Insert Clip Art task pane

3. Drop down to the Picture option and select the option for Clip Art . . . (**Insert>>>Picture>>>Clip Art . . .**). The *Insert Clip Art* task pane will appear on the side of your document (see Figure 2.6).

MAC USERS

Same procedure as the PC; however, a Clip Gallery window will appear and you can select from the gallery's categories and available clip art.

4. In the Search text box, enter a key word that describes the type of clip art you are searching for (e.g., "sports") and then click the Search button. Various small versions of the clip art should appear in the task pane.
5. Scroll through the alternatives presented in the task pane. Use Other Search Options to refine your search if needed (e.g., where to search, types of media to search for).
6. Select the clip art, and the picture will automatically be inserted within your document.

Note: Some of your selected pictures may not be stored on your hard drive or server. In that case, a window will appear and state that your selection was not found. To solve this dilemma, you can do one of several things. Find the CD-ROM that contains the library of clip art and insert it. Retry the insertion process and the clip art should be retrieved from the CD. Another option is to go directly to the Microsoft Clips Online site. There should be a direct link located at the bottom of the Insert Clip Art task pane. Once you arrive at that site, follow the directions for selecting and using their clip art.

7. If your inserted clip art is the perfect size for your document, great—leave it as it is. However, in many cases, the size will not be perfect. So point your mouse at the picture and left click once. You'll note that a box is drawn around the picture and small dark squares are placed at each of the corners and in the middle of each of the sides. These are called *handles*. You can grab a handle by putting your mouse pointer on the handle (note that your pointer changes into a double-headed arrow), left click, and hold it. Dragging a handle causes the picture to be altered. Try different handles and see what happens to the shape and size of the picture.

Selected clip art with handles

No.	To Do	How to Get It Done
		8. Once your picture is inserted and sized appropriately, you can align it by clicking it once (the handles should appear), and then selecting from the alignment icons on the Formatting toolbar.
		Note: Working with clip art and other graphic files may take a bit of practice. Some won't look as pleasing when their size is changed to a drastic degree—others work great. You'll also find that access to the Internet gives you an endless supply of clip art that you may want to insert within your documents.
7.	**Page border**	**Goal:** Set a fancy border around an entire document page.

Steps:
1. Click **Format Menu>>>Borders and Shading . . . .**
2. The Borders and Shading window appears (see Figure 2.7). Click the **Page Border** tab.
3. Under the section of Settings, click the Box option. Note what happens in the Preview section on the right-hand side of this window.
4. Under the section of Art, click the down arrow and scroll through the different borders that can be selected. Select one that you think would look cool. Look at the Preview box to see what has occurred.
5. Explore this window and try several settings. See what appeals to you by watching how the changes impact the Preview box. When you have made your final set of selections, click OK.

Note: Under the Format drop-down menu the Borders and Shading . . . window will be used a lot. Make sure you take time to go back there and try the different options under the Borders tab and the Shading tab. You can learn to draw boxes around specific bits of text, color the boxes, or even shade the backgrounds within the boxes.

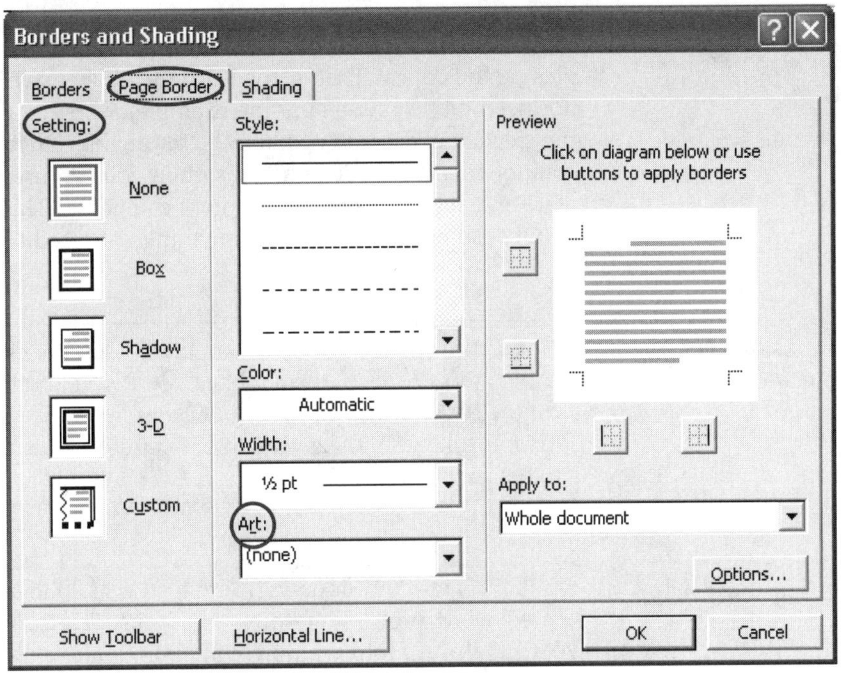

Figure 2.7 Borders and Shading window

continued

No.	To Do	How to Get It Done
8.	**Spell check**	**Goal:** Create a document free of misspelled words. **Steps:** 1. When the document is nearly finished, click on the spell checker icon on the Standard toolbar. 2. Check any misspelled words or suspect grammar indicated by the checker. If you want it left alone, select Ignore; if you want to change according to the suggestion, click Change and the change is made automatically for you. **Note:** Word concurrently checks all spelling and grammar as you are inserting text within your document. A suspected misspelled word will have a squiggly red line under it to indicate that it should be checked. Questionable grammar will have a green squiggly line under the text. You can turn this off if it bothers you.

Level 2: Tables, Templates, and Other Good Stuff

What should you be able to do?

At Level 2 you learn to recognize additional word processing features and gain confidence using Help to create, edit, and format several original documents.

The key here is not to memorize all that the word processor is capable of—it is better to know some of the basics and when, where, and how to find assistance for everything else.

The little story continues . . .

Remember, Brinna from the opening story had actually given Sally three different documents to take home. The second and third documents are presented Figures 2.8 and 2.9. These figures have various formatting features highlighted for easy identification.

One thing that an experienced teacher like Brinna knows is that the use of examples can be critical. That is, the lesson plan she gave Sally is about blubber. Sally may not need that content—but the example of how to use the word processor to help in the creation of a lesson plan may be invaluable. Once you have determined the needed components of your lesson plans, then you can use the blubber document as a template and cut and paste new content as needed. This can quicken the overall process, and it ensures you don't forget anything you need to consider within your plan.

CD ACTIVITY

Note: For the full blubber lesson plan, open the chp2_WP folder on the CD, then launch (double click) the "blubber" file. If you find this a useful template, select and cut the content, and add your own content to the structure that is already designed for you. Likewise, a text version of Figure 2.9 is also available in the same chp2_WP folder (open "station").

Getting some Help

Similar to **Help** in Windows, there is also Help in MS Word and most other sophisticated word processing software. To use **Help**, click **Help menu>>>Microsoft Word Help.** A **Help** window will open, and by clicking the *Answer Wizard* tab you can type in your question and Help will respond with a variety of potential answers for you to investigate. To get a general overview of what **Help** has to offer, click on the Contents tab.

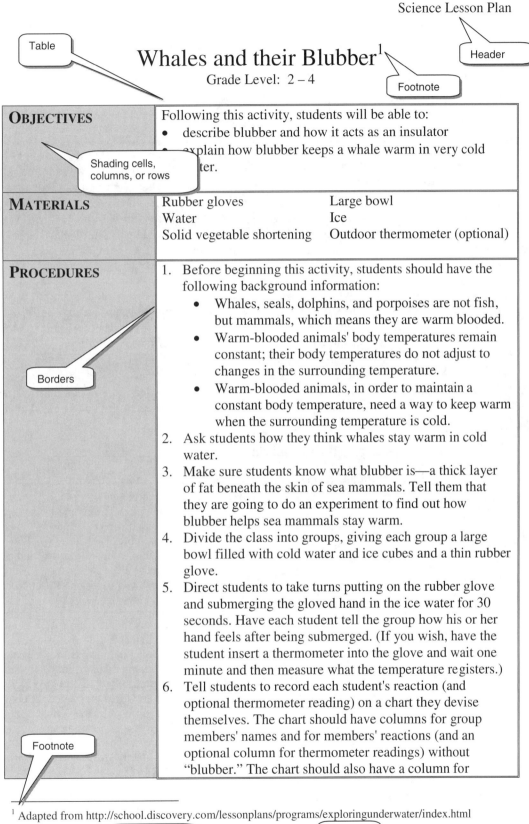

Figure 2.8 Lesson plan with highlighted formatting features

Help generally *does not* have all of the answers—but it will have a lot of them. Make sure you become familiar with how it works and how often it can be of assistance.

> **Note:** Check out the Getting and Using **Help**, Crib Note 6, in appendix A for more information and insights on using the **Help** feature.

Explore: "Blubber"— the lesson plan

Within Level 2 of this software application, "blubber" isn't all that important—what *is important* are the formatting features presented within this lesson plan. Look closely at Figure 2.8 (lesson plan) and note the major features we have included: tables, footnotes, headers and footers, page numbers, borders, and shading. Are these features critical for you to become a good teacher? Probably not. But they will help you organize your documents and make them more readable and understandable. That is important for your students.

Workout: Stretching with a little Help . . .

You may already have a favorite lesson plan that you can use at this point or you may have a desire to create a lesson plan about a topic that you haven't had the needed motivation or time to get to—until now. Either way, select a topic and create something that is of value to you and your teaching (or future teaching).

Use Figure 2.8 as a template for your plan. As you include your content, make sure you can grasp the following formatting features. We won't explain exactly how to do each, but we will provide you with an example of the feature, and pose critical questions you can ponder and investigate (via Help/Office Assistant) to find the needed answers.

Feature	Ask the Office Assistant (Help)
Table	• **What is a table?** Study closely the section "About tables." Important information can be gleaned here (i.e., creating, formatting, and using). • **How do you resize a table?** This shows you how to expand or shrink column width, row height, and so on, according to your specific needs. • **Also investigate:** Table menu (click Table button on Main Menu).
Borders and Shading	• **What is a border?** Look for the option "About borders." Around the edges of the table (and also selected text) you have the capability of putting a border (e.g., line). Check out how borders are created, the different types of borders available, and so forth. Borders are a great way to highlight text and focus the reader's attention. • **What is shading?** Look again at the option "About shading." Scan through the information and look for topics specific to adding or changing shading. • **Also investigate:** Format menu (**Format>>>Borders and Shading . . .**).
Footnote	• **What is a footnote?** Look for the "About footnotes and endnotes" to learn about what footnotes are, and how, when, and why they are used. You may also discover something about "endnotes." • **How is a footnote inserted?** Check the section on "Insert a footnote." • **Also investigate:** Insert menu (**Insert>>>Footnote...**).

Feature	Ask the Office Assistant (Help)
Headers and Footers	• **What are headers and footers?** Review the overview section about these descriptive titles. This will give you the basic background information. • **How do you create a header or footer?** This is a simple procedure. Note that page numbers, time, and so on, can be added easily to the header or footer. • **Also investigate:** View menu (**View>>>Header and Footer**).
Page numbers	• **How do you insert page numbers?** Page numbers can be added readily to headers and footers (see Help on creating headers and footers for information). Additionally, you can add page numbers by selecting the "Add page numbers" option and following the directions given by Help. • **Also investigate:** Insert menu (**Insert>>> Page Numbers . . .**).

With this information and example, create or adapt a lesson plan that you can use. Use the Table feature, but adapt it as needed, formatting it with borders and shading, and so forth. See if it's possible to add headers and footers with page numbers to your document. Adapt the lesson plan to meet your needs. Add sections that you find valuable and eliminate those that you feel are not helpful.

You may find it helpful to go to the CD, look within the chp. 2 folder, and open the document named "blubber." You can adapt this document by adding rows to the table, altering the shading, borders, headers, and content to fit your needs. Use this as a beginning template that you can adapt as you become more comfortable with these formatting features.

Note: Remember and implement the first Rule to Live By: "Save, Save, Save, and then Save your work again." This is a key principle mentioned in the introduction. Make sure you Save—or it will come back to haunt you sometime down the road.

Also think about rules 3–5. Keep it simple, watch for how others accomplish what we have described above, and think about saving the lesson plan as a template that can be adapted and used later as needed.

Explore: "The Station"

The final document that Brinna gave Sally was "The Station" by Robert J. Hastings. For us, this word-processed document shows a few other formatting features that will be beneficial. Figure 2.9 shows the printed document and highlights the formatting features used. It is given here as an example of the possibilities available to you or your students with word processing software.

As you explore this example, note how the title and author's name are centered at the top of the page, but directly underneath all lines of the quote are placed within two columns. This requires the document to be divided into sections so that in one section something can occur that you may or may not want to occur in other sections. Also note that we have inserted a picture of a railroad station, but in this case we have created it as a watermark, enlarged it, and used it as a background to the words in the quote. This requires the use of the Picture toolbar located within the **View >>> Toolbar** menus.

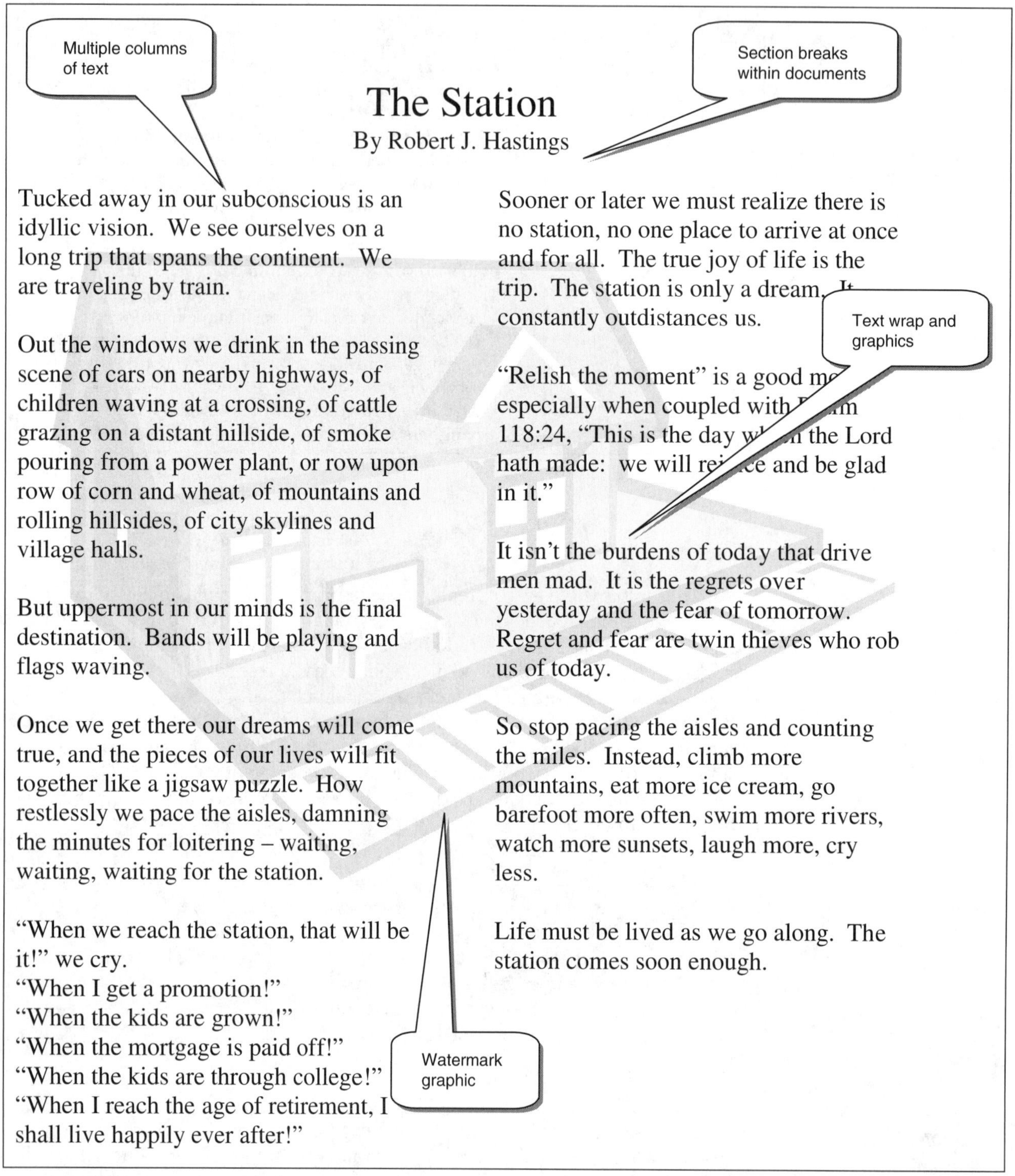

Multiple columns
of text

Section breaks
within documents

The Station

By Robert J. Hastings

Text wrap and
graphics

Tucked away in our subconscious is an idyllic vision. We see ourselves on a long trip that spans the continent. We are traveling by train.

Out the windows we drink in the passing scene of cars on nearby highways, of children waving at a crossing, of cattle grazing on a distant hillside, of smoke pouring from a power plant, or row upon row of corn and wheat, of mountains and rolling hillsides, of city skylines and village halls.

But uppermost in our minds is the final destination. Bands will be playing and flags waving.

Once we get there our dreams will come true, and the pieces of our lives will fit together like a jigsaw puzzle. How restlessly we pace the aisles, damning the minutes for loitering – waiting, waiting, waiting for the station.

"When we reach the station, that will be it!" we cry.
"When I get a promotion!"
"When the kids are grown!"
"When the mortgage is paid off!"
"When the kids are through college!"
"When I reach the age of retirement, I shall live happily ever after!"

Sooner or later we must realize there is no station, no one place to arrive at once and for all. The true joy of life is the trip. The station is only a dream. It constantly outdistances us.

"Relish the moment" is a good motto, especially when coupled with Psalm 118:24, "This is the day which the Lord hath made: we will rejoice and be glad in it."

It isn't the burdens of today that drive men mad. It is the regrets over yesterday and the fear of tomorrow. Regret and fear are twin thieves who rob us of today.

So stop pacing the aisles and counting the miles. Instead, climb more mountains, eat more ice cream, go barefoot more often, swim more rivers, watch more sunsets, laugh more, cry less.

Life must be lived as we go along. The station comes soon enough.

Watermark
graphic

Figure 2.9 "The Station" with highlighted formatting features (Originally published in *A Penny's Worth of Minced Ham* by Robert J. Hastings © 1986 Southern Illinois University Press. Reproduced by permission of the publisher.)

Implement

Again, here is some guidance on where to find the needed information to create a document similar to "The Station." We would like you to select your own document or content on which to practice these formatting techniques.

Feature	Ask the Office Assistant (Help)
Sections	• **What are sections?** Click on the section titled "About *sections* and *section breaks*." Also look closely at how to insert and delete a section break. • **Also investigate:** Insert menu (**Insert>>>Break**). Look for "Section break types."
Columns	• **What are columns?** Click and read the option that begins "Create newspaper-style columns. . . ." Note that there are directions on how to get the full document to change into columns or just specific sections of the document. Also note that various numbers of columns can be selected.
Picture: watermarks	• **How do you insert a picture or graphic?** This is discussed in Level 1, but Help will give you guidance on doing this and on getting additional clip art if needed. • **How do you edit a picture or graphic? Help** will direct you to the Picture toolbar (**View>>>Toolbars>>>Picture**). Display this toolbar on your workspace and then play with the options. One such option is "Watermark." • **How do you create a watermark?** Check out the section on "About watermarks." This should give you good ideas on what can be done to your document.
Picture: text wrapping	• **What is text wrapping?** Look over the section called "Change the text wrapping style for a picture or graphic object." There are several options on how the text can work around, over, or through a picture. • **Also investigate: View Menu >>> Toolbars >>> Picture**.

Workout:
Create your document

Now you try it.

1. Find a favorite quote that you have wanted to give to someone else or hang in your room, or whatever.
2. Enter the document into the word processor.
3. Divide it into appropriate sections.
4. Put some of the document into columns.
5. Align and format the title and all key headings.
6. Insert an appropriate picture, clip art, or graphic, and place it within the document so that the words are wrapped correctly.

> **Note:** Invoke Rule 1: Save your work.

Level 3: Integration and Application

What should you be able to do?

Here you need to think of how to use word processing both in terms of yourself and your students. You should be able to apply the examples given to generate ideas on how to integrate and apply the word processor to improve personal productivity as well as student learning.

Introduction	Within Levels 1 and 2 of this chapter, we focus on word processing from the perspective of learning to use it. However, to extend its use, you need to look at word processing as a means to enhance the learning experience of students. There are times when integrating word processing within a learning situation may improve the learning opportunities and possibilities of the learners. However, there are other times when such integration would be more of a hassle than potential benefits warrant. Learning to tell the difference can help you be successful in what you develop and use in your classroom.

Word processing integration

Creating the enhanced learning experience: A partial lesson plan

Topic: A study of the people, places, and culture of an African country.

Overview: Mr. Carpenter is an eighth-grade social studies teacher at Lowell Middle School. He constantly searches for ways to increase his students' interest in the topics they explore and learn in his classes. Recently, he had the opportunity to speak with one of his past students, Jonathon Rogers, who had attended Lowell a number of years ago. Jonathon is now a graduate student at a nearby university.

During their discussions, Jonathon explained to Mr. Carpenter that during the coming school year he was going to work on an internship for an international health organization. He would be traveling to the country of Zimbabwe in southern Africa to help with the organization's distribution of health supplies and educational materials. He would live and work with the Zimbabwean people throughout the next school year.

Through a little brainstorming, Mr. Carpenter and Jonathon determined that with mail and possibly e-mail they could establish a connection between Mr. Carpenter's social studies classes and some of the culture, politics, education, and geography that Jonathon would be experiencing. The students at Lowell could perhaps come to learn vicariously through the eyes and ears of Jonathon as he explored another country half-way around the world.

Specific learning task: To begin the course of study on Zimbabwe, the students in Mr. Carpenter's classes were to make simple comparisons between Zimbabwe and their own country. Members of the classes were divided into smaller cooperative research groups. Each group selected a major topic of interest (e.g., education, geography, politics, health, culture) that they would investigate to make their comparisons.

Sample Learning Objectives: Students will be able to do the following:

1. Compare and contrast the key similarities and differences between the countries of Zimbabwe and the United States.
2. Identify and explain several common issues impacting the people of both countries, as well as issues isolated within one country or the other.

Procedure:
1. Break into the groups and brainstorm the key questions to investigate about the selected topic.
2. Research answers for the questions from the view of both Zimbabweans and U.S. citizens.
3. Create a comparison table that lists the questions and potential answers determined through research. Reference the answers to the questions that were found within the research.
4. Write a reflection paper about the salient findings reported within the comparison table. Explain the major similarities and differences noted between the two countries.
5. Send the comparison tables to Jonathon and have him select several of the questions to ask people he encounters in Zimbabwe. Have him respond and enter those responses within a new column on the comparison table.

6. Based on the full findings of the group and the responses by Jonathon, the group will develop a final written executive summary of their findings to be distributed to all members of the class. The final version should include additional questions that the group may wish to investigate if given the opportunity to do so.

Questions about word processing integration

Obviously, this lesson could be completed with or without the use of word processing software. Use these reflective questions to explore the value of potentially integrating word processing within such a lesson as outlined by Mr. Carpenter.

- Within this lesson, in what way could word processing be used by Mr. Carpenter, by Jonathon, and by the members of the social studies classes?
- How could word processing help with the development of the initial group brainstorming of the key questions?
- How could word processing be used to complete research on the selected topics? Could word processing increase the potential creativity and/or the breadth of the research of the students?
- In what way could the use of word processing be helpful in the design and development of the comparison table? Would its value increase as information was input and periodically updated?
- How could word processing facilitate the development and production of the assigned reflective paper? Could word processing allow for additional insights and levels of creative thought and/or comparison?
- Could word processing facilitate increased levels of communication between Jonathon and the classes of social studies students?
- Could word processing impact the creation, production, and dissemination of the final executive summary report?
- Are there potential problems and pitfalls if word processing is integrated within this lesson and its respective assignments?

Workout: Integrating word processing

Now it's your turn. Complete the following steps to this Workout as you think about the future use of word processing within an applied setting.

1. Read each of the following situations. Imagine being directly involved in the planning for each of these projects. Select one (or more if you wish) for further consideration.

Roller Park Proposal:

The mayor of Billingsburg has asked the city parks engineers to create a proposal for a park that would focus on roller blade activities for city youth. The park can be located on city land adjacent to the new city swimming pool. To accomplish this task, the city engineers have contacted the local middle schools and high schools, and asked the students to make recommendations for the proposal. They want students to suggest layouts of the parks, types of jumps, obstacles, and activities that should be integrated, proposed fees for the use of the park, and so on. They have even asked the students to propose the types of safety features that should be included.

The Greatest Decade:

During the twentieth century many wonderful, sad, horrifying, and satisfying events occurred. But was there one decade that shines above the rest as making the greatest impact? How and why should one decade be selected over the others as being the "most significant" decade of the twentieth century? How can the strengths and weaknesses of each decade be effectively exposed, compared, and debated?

Senior Citizens and Young Mentors:

The activities chairperson at Heritage Retirement Center is constantly being asked for lessons on basic computer skills. Many residents of the Center desire to use the available computers to type letters, send e-mail, and surf the Internet. The activities chairperson contacts a neighborhood elementary class of fourth and fifth graders to come to Heritage and mentor the residents. Her thoughts are to have the children and the residents work together to produce a newsletter that could be published and distributed. The contents of the publication could be stories from the lives of the residents.

Making a Copy:

The high school media specialist is worried that many of her students may not fully understand the ramifications of copyright infringement. She notes that they seem to freely copy and distribute music CDs, pictures from the Internet, and even papers for various school class reports. She decides that perhaps a discussion is in order where small groups of students can debate the pros and cons of copyright law in today's digital world.

2. Based on your selected project, consider the following questions found within the Integration Assessment Questionnaire. Mark your response to each question.

Integration assessment questionnaire (IAQ)

Will using **WORD PROCESSING** software as a part of the project:			
Broaden the learners' perspective on potential solution paths and/or answers?	___ Yes	___ No	___ Maybe
Increase the level of involvement and investment of personal effort by the learners?	___ Yes	___ No	___ Maybe
Increase the level of learner motivation (e.g., increase the relevance of the to-be-learned task, the confidence of dealing with the task, and/or the overall appeal of the task)?	___ Yes	___ No	___ Maybe
Decrease the time needed to generate potential solutions?	___ Yes	___ No	___ Maybe
Increase the quality and/or quantity of learner practice working on this and similar projects?	___ Yes	___ No	___ Maybe
Increase the quality and/or quantity of feedback given to the learner?	___ Yes	___ No	___ Maybe
Enhance the ability of the student to solve novel, but similar, projects, tasks, and problems in the future?	___ Yes	___ No	___ Maybe

3. If you have responded "Yes" to one or more of the IAQ questions, you should consider the use of word processing to enhance the student's potential learning experience.
4. Using the example lesson plan, develop a lesson plan based on your selected project. Within the plan, indicate how and when the learner will use word processing. Additionally, list potential benefits and challenges that may occur when involving this software within the lesson.

Workout: Exploring the NETS Standard connection

Developing a lesson plan, as suggested in the previous Workout, which integrates the use of word processing, directly addresses several of the NETS Standards for both teachers (NETS*T) and students (NETS*S). For a full listing of the standards, refer to appendix B.

Part A: In a straightforward manner, NETS*T Standard V.C. for teachers and NETS*S Standard 3 for students indicate that you should be able to apply technology to increase productivity. With the use of word processing it is relatively simple to demonstrate the increased productivity you can achieve (e.g., rapidly editing and reproducing a saved lesson plan). However, reflect on the following questions and consider how the integration of word processing may impact other areas addressed by different technology standards:

- How can the use of word processing help develop students' higher order skills and creativity? Is there something about the use of the word processor that may enhance the exploration of alternative ideas, thinking patterns, solutions, or that may positively impact overall student creativity? (NETS*T III.C.; NETS*S 3)
- In what ways could word processing be used to facilitate the communication and collaboration between teachers, students, parents, and subject matter experts on specific projects that ultimately impact student learning? (NETS*T V.D.; NETS*S 4)
- How can word processing improve how the collection, analysis, and assessment of student work or data are completed? Can this increased information be used to improve the learning environment and experience? (NETS*T IV.B.;V.B.; NETS*S 5)

Part B: Go to the International Society for Technology in Education (ISTE) *Web site* http://cnets.iste.org. Within that site, select to review either the student or the teacher NETS Standards. Once you have selected the standards to review, select either the student or teacher profiles and look for the corresponding scenarios. Review the scenarios and determine how the word processor can be used within several of those situations.

While visiting the ISTE Web site and exploring the scenarios, go to the lesson plan search area and select a number of different lesson plans of interest. Review those and determine the role (if any) of word processing within the development, implementation, and assessment of the lesson. Note this both from the perspective of the teacher developing the lesson and from the perspective of the student participating in the implemented lesson.

Workout: Comprehensive integration

You need to understand that in most practical learning situations, one type of software generally doesn't stand alone as *the* solution. That is, full integration may mean that you use word processing *and* other software such as Web development, spreadsheets, and data management. For this Workout:

1. Read through the lesson plan you designed within the previous Workout.
2. Identify how your suggestions for the integration of word processing may be enhanced by the use of other software (e.g., Web development or presentation software).
3. Describe the benefits and the problems that may be associated with the integration of other software within the same project.
4. Describe how additional technology standards (e.g., NETS*T II.A.: "...design developmentally appropriate learning opportunities that apply technology-enhanced instructional strategies to support the diverse needs of learners") can be addressed by the integration of various types of applications software.

Further ideas on using word processing as a learning tool

When students are involved in using the word processor, the task frequently revolves around generating a written report of some kind. The word processor is a great tool to facilitate reflection, generation, and editing of materials.

> **Note:** These ideas are to help you generate your own ideas of what can be done. Don't let it bother you if they are not the right content or grade level—use the idea and adapt it to be helpful within your own situation. These are meant to be stimuli for additional ideas.

Here are a few ideas that may help you see how the word processor might be beneficial:

1. Create a table and have the students fill in the blanks, or have them create the frame themselves. For example, on the axis on the left side include different types of Native Americans and where they lived. Along the top table row or axis, put categories of clothing, shelter, tools, or food sources. Have the students fill in the cells of the table and make predictions about the relationships between climate and their tools, shelter, and so forth.

2. Compose and format different types of letters (e.g., business, personal, memo, cover letter, persuasive communication, and letter to the editor) and then compare the different styles of writing.

3. Have students conduct research by generating data gathering instruments (e.g., questionnaires), describing procedures, and then summarizing the results.

4. Have learners create an assessment rubric that outlines all criteria for a group project presentation.

5. Have students write a group report using comments and tracking in the word processor to monitor who makes which comments and suggestions within the document.

6. Have students develop a brochure about a specific historical topic (e.g., colonial America), their personal work history and skills (e.g., jobs they have held and what they have done), or places they may someday travel (e.g., Australian Outback).

7. Have learners use the word processor's outlining function, and brainstorm and design a required group presentation.

8. Given specific paragraphs from the writings of famous authors, have students identify and highlight nouns, verbs, adjectives, and so on, in various electronic highlighter colors.

9. Have students review a paragraph or document that contains highlighted target words. Have them use the thesaurus and change the words to add clarity to the document.

10. Have students work in groups to develop divergent viewpoints about historical controversies (e.g., American Japanese internment camps; Star Wars Defense System; Antitrust settlements of AT&T and/or Microsoft). Their written points and counterpoints can then be summarized, shared, and discussed within a single document.

11. Have students evaluate a set of instructional materials (e.g., a biology CD) and give their opinions on its value, what they felt was worthwhile, and what they felt could have been improved to make it more effective.

12. Have students develop (or complete) a matching game that consists of a table of anatomy terms in one column and a picture of various anatomical structures in the other column.

13. Have learners create original poetry and combine it with an inspirational photo as a background to their written work.

14. Have students use voice recognition software and compose a short story about living in a world without the use of one's eyes and/or hands.

15. Have students identify three college scholarship applications that require short essays as part of the application process. Have them create word-processed responses to those essay questions.

Additional ideas on using the word processor as an assistant

1. **School Conduct Report.** Create a table that highlights all of the rules of class conduct and provides cells to report when the rule was not followed.
2. **Communication Report.** Create a template that allows you to monitor how often notes are sent to parents or supervisors about a student.
3. **Certificates.** Create certificates for extra effort and merit.
4. **Progress reports.** Develop reports to keep students (and parents) informed of what has been accomplished and what is still needed.
5. **Work sheets.** Construct various types of worksheets and/or directions for projects.
6. **Individual Education Plans (IEPs).** Develop IEP templates that can be altered and adjusted for each individual student.
7. **Calendars.** Develop and use daily, weekly, and/or monthly assignment or work calendars.
8. **Weekly lesson planning.** Develop a table template of all weekly planning for lessons and subjects.
9. **Badges and labels.** Produce name badges for students, class helpers, and parents and/or labels for files, folders, and so forth.
10. **Programs.** Develop programs and handouts for school productions.
11. **Newsletters.** Write weekly or monthly classroom newsletters containing relevant information for students and parents.
12. **Permission slips.** Develop permission slips for events such as field trips, bus rides, and authorized school activities.
13. **Makeup work assignments.** Develop a template for helping students who have missed school so they know what was missed and when it should be completed.
14. **Volunteer schedules and job responsibilities.** Create a document that explains job responsibilities and schedules for individuals who volunteer at the school.
15. **Reminders.** Write memos to remind students about their assignments or to sign up to complete tasks (e.g., bring snacks or give a report).
16. **Class activities.** For example, develop a short script for a play that includes text columns for sets, narration, costumes, and scenes. Use graphics to draw basic areas of the stage, and show where actors and scenery will be placed.

Word Processing References

Teachers using word processing

Online tutorials and Web sites *are not always reliably available*: therefore, going to a search engine (e.g., www.google.com) and then using productive search terms is very important. If you need more help with how to search the Web effectively—check out Crib Note 10 on Simple Web Search Procedures (appendix A).

Search terms for finding sites that have lesson plans for school topics that involve using word processing:

- **Word processing lesson plans**
- **"Lesson plans," "word processing"**

Examples of such sites include the following:

http://www.teach-nology.com/teachers/lesson_plans/computing/

Lesson plans that focus on the use of the computer are found at this site. As you look through the list, those that focus on word processing are easily identified.

http://www.dpi.state.nc.us/Curriculum/Computer.skills/lssnplns/wordproc/wp_toc.htm

This is a collection of word processing specific lesson plans for grades two through eight.

http://desktoppub.about.com/cs/wordprojects/

Here you can find ideas and tutorials on how to use word processing for different projects.

Tutorials and other resources

Search terms for learning how to use word processors and other useful tips:

- **Word processing tutorials**
- **Word processing tips**

Example tutorial sites that should prove helpful:

http://www.jegsworks.com/Lessons/words/index.html

Excellent Web site that has tutorials to introduce the basics of word processing and outlines three different projects that include using advanced tools, as well as making brochures and reports.

http://www.fgcu.edu/support/office2000/word/

This is Florida Gulf Coast University's Online Tutorials. Well-designed tutorials detail how to work with text, format paragraphs, use styles, and so on.

http://www.microsoft.com/education

Select tutorials and other instructional materials for all Microsoft products across various grade levels and subject areas can be found here.

http://www.findtutorials.com/

This is a Web site that helps you find specific tutorials. Once the welcome page appears, click the *Tutorials* tab and then insert the term *word* in the search function. All kinds of tutorials for how to do things with MS Word and other word processors will be identified and highlighted.

	Desired task to accomplish	Reference menu or toolbar*
Basic Tools	Create a new document	**File>>>New . . .**
	Access toolbars	**View>>>Toolbars**
	Access task panes	**View>>>Task Pane**
	Adapt view of workspace	**View>>>**[normal, web layout, print layout, outline]
	Insert text	**Click on workspace, begin typing**
	Insert picture	**Insert>>>Picture**
	Insert table	**Table>>>Insert>>>Table**

Desired task to accomplish	Reference menu or toolbar*
Formatting Features	
Text (font type, color, size, effect)	**Format>>>Font . . .**
Paragraph (alignment, indention, line spacing)	**Format>>>Paragraph . . .**
Picture (text alignment, contrast, color, size)	**View>>>Toolbars>>>Picture**
Tables (alter rows, columns, cells, properties)	**Table>>>**[insert, delete, merge cells, table properties]; *also* **View>>>Toolbars>>>Tables and Borders**
Columns	**Format>>>Columns . . .**
Page and section breaks	**Insert>>>Break . . .**
Page numbers	**Insert>>>Page Numbers . . .**
Tabs	**Format>>>Tabs . . .**
Headers and footers	**View>>>Header and Footer**
Margins	**Format>>>Paragraph;** *also* **View>>>Ruler**
Lists	**Format>>>Bullets and Numbering . . .**
Borders	**Format>>>Border and Shading . . .**
Shading	**Format>>>Border and Shading . . .**
Additional Features	
Text special effects	**Format>>>Font . . .>>>tab: Text Effects**
Themes	**Format>>>Theme . . .**
Symbols	**Insert>>>Symbol . . .**
Thesaurus	**Tools>>>Language>>>Thesaurus**
Comments	**Insert>>>Comment**
AutoShapes	**Insert>>>Picture>>>AutoShapes**
WordArt	**Insert>>>Picture>>>WordArt**
Track changes	**Tools>>>Track Changes**
Forms	**View>>>Toolbar>>>Forms**
Word count	**Tools>>>Word Count . . .**
Envelopes and labels	**Tools>>>Letters and Mailings>>>Envelopes and Labels . . .**
Text direction	**Format>>>Text Direction . . .**
Linking to the Internet	**Insert>>>Hyperlink . . .**
Readability statistics	**Tools>>>Options>>>tab: Spelling and Grammar>>>check "show readability statistics"**

*NOTE: The first item listed is the Main Menu or toolbar. As explained earlier in chapter 1, the >>> indicates the selection to be made once a drop-down menu has been revealed. For example, **View>>>Task Panes** means to click on the View option of the Main Menu bar. This exposes a drop-down menu, and from that menu you can click the Task Pane option. This activates the relevant Task Pane window.

Chapter 3
SPREADSHEETS
MS Excel: The Basics of a "Number Cruncher"

Introduction

What should you know about spreadsheets?

Spreadsheets are designed to help you work with numbers—not just for normal adding, subtracting, and so on, but also for comparing, predicting, and evaluating. Beyond numbers, this software deals with text in a way that teachers can find very helpful. Within this introduction to spreadsheets, we want you to discover

- what a spreadsheet is, what it can do, and how it can help in teaching and learning;
- how to justify the use of the spreadsheet as an effective tool—by knowing when and why it should or shouldn't be used.

Terms to know

cell	*row*	*column*
formula	*function*	*chart*
worksheet	*View menu*	

What is a spreadsheet and what does it do?

Spreadsheets are remarkable tools that allow you to organize, calculate, and present data (generally, this data has to do with numbers—but not always). These tools organize the world into a grid of rows and columns.

A grade book is a familiar example for most teachers. Within an electronic spreadsheet grade book, you not only can quickly find and organize data for each student, but the spreadsheet can be set up to do the needed calculations automatically. Just as quickly, you can rearrange how the grade book looks and how grades are calculated. Figure 3.1 shows a very simple form of such a grade book.

Student's Name	Project 1	Project 2	Project 3	Total
Andersen, Adam	13	14	13	40
Butler, Julie	14	15	15	44
Jersey, Sara	12	11	13	36
Johnson, Billy	15	14	15	44
Nesbit, Brayden	11	10	9	30
Rendolf, Kelsy	15	15	15	45

Figure 3.1 Simple grade book spreadsheet

What are some commonly used spreadsheets?

- Microsoft's Excel
- Lotus 1-2-3
- Corel's Quattro Pro
- Sun Microsystems' StarOffice Calc
- The spreadsheet program within Microsoft's Works
- The spreadsheet program within Appleworks (formerly Clarisworks)

> **Note:** We focus on Microsoft's Excel in this book. However, **what we present can be done in any of the other spreadsheets listed.** So if you don't have access to MS Excel, don't be alarmed—you can still complete the projects and learn the basic skills.

Why bother learning how to use a spreadsheet?

- **To cut your time.** Just think about it—if you have six class periods in a day with twenty to twenty-five students in each period, and over the course of the grading period you record a dozen assignments, three quizzes, and two tests, you have over two thousand scores to record! Think of the time it takes to calculate totals, subtotals, averages, and so forth, during the course of a semester. The spreadsheet can calculate automatically for you.
- **To cut your mistakes.** If you are continually entering and reentering the same data over and over, you will eventually punch in the wrong number. Having the computer do the calculations can overcome many of the little problems that creep in because of fat fingers, tired eyes, and low power cells (yours and the calculator's).
- **To use the work of experts.** Maybe you don't know much about certain statistical, accounting, or other mathematical formulas and functions. Many of these are built into an electronic spreadsheet. Instead of creating the formula, you just make a selection and the computer completes the calculation.
- **To allow predictions.** This software allows you to imagine what the possibilities are if the current course of action continues or if some changes are made ("What if . . . .").
- **To allow for quick repurposing.** Instead of constantly rebuilding from scratch (e.g., creating a new grade book for next semester's class), you can use a spreadsheet that is similar and just needs some quick adaptations. This is often faster than starting over.
- **To help you adapt your point of view.** Through the use of charts that can be quickly and easily generated from the spreadsheet, what was once a bunch of rows and columns of numbers can now be seen as simple, understandable trends and answers to problems unnoticed before.

How can spreadsheets be used at school? A brief list of ideas

By the teacher:

- Grade books
- School class expense budget
- Track fund-raiser sales
- Highlight relationships and trends graphically
- Create class seating charts

By the student:

- Math assignments
- Assignment planners
- Personal budgets
- Science reports for calculating and reporting results
- Chart personal goals and progress

Workout

Think about Bob Cratchet from *A Christmas Carol* by Charles Dickens (or imagine watching one of a dozen animated videos, including *Mickey's Christmas Carol*, based on Dickens' story). Bob spends a lot of time working in a huge account book for

Mr. Scrooge. That book is actually a spreadsheet (the old-fashioned kind that doesn't automatically complete the calculations). If there had been an electronic version at Bob's disposal, he probably could have left work early on Christmas Eve.

Generally, when using spreadsheets we think about what an accountant would use it for. For teachers, that accounting would focus on things like the course grade book. Look closely at the following subjects and be creative about how the electronic spreadsheet might allow you to do what might be impossible otherwise. Write some of your thoughts in the space provided.

Science: _____

_____

Math: _____

_____

Consumer and Family Science: _____

_____

_____

History: _____

_____

Geography: _____

_____

Orientation

What's the workspace look like?

Figure 3.2 depicts the workspace of a common spreadsheet (MS Excel). Note the workspace consists of designated *rows* and *columns* (where they intersect is known as *cells*). Similar to other programs, there are toolbars and menus placed around the workspace.

Those grids of rows, columns, and cells

Spreadsheets are designed to maximize organization. Think about it—everything on the sheet can be identified based on which row and/or column it resides within.

For convenience, numbers generally designate rows and letters designate columns. So if in your grade book you want to know how well Billy Johnson did on his third project, you can look for the row with Billy's name under the student name column, then locate the column that lists the third project. Where the row with Billy's name (row 5) and the column with the Project 3 scores (column D) intersect, that's where Billy's third project score (cell D5) is located.

A spreadsheet is a great way to organize certain parts of your world. Mapmakers use this system to help you find exact locations—city planners may call them streets, avenues, and blocks—but they have the same idea. And of course, accountants know all about such grids for keeping track of income, expenses, and totals.

What can go in the cells?

In an electronic spreadsheet, something interesting happens. Within any one cell you can insert words (*Project 1*, *Student's Name*, etc.), numbers (actual scores on projects), variables (=B5, which tells the spreadsheet to find cell B5, copy what it finds there, and insert whatever it finds into the current cell), or even mathematical formulas or functions (*B5 + D5*, which instructs the spreadsheet to add the number found in cell B5 to that found in cell D5).

This opens up all sorts of possibilities. Pretty soon you can envision a grade book that has your students' names in one column, as well as a set of cells that includes scores for all of their assignments, projects, and so on. Additionally, you should begin to see that there may be cells containing formulas that add up all the scores for individual students,

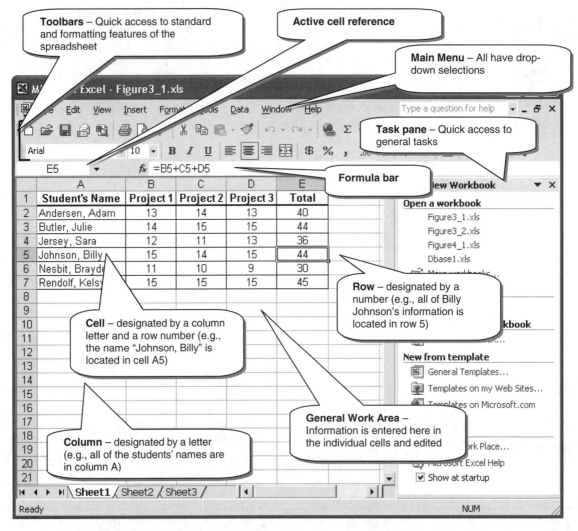

Figure 3.2 View of Microsoft Excel spreadsheet work area with simple grade book

provide averages, show high and low scores, and so forth. All of these can be accomplished simply by controlling what happens in the cells.

The "power of manipulation": Using functions and formulas

The power of the spreadsheet is in how it manipulates numbers. Within those cells it is possible to write formulas or equations that complete calculations on the data recorded in the spreadsheet. So not only does the spreadsheet organize, it can also manipulate the data through addition, subtraction, and so on.

Look at the simple grade book example in Figure 3.2. In cell E5 we have inserted a simple addition formula to add up all Billy Johnson's scores. When the cell is highlighted, a formula (=B5+C5+D5) can be inserted on the formula bar line; however, once activated, cell E5 automatically (and very quickly) reveals the total of those scores. Once that formula is inserted, if a change to any of Billy's scores occurs, the total found in cell E5 *automatically updates*.

The "power of 'what if . . .'"

Sometimes it helps if you can imagine what would happen if ____ (you fill in the blank). What if . . . I had married my high school boyfriend? What if . . . I decreased my calorie intake of food by 20 percent for the next two months? What if . . . I made 10 percent more than I do now? What if . . . Billy Johnson had scored a 15 on Project 2?

We doubt that the first "What if . . . "will be helped by a spreadsheet; however, for the last three it can play an important part. Because it can calculate quickly with relative ease, you can plug in formulas and then readjust those formulas to see immediately different types of results based on certain variable factors. That is, you can make projections or estimations of how things would be "if . . . ."

Imagine what you can do with your students, then, when you discuss world populations and the impact of a population growth that increases by 6 percent instead of 3 percent over the next ten years. Perhaps you could get them to understand the mindset of those in a third world nation who attempt to leave their country when inflation hits an all time high and the value of their country's money drops by 30 percent over a short period of time.

It's very powerful to be able to "see into the future." Most individuals can't do this (although some profess to have this ability—call 1-900-ICANSEE). However, with a spreadsheet some different scenarios can be played out so that predictions can be made accurately if specific situations occur.

Seeing the possibilities

Spreadsheets are the darlings of number manipulators. However, some of us can't see everything we need when given a big grid of numbers. Another wonderment of spreadsheets is that they can take the numbers and convert them to various graphs and charts with relative ease. (For help in creating charts, see Crib Note 8, Charting Excel Data, in appendix A.) In this way, instead of seeing a column of numbers, you can see a bar, line, pie, or column chart. Magically, the numbers turn into revealing pictures.

Sometimes looking at data differently allows important correlations to stand out. For example, for a middle school student, a list of all the average weekly temperatures for Indianapolis, Indiana; Bahrain, Saudi Arabia; and Santiago, Chile, may not mean much other than a big bunch of numbers. Showing those same numbers as overlapping different colored line graphs, however, may suddenly turn on light bulbs about how temperature can vary across these widely dispersed cities. You could do the same for personal budgets, speeds on the 100 meter dash, cars crossing various bridges over the same river in downtown Chicago, and the growth of a classroom of students over the course of a semester.

> **Note:** It doesn't take a brain surgeon to figure out that by combining the "What if . . . " function with the graphing function, you can perceive possible relationships and how you can prepare for those possibilities.

Workout: Explore the territory

Turn on the computer and launch your spreadsheet program. Once it's running, try the following:

1. Examine the Main Menu (usually found across the top of the screen). Click each Menu title (e.g., File, Edit) and note the various selections available under each. You won't need all of these, but it's a good idea to know where to find them. Pay special attention to where the Help menu is located.

2. Under the View menu, drop down to the Toolbar selection and make sure the Standard and Formatting toolbars are checked (**View>>>Toolbars>>>Standard or Formatting**)—see Figure 2.2. These are the common toolbars you will use (also note that there are several others available and later we access and use those).
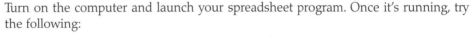

3. Note that the tools on the toolbars show icons representing what the tool is for. If you lay the mouse pointer over any specific tool (don't click), the name of the tool appears. Use of the toolbars is a fast way of accessing commonly used tools.

4. Click any cell in the spreadsheet workspace. Enter a word or a number into the cell. Highlight some or all of the words you enter, and then click on various tool icons on the Formatting toolbar. Note how your highlighted words change based on the tool that you have selected. Also note the Formula bar and how it reflects which cell is currently selected (active) and what is in that cell.

5. Play with it for a few minutes so you get a feel for what can be done and how easy it is to use.

Level 1: Designing, Creating, and Producing a Grade Book

What should you be able to do?

At this level, the emphasis is on using various tools and techniques of the spreadsheet software to create a document given specific guidelines and step-by-step procedures.

The situation . . .

John Rena has just arrived at the newly constructed Heaton Middle School. It's great being in a new school, but the network to the school PCs is not on line yet, and it may be some time before it is. John has access to his class computer, but he really needs to begin to set up and store his grades for his various classes. He has never created an electronic grade book on his own, but he has heard that it isn't all that tough, so he's willing to give it a try. To help, he pulls out last year's printout of one of his class grade book pages completed on the school's special grade book program (see Figure 3.3). To begin, he just wants to reproduce it exactly on his PC's spreadsheet program.

The plan

- Take a close look at Figure 3.3. This is an example of John's grade book page. Figure 3.4 displays the same data, but it highlights all the unique features that have been added to the spreadsheet so it looks and works like a professional product.
- We want you to follow the step-by-step procedures and reproduce the grade book page with all of the key features included. It doesn't have to be an exact replica, but we want you to demonstrate that you can carry out the highlighted functions.

	A	B	C	D	E	F	G	H	I
1									
2									
3									
4									
5									
6									
7				Science - 3rd Period					
8									
9	Last Name	First Name	Assign 1	Assign 2	Quiz 1	Quiz 2	Final	Overall	
10	Barrymore	Cade	15	12	24	29	85		
11	DeFore	Alexis	15	15	29	30	97		
12	Drury	Landon	9	8	22	20	65		
13	Jeski	Robert	10	11	22	25	78		
14	Moreno	Elizabeth	11	12	20	28	82		
15	Packard	Dale	12	14	27	25	90		
16	Polk	Madison	13	14	26	27	88		
17	Saterwaite	Kimberly	13	10	26	26	80		
18	Smith	Fiona	15	14	27	28	92		
19	Washington	Violet	6	12	18	26	73		
20									
21	Class Average								
22	Highest Score								
23									

Figure 3.3 Mr. Rena's third-period science grade book unfinished and unformatted

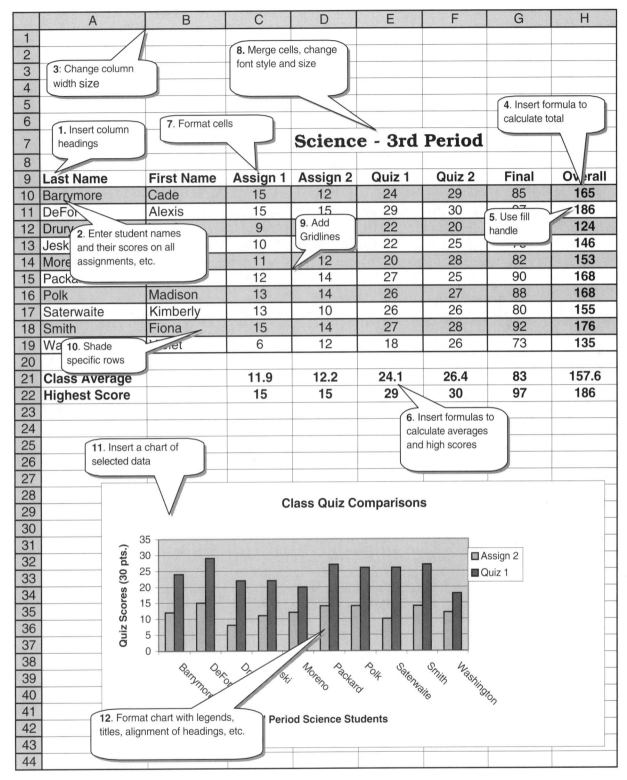

Figure 3.4 Third-period science grade book spreadsheet with finishing and formatting steps highlighted

Workout: By the numbers . . .

CD ACTIVITY

1. Launch your spreadsheet application program (e.g., Microsoft Excel).
2. Open the existing unformatted version of the document on the CD (**File >> Open . . .**). Then navigate to the CD, view the CD contents and open the chp3_SS folder, launch (double-click) the "grades1" file within that folder), or if you like, you can open a new worksheet and type in the information yourself. Once opened (or once you have typed it in), your spreadsheet should look something like Figure 3.3.

> **Note:** If you need some help launching a program and/or accessing files on another drive such as a CD, check out the Crib Notes in appendix A for a little extra guidance.

3. Look again at Figure 3.4. Note the numbers. Those numbers correspond to Figure 3.3, and what you will do to complete the grade book.

No.	To Do	How to Get It Done
1.	**Insert column headings**	**Goal:** Design the basic grade book with the proper column headings. **Steps:** 1. To insert a column heading, click the cell where you want to begin. For our example, click cell A9 and then type the words *Last Name*. Hit the tab key and cell B9 is highlighted. Type in *First Name*. Hit the tab key and continue until all of the headings have been entered. > **Note:** It's not necessary to leave blank rows at the top of the spreadsheet workspace. If you want to add or delete rows (or columns) later, that can be easily completed. 2. To navigate from one cell to the next, use the mouse and click the desired cell destination, use the tab key, or use the arrow keys. > **Note:** If you make a mistake, don't panic. Click the cell that you want to change, then go to the Formula bar at the top of your spreadsheet (usually just under the toolbars) and make your changes there. 3. Copy, cut, and paste work fine in this application. If you find you need to enter in headings that are similar (e.g., *Assignment 1, 2, 3, 4, . . .*) and you don't want to type the words over and over, you can copy the heading and then continually paste it into the cells as needed. For more information on Copying, Cutting, and Pasting, see Crib Note 4 in appendix A.
2.	**Enter student names and main data of the spreadsheet**	**Goal:** Enter in all of the main data for the spreadsheet. **Steps:** 1. Click cell A10 and enter in the last name of one of the students. Click the tab key and enter that student's first name (cell B10), click the tab key and enter the score for the first assignment (cell C10), and continue until all names and data have been entered. Leave the "Overall" column empty of all data. Additionally, don't put any data in for the "Class Averages" or the "Highest Score" rows. We'll do that in a moment. 2. If any entry errors are made, click on the cell and go to the Formula bar and make the needed editorial changes. Once finished with the editorial change, click the Enter key and the change occurs within the proper cell.

No.	To Do	How to Get It Done
3.	**Adjust column width (or row height)** 	**Goal:** Adjust column or row widths and heights. **Steps:** 1. Directly beneath the Formula bar, each column is labeled with a letter. Put your mouse pointer on the column border that divides column A and column B. The pointer changes into a two-headed arrow. 2. With the two-headed arrow showing, click and hold the mouse and drag it to the right or left. You will notice that as long as you have the mouse button held down, the width of column A will change based on your mouse movement. 3. Drag the mouse to the right and column A expands in size. Note that you want it wide enough to hold the longest last name of all your students. 4. When you have determined the correct size, release the mouse and the column size is altered. If you don't like it, you can immediately repeat the process and produce a different size.
4.	**Inserting a formula to calculate a total**	**Goal:** Learn to enter formulas. **Steps:** 1. Click cell H10. This is the cell where the overall score (sum of all other scores) should be calculated. 2. Instead of manually entering the total here, we enter a formula that instructs the spreadsheet how to complete the calculations and then post the result in this cell. 3. On the Formula bar enter the following equation: = Sum (C10:G10). This translates into: Sum up all of the totals found in cells C10 through G10 and put the total in cell H10. $$\boxed{\text{H10} \quad \blacktriangledown \qquad f_x \quad \text{=SUM(C10:G10)}}$$ **Note:** The equals sign (=) plays a key role. It tells the spreadsheet that what follows is an equation to be calculated. If you forget this, it will treat the equation as a simple set of text and it won't do any calculations. This is a common mistake—at least it is for me. **Note:** There are generally a number of ways to write these equations. A different way that also works is: =C10+D10+ E10+F10+G10.
5.	**Use the fill handle** **Overall** **165** Normal selected cell **Overall** **165** Mouse cursor overlaying the handle on a selected cell	**Goal:** Learn how to use the *fill handle* to incorporate the formula to other relative cells. **Steps:** 1. Once one formula has been constructed as in H10, you can use the same one for all the other totals that need to be calculated in the Overall column (H10 through H19). It's very simple and doesn't take much time. Click on cell H10. 2. A box is drawn around the total that now appears in that cell. Note that in the lower right-hand corner a small black square (known as a **handle**) appears. Place your cursor over that small handle and it will turn into a thin cross. 3. Click and hold the mouse and drag it from cell H10 to H19. Release the mouse—and behold what you have done. Totals have now been calculated for each student, using the correct scores for each. Actually, the formula that you created in H10 has been filled into all the other cells below it relative to the data in each cell's respective row. That is, the total for Cade Barrymore is based on his grades (found in cells C10 through G10), but Madison Polk's total is based on her scores found in C16 through G16.

continued

No.	To Do	How to Get It Done
		Note: Another way of completing this *"fill"* command is to enter the formula (or whatever you want to fill) into the cell (e.g., H10 in our example), select that cell and all other cells that you want to "fill," then go to **Edit>>>Fill>>>Down** (or Right, Up, Left). This eliminates the need to use the fill handles. This is also the more common way of completing a fill in other spreadsheet programs beside Excel.
6.	**More formulas and filling**	**Goal:** Practice using formulas and filling in those formulas. **Steps:** 1. Click cell C21 and enter the following formula on the Formula bar: =Average(C10:C19). Hit the Enter key and see if the average of Assign 1 is now reported in cell C21. 2. Click C21, find the handle, click, hold, and drag to the right. This should efficiently fill in the averages for all of the rest of the Assignments, Quizzes, Final, and Overall. 3. Repeat this procedure for the Highest Score row. Use this formula: =Max(C10:C19). 4. Use the fill handle to fill the formula across from C22 to G22. **Note:** The spreadsheet has lots of built-in functions. To view these, go to the Insert menu on the Main Menu bar and drop down to "Function . . ." **(Insert>>>Function . . .).** An Insert Function window (see Figure 3.5) appears that will help you select an appropriate function. You can also view the structure of the formula and if you desire you can have a wizard walk you through the setup and use of the formula.

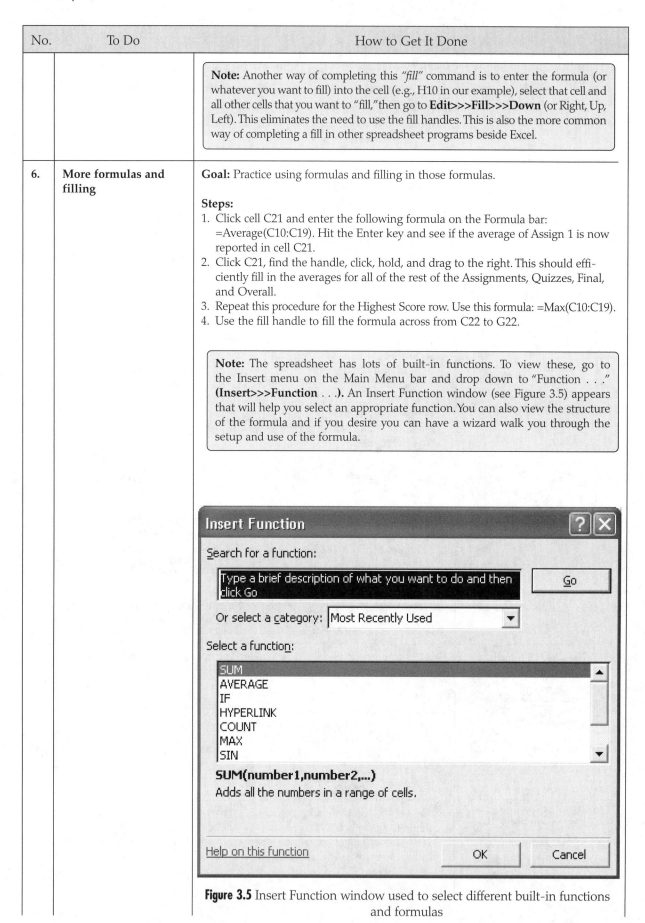

Figure 3.5 Insert Function window used to select different built-in functions and formulas

No.	To Do	How to Get It Done
7.	**Formatting cells (and their data contents)**	**Goal:** Format text and data (e.g., alignment, change font style) as needed.

Steps:

1. To change the alignment of column headings, cell data, and so on, select the cells that you want to affect. For example, select all the headings from cell A9 to H9.
2. On the Main Menu bar, select **Format >>>Cells . . . .** The Format Cells window opens. Examine all the possibilities within this window (note the tabs along the top of this window—click on a tab and it shows you what else can be done). See Figure 3.6 for a peek at what you can play with.
3. To change font style: (a) click the Font tab, and (b) select the type, style, size, color, and other effects you desire. Click the OK button and what you selected is applied to all selected cells.
4. To change the alignment (center, left, right, and so forth) or to change the direction of the words within your selected cell(s), click on the Alignment tab within the Format Cells window.

> **Note:** At times you may wish to have certain cells (e.g., column headings) enter the words vertically or at a slant. This Format Cells window is where you make such changes occur.

5. Other cell formatting functions include choosing borders for the cells, adding patterns to the cells, and protecting the cells in certain ways. All these functions are completed through this Cell Format window.

> **Note:** Selecting the cell(s) and then clicking the appropriate icons within the Formatting toolbar can accomplish similar formatting changes.

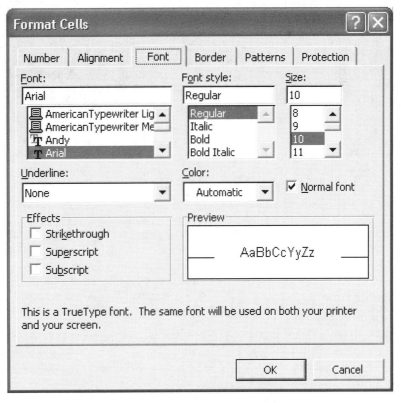

Figure 3.6 Format Cells window (Font tab is selected)

continued

No.	To Do	How to Get It Done
8.	**Cell merging and formatting**	**Goal:** Bring together (merge) several cells so that headings, for example, can be displayed. **Steps:** 1. At times it is appropriate to have several columns merge together to display data that would normally go beyond the single cell size. To do this, begin by selecting all the cells you want to merge. *Note:* The cells must be next to each other in the adjoining row(s) or column(s). 2. On the Formatting toolbar, click the Merge and Center icon. The cells are automatically merged. 3. To format the data in the cell, return to the Cell Format menu mentioned in Step 7 and use the same formatting functions listed there.
9.	**Add gridlines**	**Goal:** Add lines between selected rows and columns of data. **Steps:** 1. Select all the cells where you want borders displayed. 2. Again, return to the Cell Format window (**Format Menu >>> Cells . . .**) and select the Border tab. 3. Select the type of gridline, color, and location you want the line to be drawn. Then click the OK button to see what has happened. **Note:** There is also a border icon on the Formatting toolbar that can speed up this process. The down arrow indicates the different selections for border types.
10.	**Shading**	**Goal:** Shade in specific areas of the spreadsheet for emphasis or clarity. **Steps:** 1. Select the row(s), column(s), or cell(s) you wish to shade. **Note:** To select a whole row (or column), click the number associated with that row (or the letter for the column). The full row highlights all at once. To select more than one row, press and hold the Control key as you select the various rows you wish to highlight. In this way, multiple rows can be selected at any time. 2. Return to the Cell Format window (**Format>>>Cells . . .**) and select the Patterns tab. Select the color and/or pattern that you wish this row, column, or cell to contain, and then click OK.
11.	**Creating a chart of specific data**	**Goal:** Select any part of the data displayed in the spreadsheet and have it displayed in a visual chart format. **Steps:** 1. Select the data that you want to be displayed within the chart. In our example we selected cells A9–A19 [name of all students in the class *and* the title of that column (i.e., "Last Name")]. We did this by holding down the Control key, and clicking and holding the mouse key down while dragging the pointer from cell A9 down to cell A19. With the Control key continuously held down, Quiz 1 scores (Cell E9–E19) followed by Quiz 2 scores (Cell F9–F19) were selected. At this point, selected data (and headings) in column A, D, and E were highlighted. 2. On the Standard toolbar, click the Chart icon. A Chart Wizard appears and walks you through a step-by-step process of creating a chart for your data. Examine and explore what occurs as you try different alternatives within this Chart Wizard. 3. If you don't like your results, click anywhere on the chart itself, and a line and little black handles appear surrounding the chart. Click the Delete key and the chart is gone.

No.	To Do	How to Get It Done
		Note: A frequent mistake is not highlighting the heading of the column (e.g., Last Name, or Quiz 1) as the rest of the data is being selected. The spreadsheet may still create the chart, but without the headings the Chart Wizard will input its own set of titles that may or may not make sense to you.
12.	**Format changes on the chart**	**Goal:** Alter the appearance of the chart once it has been created. **Steps:** 1. If there are formatting changes that you would like to do on your chart, begin by clicking once anywhere on the chart so that the handles (small black squares) appear surrounding the chart. 2. To alter the size of the chart, click, hold, and drag one of the corner handles. The size alters based on the direction of your mouse drag. 3. Note that when the chart is selected (handles are revealed), a new alternative appears on the Main Menu—it is called "Chart." 4. Click on the Chart menu of the Main Menu bar and select "Chart Type . . ." if you want to alter the type of chart you have created; select "Chart options . . ." if you want to alter titles, location of the legend, and so on. 5. If you want to alter any of the individual pieces of information on the chart, point your mouse pointer on that individual piece (e.g., the individual name of a student) and double-click. A window pops up that allows you to format that piece of the chart (e.g., *x*-axis, *y*-axis, legend, titles, data points). **Note:** For more help with creating and formatting charts within spreadsheets, review Crib Note 8 on Charting Excel Data in appendix A.

Level 2: "What If's . . . ," Formatting, and Functions

What should you be able to do?

In this section we want you to learn to recognize and use additional spreadsheet features, as well as to understand how to use the **Help** feature of the software effectively.

With this instruction, you should be able to create, edit, and format several original data sets into a spreadsheet format and use formulas to compare, analyze, and summarize the data.

A little story . . .

Barry Pfleger couldn't believe what he had just been "volunteered" for. As an assistant soccer coach, he was "asked" to take charge of the Woodrow High School "Gotta Have It" Spirit Store. Originally, the store's inventory had been helpful in getting students to purchase and use items like pencils, paper, flags, and clothing all with the school Whippoorwill logo engraved or embossed. Additionally, the extra revenue, although not great, had been used to purchase a few extra pieces of equipment for various "Fightin' Whipper" athletic teams.

Over the course of the last few semesters, however, the inventory had gotten old, products weren't ordered correctly, and the store hadn't been open for regular "business."

Barry was a pretty good English teacher, but he wasn't too sure about learning the retail business. Perhaps Joan Sanchez in the business department could help him. She snickered when she heard of his new responsibilities, but she promised to help.

"First," she began, "you really need to determine where you are. So, get into the store and count everything that's there. Record what the item is, how many you have, and if possible how much it originally cost." She quickly drew a grid on the chalkboard (see Figure 3.7) and labeled the rows "*Item*"; her columns had labels of "*Quantity*" and "*Original cost.*"

"When you get the inventory counted," she stated, "come see me again and I will help you with projections. That should give you some notion of what you have, what you need, pricing—whatever."

Item	Quantity	Original cost
#1		
#2		
#3		
...		

Figure 3.7 Start of a simple inventory spreadsheet

Getting some Help

Similar to **Help** in Windows, there is also **Help** in MS Excel and most other sophisticated spreadsheet software. To use **Help**, click the **Help menu>>>Microsoft Excel Help**. A **Help** window opens, and by clicking the Answer Wizard tab you can type in your question and **Help** will respond with a variety of potential answers for you to investigate. To get a general overview of what **Help** has to offer, click on the Contents tab.

Help generally *does not* have all of the answers—but it will have a lot of them. Make sure you become familiar with how it works and how often it can be of assistance.

> **Note:** Check out Getting and Using **Help,** Crib Note 6, in appendix A for more information and insights on using the **Help** feature.

Explore: Inventory of the "Gotta Have It" Spirit Store

Within Level 2 of this software application, the inventory sheet of the Fightin' Whippers may not seem all that relevant to you. That's OK. However, we do want to point out a few things so that you can attempt to incorporate them on other more relevant projects.

Look closely at Figure 3.8 (inventory) and note what we have included: "spirit" items, how many of each, the cost of each, and so on. We have also implemented various formatting functions (such as style of numbers, word wrap within cells, merging of cells). There are also a number of ways that this spreadsheet could be expanded.

Workout: Stretching with a little Help . . .

After Barry completed this inventory sheet, he returned it to Joan. Upon quick examination, she suggested that the next step would be to recreate it as an electronic spreadsheet; then a formula could be used to calculate the wholesale subtotal. In addition, she suggested adding some columns. These extra columns could reveal some subtotals for how much the inventory was worth now (wholesale price × the quantity of a specific item). Additionally, columns could be set up to show what the cost of each item would be if it were sold for a markup of 25, 50, or 60 percent.

We aren't explaining exactly how to do each, but we do give you the example of the feature and critical questions you can think about and investigate (via Help/Office Assistant) to find the needed answers.

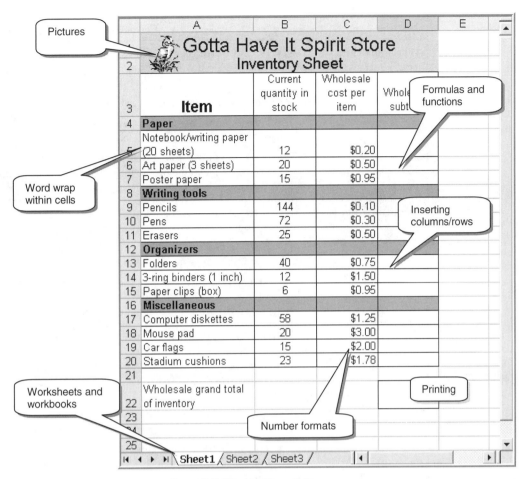

Figure 3.8 "Gotta Have It" inventory

Feature	Ask the Office Assistant (Help)
Formulas and functions	• **What is a formula?** Look in the sections about calculating with formulas and the section dealing with constructing a formula. • **What is a function?** This is related to formulas and understanding one will facilitate your understanding of the other. You need these for the spreadsheet to complete the needed number calculations. • **How do you format formulas?** • **Also investigate:** How to use formulas/functions.
Insert columns and/or rows	• **How do you insert a column, row, or cell?** Select the section on adding rows and columns. It's a very simple procedure.
Word wrap within cells	• **How do you get multiple lines of text to be displayed within a single cell?** • **Also investigate:** Troubleshoot formatting cells.
Number formats	• **What are the different ways numbers can be formatted?** At times you will need to display numbers with varied amounts of decimal places, as currency, as a date or time, or in some customized manner. These all can be handled automatically. • **Also investigate:** Troubleshoot numbering formats.

continued

Feature	Ask the Office Assistant (Help)
Workbooks and worksheets	• **What are workbooks and worksheets?** Check out the section, "About workbooks and worksheets." These are helpful when you have several related spreadsheet files. • **How can a worksheet be used?** • **How do you create a new worksheet?** Select the section on "Inserting a new worksheet." • **How do you rename a worksheet?** This guides you in how to change the name on the tabs to indicate which worksheet you are working on.
Inserting graphics or pictures	• **How do you insert a picture?** Pictures or graphics can be added to spreadsheets. • **How do you edit a picture?** If you need to change the size, crop it in some way, and so forth, Help can help. • **Also investigate:** Another good location for information is asking Help, "How do you edit a graphic in a chart?" Lots of good links of information are revealed.
Charts	• **How do you format a chart?** Select the section on "About formatting charts" and some good basic information about charts becomes available. It explains how to change the appearance of the chart and alter various pieces of information within the chart. • **How do you edit a chart?** Subtle wording change, but Help changes the type and quantity of the information it provides. • **Also investigate:** See Crib Note 8, Charting Excel Data, in appendix A for more detailed information on how to develop and edit an Excel chart.
Printing	• **How do you print a worksheet on one page?** Select the section, "Print a worksheet to fit a paper width or a number of pages." • **Also investigate:** Select the section, "About printing," to get further information on how printing in Excel is accomplished and what can be done to alter the way in which worksheets are printed.

CD ACTIVITY

Before moving on to your own work, you might want to have some fun with the "Gotta Have It" Store.

1. Go to the accompanying CD, open the chp3_SS folder, and then launch (double-click) the "gotta1" spreadsheet file.
2. Develop a formula in cell D5 that automatically calculates the subtotal wholesale cost of all notebooks currently in stock.
3. Fill down the cells under D5 so that a similar formula calculates all wholesale costs for the entire inventory.
4. In cell D22 develop a formula that calculates the grand total of the wholesale cost of the current inventory.
5. Create a new column (E) and put in the following heading: "Retail Price—25% Markup."
6. Develop a formula that takes the wholesale price of an object and raises it by 25 percent (*Hint:* Multiply the wholesale price by 1.25) and then multiplies that total by the listed number in the inventory.
7. Fill down this 25 percent markup retail for all items in the store.

8. Answer the following:

- What if the markup was 50 or 60 percent?
- How can the spreadsheet be used to make such comparisons?
- Can you create a chart that compares profits for the school given the different retail markup levels?
- Can you see how such "What if . . ." information can be used to help make projections and estimations of future needs and profits?
- Can you also see how this could be used with a grade book to monitor current progress of students and project what will be needed in order for specific levels of achievement to be attained?

Now that you have seen a couple of examples of spreadsheets and how they are constructed and formatted, it's time to try your hand at it.

Workout: Create your spreadsheet

With this information and example, go ahead and create a spreadsheet you can use. Keep it simple in the beginning. Perhaps it can be something to do with fund-raisers, book orders, a home budget, car expenses, or exercising.

Adapt the spreadsheet so that it is something you can use. Make sure you include formulas or predefined functions that help with the calculations. Try to include a "What if . . ." within your spreadsheet to give you an idea of the possibilities (e.g., What if your school district gave you a 40 percent raise next year—how would that impact your personal budget?).

Don't forget one of the Rules to Live By: **Save your work.**

One final note: After you work on your spreadsheet, think about different ways that it could be used for other similar types of projects. Make a note of how it can be adapted, and then use it as a "template" to guide the development and use of other spreadsheets that may be needed.

Level 3: Integration and Application

What should you be able to do?

This is where you can use this software to help yourself and your students. This section will aid you in discovering the many applications possible by using a spreadsheet. You can use these examples as a springboard to launch ideas on ways to improve levels of student learning and your personal productivity.

Introduction

For many of us, thinking of spreadsheets generally conjures up thoughts of a fancy grade book. That's fine. However, it's time for you to expand—and perhaps to see this as a tool for a wide variety of tasks, as well as a tool to help your students learn. Read and reflect on the examples given below. Think about ways you can integrate spreadsheets into your life and into your curriculum. There will be times when integrating Excel or some similar spreadsheet will enhance the overall learning of the student.

Spreadsheet integration

Creating the enhanced learning experience: A partial lesson plan

Topic: A study of the people, places, and cultures of an African country.

Overview: As we explain in chapter 2 ("Word Processing") Mr. Carpenter is an eighth-grade social studies teacher at Lowell Middle School, and he is beginning a unit of study on the African country of Zimbabwe. One of his past students, Jonathon Rogers, is a graduate student working on an internship for an international health and education organization located in Zimbabwe. During the school year, Mr. Carpenter wants his students to gather and exchange information about the Zimbabwean people and country with the help of Jonathon. Through Jonathon's work assignment, he will be visiting many schools, as well as health facilities. Hopefully, Mr. Carpenter's classes will be able to contact Jonathon through both the mail and e-mail to gather their desired information.

One goal of this instructional unit is for the students to discover what life is like in another country and culture. Through various discussions, Mr. Carpenter's classes identified several relevant points of interest that they desired to examine and compare.

Specific Learning Task: One specific area of interest is that of the types and amounts of food eaten by similar aged students in the two countries. The goal is to gather data from students in both countries on what they commonly eat. Once gathered, cross-country comparisons can be examined and compared with U.S. governmental nutritional guidelines.

Sample Learning Objectives: Students will be able to do the following:

1. Describe the most common foods eaten by the sample of students from the two different cultures.
2. Identify and describe foods common between the two cultures.
3. Based on the collected data, identify potential discrepancies between U.S. governmental nutritional needs of students in both countries.

Procedure:

1. Subdivide each of Mr. C's eighth-grade classes into three research groups:
   • **Research Group A:** This group will gather and report data on common food eaten by a sample of students in Mr. C's class.
   • **Research Group B:** This group will work with Jonathon and gather data on common food eaten by a similar sample of same-aged Zimbabwean students.
   • **Research Group C:** This group will research governmental suggested nutritional information on the types and amounts of food that should be eaten by similar-aged students.

2. Create small data journals to collect data on foods eaten. Each journal should have a place to record the type and amount of food eaten during the morning, afternoon, and evening of each day for a fourteen-day time period. Also include instructions for the students to describe foods that individuals from other cultures may not recognize.

3. Randomly select ten students (five girls and five boys) from Mr. C's class, and contact Jonathon to see if he can likewise get ten participants from one of the schools he's working with.

4. Have Jonathon review the journals and ask for any needed clarification on food types and so on, and then mail the completed journals to Lowell Middle School. Members of Groups A and B will examine their respective journals and enter the data received.

5. Group C will record the suggested governmental types and amounts of food.

6. Students will compare the data from the two countries and the suggested governmental standards and
   a. determine the most common food eaten within each country,
   b. determine foods commonly eaten by students in both countries,
   c. determine general nutritional value of the common foods eaten by the individual students in both countries, and
   d. present a data chart that illustrates the comparisons between countries and the standards.

7. Write a short paper about a proposed visit to Zimbabwe and what types of food they could expect to encounter. Use the data chart to identify which foods they would be excited about tasting and what foods they probably would try to avoid.

Question About Spreadsheet Integration

This lesson could be completed in a number of ways. One specific method would be to use a spreadsheet, such as Excel, to help gather, analyze, and report the results of the collected data. Use these reflective questions to explore the value of potentially integrating a spreadsheet within such a lesson as outlined by Mr. Carpenter.

- As outlined within this lesson, in what way could a spreadsheet be used?
- For each of the groups, how could the spreadsheet be used to gather and archive the data that they received?
- Once the information is entered into the spreadsheet, are there ways to manipulate the data to highlight specifics that otherwise might not be seen by the students? For example, could you readily identify those foods with the highest and lowest nutritional content? Could foods be identified that are most regularly eaten (and perhaps eaten at the most regular times of the day)?
- Through the construction of a data chart, would students be able to draw relevant cross-cultural comparisons? Could a number of different chart types be used (i.e., pie, bar, line) in order to get the best view and analysis of the data?
- Could students see benefits and problems that are evolving in the eating habits of individuals from the different cultures? Could they make predictions on what would happen if similar eating habits continued throughout each student's life?
- Through nutritional comparisons, could students problem solve and create menus of combined foods between the two countries to supply the needed nutritional values that both sets of students can optimally use?
- In what ways can the spreadsheet help highlight the similarities and differences with the foods eaten within the two cultures? Can manipulations within the spreadsheet allow students to predict what would happen if certain changes were made within the diets of either group of students?
- Could the reported data and spreadsheet results be used by Jonathon in his work with his international health organization internship?
- If Jonathon isn't able to help gather data from students in Zimbabwe, is there another way to get similar types of data (e.g., from the Internet) that will allow some comparisons to be made? Could a spreadsheet be used to store, analyze, and present this type of data?

Workout: Integrating spreadsheets

This is a good time for your practice. First, reflect on the partial lesson plan given above. Next, think about the use of spreadsheets within applied classroom settings. Finally, work through each of the following steps.

1. Read each of the following situations. Imagine being directly involved in the planning for each of these projects. Select one (or more if you wish) for further consideration.

Favorite Color

A third-grade teacher at Johnson Elementary asked his kids to tell him which color was the most preferred. To investigate, he had his students go out after school for ten consecutive days, and identify and record twenty different human-made items that they encountered (e.g., vehicles, houses, clothes). They were to report each item and its main color. From their findings they were to determine which was the most recorded color, the least used color, and if certain items were colored more frequently one color than another.

Holiday wrap

For a school project, the seventh-grade students of Mayflower Middle School have decided to open a gift wrapping business at one of the small center shops in the local mall.

They need to project their costs for the coming months of September through December. They need to show how many volunteers need to be working at any one time for all of the shifts. Additionally, they need to show the amount of projected money they will earn based on the number of boxes wrapped, size of the box, and time required to wrap. Additionally, they need to consider the impact of competition from other gift-wrapping stores and how this competition should determine their overall prices.

Utilities Manager

How much raw sewage is processed each day at the local water or sewage treatment plant? Which days of the week produce the highest and lowest amounts of sewage? Are there typically high and low months or weeks of the year? Based on charts of processed sewage, identify potential causes of the fluctuations in the amount of sewage that is treated.

Growth Rate

Is there a way to compare the population growth rate of different countries of the world and then predict which ones may have problems in the future based upon rapid, stagnant, or decreasing growth rates? Which areas of the world would you predict would have the greatest amount of worry in the next few decades based on their current level of population growth?

2. Based on your selected project, consider the following questions that concern the integration of spreadsheets. Mark your response to each question.

Integration assessment questionnaire (IAQ)

Will using **SPREADSHEET** software as a part of the project			
Broaden the learners' perspective on potential solution paths and/or answers?	_____Yes	_____No	_____Maybe
Increase the level of involvement and investment of personal effort by the learners?	_____Yes	_____No	_____Maybe
Increase the level of learner motivation (e.g., increase the relevance of the to-be-learned task, the confidence of dealing with the task, and/or the overall appeal of the task)?	_____Yes	_____No	_____Maybe
Decrease the time needed to generate potential solutions?	_____Yes	_____No	_____Maybe
Increase the quality and/or quantity of learner practice working on this and similar projects?	_____Yes	_____No	_____Maybe
Increase the quality and/or quantity of feedback given to the learner?	_____Yes	_____No	_____Maybe
Enhance the ability of the student to solve novel, but similar, projects, tasks, and problems in the future?	_____Yes	_____No	_____Maybe

3. If you have responded "Yes" to one or more of the IAQ questions, you should consider the use of a spreadsheet to enhance the student's potential learning experience.

4. Using the example lesson plan, develop a lesson plan based on your selected project. Within the plan, indicate how and when the learner will use a spreadsheet. Additionally, list potential benefits and challenges that may occur when involving this software within the lesson.

Workout: Exploring the NETS Standard connection

Developing and executing a lesson plan that integrates the use of spreadsheets directly addresses several of the NETS Standards for both teachers (NETS*T) and students (NETS*S). See appendix B for a full listing of the standards.

Part A: Generally, the main purpose for learning and using application software is to increase your level of production—that is, to do things faster, better, or both. NETS Standards (NETS*T Standard V and NETS*S Standard 3) help us focus on these productivity objectives for both teachers and students. There are other technology standards, however, that may also be potentially addressed through your knowledge and use of spreadsheet software. Reflect on the following questions and consider the potential impact of spreadsheet integration (refer to appendix B to review the full sets of standards):

- How could the integration of spreadsheets improve the collection, analysis, and assessment of data collected by the teacher and/or the students? Could the enhanced data collection and analysis capabilities increase levels of problem solving? (NETS*T IV.B. and V.B.; NETS*S 5 and 6)
- How can the use of spreadsheet software help develop students' higher order skills and creativity? Is there something about the use of spreadsheets that may enhance the exploration of alternative problem analyses, data comparisons, predictions, and ultimate solutions? How does the "what if . . ." capabilities afforded by spreadsheets allow for increased levels of creative problem solving? (NETS*T III.C.; NETS*S 3)
- In what ways could spreadsheets be used to facilitate the communication and collaboration between teachers, students, parents, and subject matter experts on specific projects that ultimately impact student learning? Are there alternative means of displaying data (e.g., charts) that would allow for diverse audiences to better grasp the meaning of the information? (NETS*T V.D. and VI.B.; NETS*S 4)

Part B: Go to the ISTE Web site http://cnets.iste.org. Within that site, select to review either the student or the teacher NETS Standards. Once you have selected the standards to review, select either the student or teacher profiles and look for the corresponding scenarios. Review the scenarios and determine how spreadsheets could be used within several of those situations.

While visiting the ISTE Web site and exploring the scenarios, go to the lesson plan search area and select a number of different lesson plans of interest. Review those and determine the role (if any) of spreadsheets within the development, implementation, and assessment of the lesson. Note this from both the perspective of the teacher developing the lesson and from the perspective of the student participating in the implemented lesson.

Workout: Comprehensive integration

You need to understand that in most practical learning situations, one type of software generally doesn't stand alone as *the* solution. That is, full integration may mean that you use a spreadsheet *and* other software such as Web development, word processing, and data management.

For this Workout:

1. Read through the lesson plan you designed within the previous Workout.
2. Identify how your suggestions for the integration of a spreadsheet may be enhanced by the use of other software (e.g., Web development, presentation software).
3. Describe the benefits and the problems that may be associated with the integration of other software within the same project.
4. Describe how additional technology standards (e.g., NETS*T II.A.: ". . . design developmentally appropriate learning opportunities that apply technology-enhanced instructional strategies to support the diverse needs of learners") can be addressed by the integration of various types of applications software.

Further ideas on using the spreadsheet as a learning tool

> **Note:** These ideas are to help you generate your own thoughts of what could be done. Don't let it bother you if they are not the right content or grade level; use the idea and adapt it to be helpful within your own situation. These are meant to be a stimulus for additional ideas.

Here are a few ideas that may help you see how a spreadsheet might be beneficial:

1. Provide or generate a set of data, and have students analyze and summarize the data by developing different formulas (e.g., means, standard deviations) to compare the results.
2. Have the students develop a survey, then collect, record, and analyze the data using statistical functions within the spreadsheet. Moreover, use the chart feature to report the data that they collected.
3. Collect, store, and compare monthly temperature averages for key cities in strategic locations of the world. Compare those averages with the average temperatures of the students' hometown.
4. Have the students collect data on the growth (e.g., height, loss of teeth) of their classmates over the course of a school year. Compare that data with students in other classes, other grades, other schools, or other countries.
5. Have the students compare the amount of soda, juice, and water purchased from the school's machines during different times of the day, on different days of the week, and/or different months of the year. They can also calculate the amount of money earned by the school from these machines given the cost of the repair and maintenance.
6. Have students develop a personal budget for their current standard of living. Also have them budget for when they go to college, volunteer for the military, or enter the work force.
7. Have students create a sign-up chart for using specific items within the classroom (e.g., a special learning center, the computer, a special place to sit and read).
8. In a business class, have students monitor the price of specific stocks and note trends that may suggest optimal buying or selling times.
9. In a physical education class, have students create a spreadsheet that collects and analyzes weekly efforts in speed, endurance, strength, and so on.
10. Have students maintain a statistical record of their favorite professional sports star and compare performance levels across several years.
11. Have students design a judge's rating sheet for a club or sport (e.g., gymnastic, dancing, skating, diving).
12. Have students guess what the most popular color of car or truck is, and then have them count the different colors that pass on a street near the school during a twenty-minute time period. Also have them count and record the colors of M&M candies (or any other multicolored candy), socks, eyes, whatever, and analyze what they find.
13. Using the rows and columns of a spreadsheet, have the students design a sign-up sheet for use of the computer lab. This could also be converted to a work assignment sheet for various jobs in the classroom on different days of the week.
14. With the rows and columns as a guide, have students develop crossword puzzles covering key words in a history, geography, science, or other school subject lesson.

Additional ideas for using a spreadsheet as an assistant

1. **Grade book.** Student scores can be recorded, edited, sorted, summarized, and reported with relative ease.
2. **Life organizer.** With all of those columns and rows, a spreadsheet is a good tool to develop a calendar or a daily meeting or work schedule. If you need to develop a set schedule for the lab, the spreadsheet can be formatted easily to display the times in a clear manner. It also works well to create quick and easy seating charts.

3. **Estimator.** Use it to record the current state and progress, and then estimate where goals should be set. For example, a teacher in a high school weight lifting class can record a student's name, current weight, and lifting capabilities, and then project what future goals for lifting should be set. The charting function allows these goals to be shown in a visual manner. *Note:* This is also a good thing for personal weight management programs (those things we refer to as "diets" and "watching our weight").
4. **Personal budgets.**
5. **Calculator.** Calculation of mortgage rates and monthly cost of a home.
6. **Schedules.** Develop time sheets for a small business and the work schedules of the employees. This can also be adapted for work schedules for individuals on school projects.
7. **Money tracker.** Use it to account for all fund-raiser money sales, book order sales, lunch money, and so forth.

Spreadsheet References

Teachers using spreadsheets

Online tutorials and Web sites *are not always reliably available* (that is, they come and go); therefore, going to a search engine (e.g., www.google.com) and then using productive search terms is very important. Here are some search terms that can be helpful in finding lesson plans for school topics that involve using spreadsheets:

- **Spreadsheet lesson plans**
- **Teachers using Excel**

Examples of such sites include the following:

http://www.teach-nology.com/teachers/lesson_plans/computing/

Lesson plans that focus on the use of the computer are found at this site. As you look through the list, those that focus on spreadsheets are easily identified.

http://www.mwsu.edu/~educ/coe/ss/ss.htm

This is a collection of spreadsheet-specific lesson plans that are focused particularly on developing math skills.

www.essdack.org/tips/page1.htm

Look on this page for some sensible ideas on how to use the spreadsheet (and other application programs) within practical classroom lessons.

Tutorials and other resources

Search terms for learning how to use spreadsheets and other useful tips:

- **Spreadsheet tutorials**
- **Spreadsheet tips**

Example tutorial and tips sites that should prove helpful:

www.microsoft.com/education/

This site has select tutorials and other instructional materials for all Microsoft products across various grade levels and subject areas.

www.jegsworks.com/Lessons/numbers/index.html

Excellent Web site that has tutorials to introduce the basics of spreadsheets.

www.techtutorials.com/Applications/Microsoft_Office/Excel/

Various links to a wide variety of spreadsheet explanation pages and tutorials can be found here. This site also provides a short description of the sites it lists, as well as a rating on how useful individuals have found the sites to be.

	Desired Task to Accomplish	Reference Menu or Toolbar*
Basic Tools	Create a new workbook	**File>>>New . . .**
	Create a new worksheet	**Insert>>>Worksheet**
	Access toolbars	**View>>>Toolbars**
	Access task panes	**View>>>Task Pane**
	Adapt view of worksheet	**View>>>Normal** *or* **Page Break Preview**
	Insert data	**Click on workspace cell, begin typing**
	Insert cells	**Insert>>>Cells . . .**
	Insert row	**Insert>>>Rows**
	Insert column	**Insert>>>Columns**
	Insert function	**Insert>>>Functions . . .**
	Insert chart	**Insert>>>Chart . . .**
	Insert picture	**Insert>>>Picture**
	Sort data	**Data>>>Sort . . .**
	Search data	**Data>>>Filter . . . >>>AutoFilter** *or* **AdvancedFilter . . .**
Formatting Features	Cells (number type, alignment, font, border, color, protection)	**Format>>>Cells . . . >>>tab:** *select appropriate*
	Row height	**Format>>>Rows**
	Column width	**Format>>>Column**
	Text (type, color, size, effects)	**Format>>>Cells . . . >>>tab: Font**
	Text alignment	**Format>>>Cells . . . >>>tab: Alignment**
	Picture (text alignment, contrast, color, size)	**View>>>Toolbars>>>Picture**
	Page break	**Insert>>>Page Break**
	Page numbers	**View>>>Header/Footer . . . >>>tab: Header/Footer . . . Custom Header . . . button>>># button**
	Headers and footers	**View>>>Header/Footer . . . >>>tab: Header/Footer . . .**
	Borders	**Format>>>Cell . . . >>>tab: Border**
	Shading	**Format>>>Cell . . . >>>tab: Patterns**

continued

Desired Task to Accomplish	Reference Menu or Toolbar*
Text wrap, orientation, direction	**Format>>>Cell . . . >>>tab: Alignment**
Word Art	**Insert>>>Picture>>>WordArt**
AutoShapes	**Insert>>>Picture>>>AutoShape**
Symbols	**Insert>>>Symbol . . .**
Comments	**Insert>>>Comment**
Linking to the Internet	**Insert>>>Hyperlink . . .**
Track changes	**Tools>>>Track Changes**
Forms	**Data>>>Form . . .**
Hide and Unhide rows	**Format>>>Row>>>Hide** *or* **Unhide**
Hide and Unhide columns	**Format>>>Column>>>Hide** *or* **Unhide**
Hide and Unhide worksheets	**Format>>>Worksheet>>>Hide** *or* **Unhide**
Change worksheet names	**Format>>>Worksheet>>>Rename**
Freeze and unfreeze portions of the worksheet	**Window>>>Freeze Panes** *or* **Unfreeze Panes**
Split and unsplit screen	**Window>>>Split**

Additional Features (row label on left)

*NOTE: The first item listed is the Main Menu or toolbar. As explained earlier in chapter 1, the >>> indicates the selection to be made once a drop down menu has been revealed. For example, **View>>>Task Panes** means to click on the View option of the Main Menu bar. This exposes a drop-down menu, and from that menu click the "Task Pane" option. This activates the relevant Task Pane window.

Chapter 4

DATA MANAGEMENT

MORE MS Excel: The Basics of Collecting, Organizing, and Retrieving Loads of Information

Introduction

What should you be able to know and do?	In a world where we have access to a huge amount of information, having a way to organize, store, and retrieve that information is critical. Databases help you select, compare, and/or identify information that can lead to more effective learning and decision making. Within this introduction to databases, we want you to discover

- what a database is, what it can do, and how it can help in teaching and learning;
- how to justify the use of the database as an effective tool—by knowing when and why it should or shouldn't be used.

Terms to know	*database*	*record*	*field*
	sort	search	*mail merge*
	filter		

What is a database and what does it do?	Databases are exactly what the name implies—bases for specific data. They are specialized storage bins where you can place information and then later recall it. The trick is knowing how to get the information into the database so that it can be located and retrieved in the future. Databases are incredibly important in a society that needs access to all kinds of information. How that information is organized is essential—or finding it can become an extremely arduous task.

A familiar example of an old and new database can be found in many libraries. Years ago (although it really hasn't been that long ago), most libraries had a large catalogue of 3-inch by 5-inch cards that contained information about each of the books in the library. To find a book, you first went to the card catalogue and looked for a card by either the book's title, author, or subject. Once you located the appropriate card, you could get information about the topic to access the book on the proper library shelf. Today, most of those card catalogues have been replaced by a computerized database. Using the same organizational structure, the computer can be used to search the library's database according to a specific book's author, title, or subject.

What are some commonly known databases?	- Microsoft's Access - dBASE - FileMaker Pro - Paradox - Sun Microsystems' StarOffice Base

Can you use something else instead (i.e., Excel)?

Yes, many of the basic functions of the database can be accomplished by using a spreadsheet program such as Microsoft's Excel. That is, if you know spreadsheet basics, you may already know most of the needed functions to have it serve to manage your data. For this reason, we are going to concentrate on Excel as a tool that can be used to carry out simple data management functions.

> **Note**: There are times when a commercial database program is needed. If the amount of data you are working with is huge or if you need specialized forms to enter the data and/or to retrieve it, then you may want to consider learning and using a commercial database program. Our contention is that most teachers don't need that kind of power (and the accompanying headaches) for most of the tasks they will use a database for.

> **Important Note**: We made the determination that for most teachers, a thorough knowledge of a commercial database would not be as needed as other forms of software (e.g., PowerPoint, Word, Excel). This decision came about because of our experience in working with teachers and students, and how they commonly use the computer within the school setting. However, we recognize that there may be some of you who would like to know about the basics of a "normal" database. *Therefore, we have developed Level 1 and Level 2 for Microsoft Access and placed it on this text's accompanying Web site.* If you desire to learn and to have an experience working with Access, please feel free to use it.

Why bother learning how to use a database?

- **Organization is paramount.** A database can help you organize vast amounts of information—which is essential if you have access to large quantities of information.
- **Sorting with lightning speed.** Databases allow you to sort information automatically in different ways. For example, an electronic student database can be sorted to produce an alphabetical list of all students. However, with the right information, you can also sort to list all students in alphabetical order based on their grade, gender, color of eyes, and shoe size if you desire. Multiple sorts can add to the power of the database.
- **Speed searches.** By using the search mechanism, you can have the computer find information you seek in a fraction of the time and effort needed to do it manually. Have it find one specific student and his or her associated information. Or have it find all instances of a specific characteristic for a data set (e.g., all students who have birthdays in October).
- **Boolean searches.** These types of searches allow you to search for specific information that contains specific words, letters, numbers, and so forth, but ignores other bits of information that you don't want. For example, search for information on Lincoln, *not* Nebraska.
- **Grasp overwhelming amounts of information.** Using the combined features of search and sort, you can identify specific bits of information that allow you to perceive relationships not readily apparent—for example, noting the elective courses frequently taken by high school students who are successful at gaining entrance into prestigious colleges.
- **Make comparisons.** Wouldn't it be nice if you could pull out different information and have the database management system compare it for you? That is, search the electronic recipe database, and have it identify and print all recipes that (1) use chicken, (2) feed up to six people, and (3) can be prepared in twenty minutes or less.
- **Multiple uses.** It isn't too difficult to think about databases teachers might find helpful. Student information, books you own, books students have borrowed, lesson plans, supplies you have on hand versus supplies that are needed, electronic

portfolios, quotes, references, pictures—the list goes on. These can be referenced, stored, searched, sorted, compared, and retrieved—if you have a knowledge of databases and how to use them to your advantage.

How are databases used at school? A brief list of ideas	**By the teacher:**	**By the student:**
	• Student information	• References for a research paper
	• Lesson plans	• Compare information on jobs, cities, businesses, weather
	• Mail merge data	• Addresses of friends and relatives
	• Articles, books, software, and so on in a personal library	• Compiled record of all work completed
	• Electronic student and personal portfolios	• Information on scholarships, grants, loans for college

Workout

Whether you like it or not, you interact with databases every day. If you use the Internet, go to the doctor's office, look up a phone number, go to the grocery store, visit the library, look up an address in your address book, check a favorite Web site, and so on, you have in some way interacted with a database. In each case, information (e.g., personal medical history, grocery inventory and prices, addresses and phone numbers, call numbers for books) had to be accessed in order for you to get something done. Databases are what organize, store, and retrieve that information.

Look around your home, school, place of work, and identify five different kinds of databases. Some may or may not be associated with the computer. Write down your list of examples and then look for the common elements within each that sets it apart as a database. What are the elements that each database must have?

In the school classroom, what are some typical areas that could benefit from an electronic database (e.g., a database of all appropriate reading books for a specific social studies assignment)? List three or four such databases.

Orientation

What's the workspace look like?

Here is an example of a database of information on books pertaining to the use of the World Wide Web for teachers (see Figure 4.1). This database was created in Microsoft Excel and should be familiar from our work in chapter 3 ("Spreadsheets"). Instead of a focus on using the spreadsheet's capabilities with numbers, here we are using its rows and columns to store specific text information. Similar to the workspace when Excel was used as a spreadsheet, there are standard and formatting toolbars, as well as ways to adjust the cells, columns, and rows.

Databases, records, and fields

Remember the last time you went to a new doctor or dentist? On that initial visit the office administrator probably had you fill out some forms. The forms asked for your name, address, and phone number, as well as your insurance company, policy number, and health history.

Ever wonder what happened to that form you filled out? In most cases, the form was taken back and put into a folder with your name on it, and then it was placed in a filing cabinet with other patient folders. The filing cabinet that holds all of the patients' files is known as a *database*, the individual file or form that you filled out is your *record*. On that record you filled in bits of information (address, medication you currently take, and so forth) and each bit of information is known as a *field*.

Electronic databases are set up in the same manner. The database holds numerous records, and each record has specific fields of information. From our example in

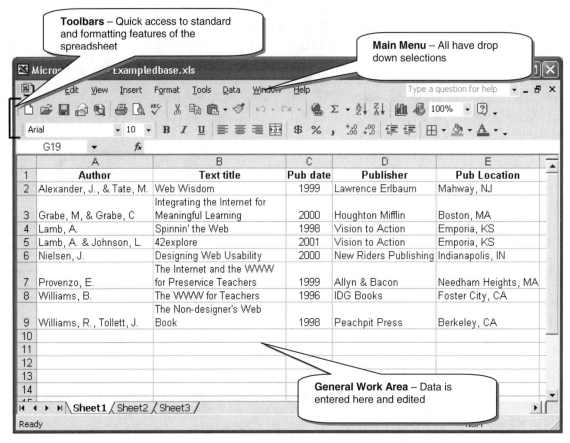

Figure 4.1 View of Microsoft Excel work area used to organize and manage textbook data

Figure 4.1, the database consists of all of the combined books listed. Each row indicates a specific record of one of those books. Each record is made up of several fields of information (e.g., publication date of a specific text, the title of a specific text).

Here is another example: Suppose your high school dance team is raising money by conducting a dance clinic for the area elementary school students. On the registration form you ask the students for their name, address, grade level, gender, t-shirt size, and years of dance experience. As the registrations come in, you develop an electronic record for each student by inputting the individuals' fields of information (e.g., name, address, grade level, and so on) for each student. Your database is the full set of all individuals who have registered. There is an individual record on each participant and you have a set number of fields of information about each participant (e.g., grade level).

What can be in a field?

Plenty. It could hold a letter of the alphabet, a name, a number, a picture, an audio or video clip, or even a whole chapter of a textbook. Some databases allow you a huge amount of space to put whatever you want within the field. In Excel, for example, in one cell (field) you can put as many as 32,000 characters of text. That is equal to about a chapter of text from a normal high school text.

The "power of 'sort and search'"

The power of the database is that it allows you to quickly sort and search information it holds. For example, you can sort all the records based on any or all fields contained within the records. Thus, you can sort each of the records alphabetically based on the name field (or gender field, or address field, or any other field) that is common within all the records.

Even more powerful is the ability to search for a subset of the records based on a specific field. So if you want to find out how many participants in your dance clinic are male, you can search based on the gender field and bring out only the records of male participants.

You can see the real power of this information when you think about a doctor who wants to examine the records of all patients aged between fifty and sixty, who have had an office visit in the last five years and have been diagnosed with diabetes. Or perhaps the teacher who desires to search and identify, from her database of hundreds of lesson plans, any and all that deal with science experiments involving copper for fourth- and fifth-grade students. Instantaneously, this information could be searched and delivered.

Workout: Explore the territory

Turn on the computer and launch your database program. Once it appears on the screen, try the following:

1. Examine the Main Menu (usually found across the top of the screen). Click on each Menu title (e.g., File, Edit) and note the various selections available under each. You won't need all, but it's good to know where to find them. Pay special attention to where the Help menu is located.
2. Under the View menu, drop down to the Toolbar selection and make sure the Standard and Formatting toolbars are checked. These are the common toolbars you will use.
3. Note that the tools on the toolbars show icons representing what the tool is for. If you lay the mouse pointer over any specific tool (don't click), the name of the tool appears. Use of the toolbars is a fast way of accessing commonly used tools.
4. Practice entering information by clicking on any cell in the workspace. Enter a word or series of words. Highlight some or all of the words you enter, and then click on various tool icons on the Formatting toolbar. Note how your highlighted words change based on the tool that you have selected.
5. Review chapter 3, Level 1, on how items are formatted within the spreadsheet. The same formatting can be employed when Excel is used as a database. Attempt to set up headings, expand the width of the columns, and adjust the word wrap to achieve some sense for how data can be inserted in this tool.
6. Play with it for a short while to get a feeling for what can be done and how easy it is to use.

Level 1: Revisiting the Grade Book

What should you be able to do?

At this level, your focus is on using various tools and techniques to store data in a database and make the data retrievable in various forms.

The situation . . .

Remember from the Level 1 exercise within chapter 3 ("Spreadsheets"), John Rena developed a grade book for his science class at Heaton Middle School. Well, John is extending that work just a bit as he has added some new information to his class's grade book. Note that now he has included personal information about each of his students (e.g., address, birthday, parents' names). These columns are not to be calculated; however, they can be manipulated. Note Figure 4.2 is a printout of John's full database with all of the rows representing individual student records and the columns representing the specific fields of information found within each record.

	Last Name	First name	Birthday	Gender	Phone	Address	City	State	Zip	Parents
5	Barrymore	Cade	10/9/86	male	478-5211	134 South 300 North	Lafayette	IN	47905	Mr. & Mrs. Barrymore
6	DeFore	Alexis	5/18/87	female	472-4578	11439 US Hwy 245	Lafayette	IN	47908	Beverly DeFore
7	Drury	Landon	12/27/86	male	447-0999	2393 W. 100 N	Lafayette	IN	47905	John and Dee Drury
8	Jeski	Robert	7/31/86	male	472-8356	4839 W. 100 N.	Lafayette	IN	47905	Mr. & Mrs. Jeski
9	Moreno	Elizabeth	2/18/87	female	424-2252	3147 St. Rd. 39	E. Lafayette	IN	47902	Barry and Elana Swartz
10	Packard	Dale	3/17/87	male	472-6854	5214 Autumn Ln.	Lafayette	IN	47905	Mr. & Mrs. Packard
11	Polk	Madison	9/7/86	female	472-7531	434 W. Monty St.	Lafayette	IN	47908	Roberta Thomas
12	Saterwaite	Kimberly	6/3/87	female	424-6587	106 Meridian St.	E. Lafayette	IN	47902	Mr. & Mrs. Tim Saterwaite
13	Smith	Fiona	11/20/86	female	424-9921	2561 Midline Ct.	E. Lafayette	IN	47902	Andrew Smith
14	Washington	Violet	9/20/86	female	478-3321	300 Main St.	Lafayette	IN	47905	Suzy and Dave Washington

Figure 4.2 Mr. Rena's full database of student information

The plan

Look closely at Figure 4.3 and compare it with Figure 4.2. In this case Mr. Rena *sorted* the records based on gender. He didn't have to retype or cut and paste to accomplish this. The computer did it automatically.

Additionally, look at Figure 4.4—in this case, Mr. Rena had the database *filter* the data to identify and show only specific records. Here he filtered the data, and now only those students living in a specific zip code (47902) are shown.

The plan now is for you to construct a database similar to Mr. Rena's. It doesn't need to be exactly the same, but you should have multiple records that have several fields of information that can then be sorted and filtered in a number of different ways.

	Last Name	First name	Birthday	Gender	Phone	Address	City	State	Zip	Parents
5	Moreno	Elizabeth	2/18/87	female	424-2252	3147 St. Rd. 39	E. Lafayette	IN	47902	Barry and Elana Swartz
6	Saterwaite	Kimberly	6/3/87	female	424-6587	106 Meridian St.	E. Lafayette	IN	47902	Mr. & Mrs. Tim Saterwaite
7	Smith	Fiona	11/20/86	female	424-9921	2561 Midline Ct.	E. Lafayette	IN	47902	Andrew Smith
8	Washington	Violet	9/20/86	female	478-3321	300 Main St.	Lafayette	IN	47905	Suzy and Dave Washington
9	DeFore	Alexis	5/18/87	female	472-4578	11439 US Hwy 245	Lafayette	IN	47908	Beverly DeFore
10	Polk	Madison	9/7/86	female	472-7531	434 W. Monty St.	Lafayette	IN	47908	Roberta Thomas
11	Barrymore	Cade	10/9/86	male	478-5211	134 South 300 North	Lafayette	IN	47905	Mr. & Mrs. Barrymore
12	Drury	Landon	12/27/86	male	447-0999	2393 W. 100 N	Lafayette	IN	47905	John and Dee Drury
13	Jeski	Robert	7/31/86	male	472-8356	4839 W. 100 N.	Lafayette	IN	47905	Mr. & Mrs. Jeski
14	Packard	Dale	3/17/87	male	472-6854	5214 Autumn Ln.	Lafayette	IN	47905	Mr. & Mrs. Packard

Figure 4.3 Mr. Rena's database *sorted* based on student's gender

	Last Name	First name	Birthday	Gender	Phone	Address	City	State	Zip	Parents
5	Moreno	Elizabeth	2/18/87	female	424-2252	3147 St. Rd. 39	E. Lafayette	IN	47902	Barry and Elana Swartz
6	Saterwaite	Kimberly	6/3/87	female	424-6587	106 Meridian St.	E. Lafayette	IN	47902	Mr. & Mrs. Tim Saterwaite
7	Smith	Fiona	11/20/86	female	424-9921	2561 Midline Ct.	E. Lafayette	IN	47902	Andrew Smith

Figure 4.4 Mr. Rena's database *filtered* to show only those students who have a specific zip code

Workout: By the numbers . . .

CD ACTIVITY

1. Launch your spreadsheet or database application program (e.g., Microsoft Excel).
2. Either open the existing unformatted version of the document on the CD [**File >> Open . . .** and then navigate to the CD, view the CD contents, open the chp4_DB folder, then launch (double-click) the "dbase1" file], or if you like, you can open a new worksheet and type in the information yourself. Once opened (or once you've typed it in), your worksheet should look something like Figure 4.2.
3. Note the row that contains the column headings. These headings represent the titles for the fields within a database. Each of the rows under the headings indicates a record for a particular student.
4. Add an additional field of information (e.g., favorite color, favorite subject in school, sports he or she plays) by inserting a new column heading.
5. Add records for several other students to the list and fill in all relevant fields of information.
6. Save the newly revised spreadsheet or database to your hard drive or to your disk. Use a specific name so that you can remember it and access it at a later time.
7. Now we'll have fun with the data, by trying different ways to sort and search the data.

No.	What We Are Working on	How You Go About Getting It Done
1.	**Sorting the records**	**Goal:** Change the order of the records based on a selected criterion. **Steps:** 1. Click anywhere within the database. 2. On the Main Menu click the Data menu and drop down to Sort (**Data>>>Sort**). The Sort window (see Figure 4.5) appears. Click the down arrow in the "Sort by" section and select your desired field to base the sort on (e.g., Mr. Rena selected "Gender" as the category). 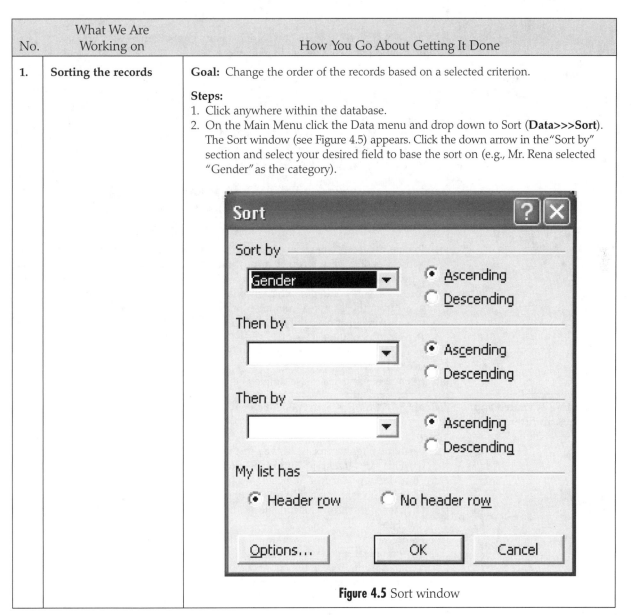 **Figure 4.5** Sort window

continued

No.	What We Are Working on	How You Go About Getting It Done
		3. Click **OK** and the sort is completed. **Note:** In the Sort window you can also select whether or not you have a header row on your database. This tells the database or spreadsheet to consider the first row as a listing of headings or as a record of data. In this case, we have a header and thus it needs to be marked as such. **Note:** In the Sort window you can also complete more than one sort at a time. For example, you can sort first by "gender" and then by "last name." In ascending order, the end result will list all of the females first, then all of the males. In addition, each of those subgroups will be in alphabetical order based on the students' last name. 4. To really get a hang of this, try sorting a number of different ways and use descending as well as ascending orders.
2.	**Filtering the records**	**Goal:** Select records based on specific criteria. **Steps:** 1. Select your full database including the column headings. 2. From the Main Menu, select **Data >>> Filter >>> AutoFilter**. 3. Note that little down arrows have now been posted by each of the column headings (see Figure 4.4). Here is an example: City ▼	Stat ▼	Zip ▼ 4. To filter the information, simply select the field title (column heading) you want to use as a filter, click its down arrow, and select the criterion on which the filter is to be based. For example, if you wanted to select students only in the 47902 zip code area, you would go to the zip code column, click the down arrow, and select 47902 from the list. Once your criterion is selected, the database only reveals those records that have the field 47902 listed. 5. To restore all of the data, simply go to **Data >>> Filter >>> Show All**. A filter, then, doesn't lose the extra data—it merely allows you to see only what you have selected to see. 6. Attempt a number of these simple filters to learn how they work.
3.	**More advanced and custom filters**	**Goal:** Select records based on a number of different criteria. **Steps:** 1. Begin the filtering process in the same way that the records were filtered in the previous steps (**Data>>>Filter>>>AutoFilter**). 2. Once the down arrows are positioned by each of the field headings, select the key criterion that you desire by selecting the appropriate column. 3. Click the down arrow for the selected column and select "Custom." A Custom AutoFilter window appears. 4. In the Custom AutoFilter window, use the down arrow button to select the comparison operator you wish to use (e.g., equals, contains, and so on). In the box next to the comparison operator, write in the criterion you wish to compare. For example, to find just those students with first names that contain the letters *al*, select the comparison operator "Contains" and type in the letters *al* in the box to the right.

No.	What We Are Working on	How You Go About Getting It Done
		5. Click OK and note how the filter has worked. **Note:** The Custom AutoFilter window also allows you to add other filters with the words *and* or *or*. So you could filter for zip codes that equal 47905 *or* 47908. This would retrieve all records with either of those two zip codes and not return any others (e.g., 47902).
4.	**Combining for even more advanced filtering and sorting**	**Goal:** Select and sort records to find very specific records. **Steps:** 1. Begin with the full database set of records. 2. Use the AutoFilter to select only the female students. 3. Use a Custom AutoFilter to select only those female students who live in either the 47902 or the 47908 zip code areas. 4. Sort the remaining list in descending alphabetical order based on first name. **Note:** As suggested here, it is possible to run a number of different individual filters to select very specific records. Now imagine if your database had 2000 potential employers and you wanted to create a list of those who were located in specific parts of the country, who had a specific beginning salary range, who allowed pets in the workplace, and so forth. If you had fields of information for each, you could filter the database to find only those potential employers who fit all of your needed requirements.

Level 2: Mail Merge

What should you be able to do?

A real time saver comes with being able to use the data stored within a database. One of the best examples of such a use is the *mail merge*. In this section, we want you to develop a database file of information and merge it with a form letter. This requires you to effectively use the Help feature of Excel.

A little story. . .

Let's imagine that John Rena is still playing with his spreadsheet and database. Now he has created a single Excel spreadsheet that contains two sheets of information. The first sheet contains students' names and all their assignment and test scores. The second worksheet has all the biographical information (the database stuff—e.g., the names, birth dates, addresses) for each of the students.

Now imagine that Mr. Rena would like to inform parents about the performance of their children on the final exam. He wants to send an individualized letter to each parent. However, that would require excessive word processing if he needed to create ten or more letters containing information relevant to each specific student. What John needs to do is create a form letter and complete a mail merge (*Note*: This is how you get "personalized" junk mail). By allowing the computer to merge information from the database with a letter written on a word processing program, letters, forms, and mailing labels can be created to use data interactively from a selected database. The end result is the best of both worlds—a single document that magically pulls specific information from the database so that it appears written personally for each student.

Getting some Help

Similar to **Help** in Windows, there is also **Help** in MS Excel and most other sophisticated software. To use **Help,** click the **Help menu>>>Microsoft Excel Help**. A **Help** window opens, and by clicking the Answer Wizard tab you can type in your question and **Help** will respond with a variety of potential answers for you to investigate. To get a general overview of what **Help** has to offer, click on the Contents tab.

    Help generally *does not* have all of the answers—but it will have a lot of them. Make sure you become familiar with how it works and how often it can be of assistance.

> **Note:** Check out Getting and Using **Help**, Crib Note 6, in appendix A for more information and insights on using the **Help** feature.

Explore: Creating a mail merge document

Within Level 2 of this software application, we want you to explore how to create a form letter or mail merge document, and then have you create one for your own use. Take a close look at the word-processed letter (see Figure 4.6). We have left _____ spaces where the merged information is to go. Once the information is merged with this form letter, then output such as Figure 4.7 can be created with little additional effort. Note that only a single word document has been created, but when printing the documents ten can be produced—each with the _____ filled in with personally relevant information drawn from the database.

March 20, 2002

Dear _____,

Greetings from Mr. Rena's Room 2206 at Heaton Middle School. After working through a major section in our math course, I thought it would be wise to let you know how well ____ did on the final exam. We have worked for a number of months on the concepts that were covered on the final exam.

_____'s score on the final was _____. If you have any questions or comments please feel free to contact me at school or through my e-mail (Renamath@isp.com)

Sincerely,

John Rena
Heaton Middle School

Figure 4.6 Sample letter that indicates where merging will occur

March 20, 2002

Dear Mr. & Mrs. Barrymore,

Greetings from Mr. Rena's Room 2206 at Heaton Middle School. After working through a major section in our math course, I thought it would be wise to let you know how well Cade did on the final exam. We have worked for a number of months on the concepts that were covered on the final exam.

Cade's score on the final was 85. If you have any questions or comments please feel free to contact me at school or through my e-mail (Renamath@isp.com)

Sincerely,

John Rena
Heaton Middle School

Figure 4.7 An example of a merged letter

Workout: Stretching with a little Help . . .

Create a simple form letter and then use the data within Dbase1.xls (on the CD) Excel document as the data source. Merge the letter and the data, and create a letter for each of the students within that course.

We aren't explaining exactly how to do each, but we do give you the example of the feature and critical questions you can think about and investigate (via Help/Office Assistant) to find the needed answers.

Feature:	Ask the Excel Office Assistant (Help):
Mail merge	• **How do you create a mail merge?** Look under the section "Create a Word mail merge with Excel data" **Note:** In Microsoft Office software, mail merges are usually completed from within MS Word. Excel's Help directs you in the steps needed to successfully complete this process—and one of the first steps is to go to Word and work from there.
Form letter	From within MS Word, ask Help the following: • **How do you create a form letter?** Look at the section on "Create form letters."

continued

Feature:	Ask the Excel Office Assistant (Help):
	Note: There are a number of steps involved in this process—all of which are carefully outlined within the Help section. Note that you will need to use the Mail Merge toolbar, as well as the Mail Merge Helper dialog box. The data source that it refers to within Help is your database or spreadsheet that you have created and saved.
	Note: You can start this form letter process with or without having first written the letter. The mail merge function either allows you to use a previously written letter stored in the computer or allows you to create one as you work through the merge process.
	Note: You can use this same procedure to address the envelopes to mail out the form letters to the students' parents.

Workout: Create your way to manage data

With this information and example, create a database (from Microsoft's Excel) that you can use. Keep it simple at first. Perhaps it can be for your CD collection, your book collection, your Christmas card address book, a bibliography of special articles, inventory of school items you have in your storage space at school, your special medications—something pertinent to your life.

Practice sorting and looking at different views of the database through the use of various filters. Finally, save your database, close it, and then open MS Word. Complete a mail merge using a new document you create and the data from the records within your database. Examine each of the merged documents, pat yourself on the back, and then begin to imagine all of the ways that this tool might help you with various bits of data that you have laying around.

Level 3: Integration and Application

What should you be able to do?

It's important for you to picture how the use of a database can be relevant to both you and your students. This section helps you see the many applications possible that involve a database. You can use these examples as a springboard to launch ideas on how to improve levels of student learning and your personal productivity.

Introduction

Within Levels 1 and 2 of this chapter, we focus on database management from the perspective of your learning to use it. However, to extend its use, you need to think about data management as a means to enhance the learning experience of students. There are times when integrating databases within a learning situation may improve the learning opportunities and possibilities of the learners. However, there are other times when such integration would be more of a hassle than the potential benefits warrant. Learning to tell the difference can help you be successful in what you develop and use in your classroom.

Database management integration

Creating the enhanced learning experience: A partial lesson plan

Topic: A study of the people, places, and culture of an African country.

Overview: Mr. Carpenter (as explained in Chapters 2 and 3) is a middle school social studies teacher determined to help his students expand their understanding of various countries of the world. For this school year, his classes have the opportunity to work with Jonathon Rogers, a university graduate student who is on an internship working for an international health and education organization in the African country of Zimbabwe. Through Jonathon, Mr. Carpenter's eighth graders are able to obtain firsthand information about the country, people, and culture of Zimbabwe.

Through research, the students have learned that Zimbabwe is a country with many exotic animals. In fact, much of its total economy is based on the tourist industry. People from all over the world travel to this African country to see elephants, tigers, and giraffes in their natural habitats.

Specific Learning Task: Zimbabwe is a country of national parks that have been set aside to protect the animals and habitats found there. Each of the parks is noted for unique animals and plants. Members of the class are to research the parks and obtain information about the location and size of the park, the types of animals and plants that reside there, and the major problems inherent with protecting, operating, and maintaining each park.

Sample Learning Objectives: Students will be able to do the following:

1. List and describe (e.g., animal and plant life, geographical features) several national parks within Zimbabwe.
2. Plan a safari through Zimbabwe in order to photograph and videotape exotic animals in their natural habitats.
3. Describe the problems and challenges that administrators and governmental officials face as they attempt to preserve the wildlife and habitats of the national parks of Zimbabwe.

Procedure:

1. Examine the following list of national parks within Zimbabwe: Chimanimani National Park, Chizarira National Park, Kazuma Pan National Park, Mana Pools National Park, Zambezi National Park.
2. Divide the class into groups, and have each group complete Internet and library research on their selected national park.
3. Have each group answer the following questions about their national park:

   a. Where is the park located (i.e., in what part of Zimbabwe)?
   b. What is the size of the park?
   c. What types of animals and plants are found within the park?
   d. What are some unique characteristics about the park? That is, if you were to visit this park, what are some key things you should really do and see?
   e. What are the chief problems/challenges facing the park in today's world?

4. Contact Jonathon to see if he can obtain further information about the parks (e.g., Has he visited one? Has he any stories? Can he suggest anyone to contact to get further information? Does he have any pictures?).
5. Have the students compile a report and/or presentation on their selected park.
6. Following the presentations, facilitate a discussion focused on the challenges facing the parks today. Potential lead questions could be as follows: (a) Should a poor country such as Zimbabwe be investing money in the parks at this time when the level of poverty of the people is so high? (b) Should outside (richer) countries help take care of the parks and wildlife found within Zimbabwe?

Question of Database Integration

This activity could be completed with or without the use of database software. Use these reflective questions to explore the value of potentially integrating database software within such an activity as outlined by Mr. Carpenter.

- If all of the information about the different national parks were to be combined, how could a database be used in this compilation process?
- Once assembled, how could the national park database be used to search and sort for specific information from all of the parks?
- Could the database be used in a way that would allow students to identify specific common elements within each of the parks (e.g., common animals, common challenges, and common solutions to those problems)?
- Could the database be used to archive pictures of each of the parks that are gathered via the Internet or from Jonathon?
- Could the database be used to generate questions for a classroom discussion or debate on current solutions to problems faced by the national parks?
- In what ways could the database be used to compile the relevant resources (Internet sites, books, articles, individuals) of information the students used to gather the needed information?
- Would it be possible to combine the key questions compiled within this database and compare these with questions about problems and proposed solutions for national parks found in other areas of Africa or even other parts of the world?

Workout: Integrating database management

Using the example lesson plan as a guide, follow the steps in this Workout as you think about the potential use of databases within various applied settings.

1. Read each of the following situations. Imagine being directly involved in the planning for each of these projects. Select one (or more if you wish) for further consideration.

Bird watchers

A fourth-grade teacher wants her students to learn how to categorize. On a field trip to the local zoo she has her students record all of the different types of birds that they see and that are identified within the zoo. Once back into the classroom, the students begin to list the different characteristics of the birds (types of food they eat, country of origin, feather colors and markings, distances and speed of flight, color and size of eggs, and so on). Once the list has been gathered, students are given novel examples and they are asked to group the bird with those from the list that are most similar based on various critical characteristics.

Internet Web sites

Do the types of favorite Internet sites frequently visited by individuals differ based on gender, age, or racial background? This was a question posed by a high school psychology teacher. To measure the potential differences, a survey was created for all elementary, middle, and secondary students in the school district. Responses asked for students to indicate what were their top three favorite Internet sites, what were their top three most useful, and how much time they spent weekly on the Internet.

Theme park comparisons

What are the "best" theme or amusement parks in the world? Mr. Ramollo wants his fifth-grade students to compare various theme parks (amusement parks) around the world to see which ones would be rated the very best. Students needed to develop a list of essential characteristics for the theme parks and then use the Internet to investigate which theme parks achieved the highest ranking for each of the categories.

Internet Cafés

An investor wants to know where would be the best place to invest in an Internet café. Such cafés are used throughout the world as places individuals can visit to rent time on a computer to use e-mail and to surf the Internet. The cafés seem to have their greatest success in those countries that have high populations, relatively low income, and poor postal systems. How can this investor determine some locations throughout the world that may be prime areas for such an investment?

2. Based on your selected project, consider the following questions that concern the integration of database management software. Mark your response to each question.

Integration assessment questionnaire (IAQ)

Will using **DATABASE MANAGEMENT** software as a part of the project:			
Broaden the learners' perspective on potential solution paths and/or answers?	_____ Yes	_____ No	_____ Maybe
Increase the level of involvement and investment of personal effort by the learners?	_____ Yes	_____ No	_____ Maybe
Increase the level of learner motivation (e.g., increase the relevance of the to-be-learned task, the confidence of dealing with the task, and/or the overall appeal of the task)?	_____ Yes	_____ No	_____ Maybe
Decrease the time needed to generate potential solutions?	_____ Yes	_____ No	_____ Maybe
Increase the quality and/or quantity of learner practice working on this and similar projects?	——— Yes	———No	———Maybe
Increase the quality and/or quantity of feedback given to the learner?	_____ Yes	_____ No	_____ Maybe
Enhance the ability of the student to solve novel, but similar, projects/tasks/problems in the future?	_____ Yes	_____ No	_____ Maybe

3. If you have responded "Yes" to one or more of the IAQ questions, you should consider the use of database management software to enhance the student's potential learning experience.
4. Using the sample lesson plan, develop a lesson plan based on this project. Within the plan, indicate how and when the learner will use a database. Additionally, list potential benefits and challenges that may occur when involving this software within the lesson.

Workout: Exploring the NETS Standard connection

Developing and executing a lesson plan that integrates the use of database management software directly addresses several of the NETS standards for both teachers (NETS*T) and students (NETS*S). See appendix B for a full listing of the standards.

Part A: Generally, the main purpose for learning and using application software is to increase your level of production—that is, to do things faster, better, or both. NETS Standards (NETS*T Standard V and NETS*S Standard 3) help you focus on these productivity objectives for both teachers and students. There are other technology standards, however, that may also be potentially addressed through your knowledge and use of database software. Reflect on the following questions and consider the potential impact of database management integration (refer to appendix B to review the full sets of standards):

• How could the integration of database software improve the collection, organization, analysis, comparison, and assessment of data collected by the teacher and/or the students? Could an enhanced capability of searching and sorting data lead to increased levels of analysis, synthesis, and creative problem solving? (NETS*T III.C. and IV.B.; NETS*S 5 and 6)

- In what ways could the use of database management software facilitate the higher order skills of comparison, synthesis, and evaluation between large sets of information? Would higher order learning of specific content area materials be increased as you develop, organize, and populate a database system? (NETS*T IV.A. and V.B.; NETS*S 1 and 6)
- Can a database be used (e.g., mail merge) to facilitate the communication and collaboration between teachers, students, parents, and subject matter experts on specific projects that ultimately impact student learning? (NETS*T V.D. and VI.B.; NETS*S 4)

Part B: Go to the ISTE Web site http://cnets.iste.org. Within that site, select to review either the student or the teacher NETS Standards. Once you have selected the standards to review, select either the student or teacher profiles, and look for the corresponding scenarios. Review the scenarios and determine how databases can be used within several of those situations.

While visiting the ISTE Web site and exploring the scenarios, go to the lesson plan search area and select a number of different lesson plans of interest. Review those and determine the role (if any) of databases within the development, implementation, and assessment of the lesson. Note this from both the perspective of the teacher developing the lesson and from the perspective of the student participating in the implemented lesson.

Workout: Comprehensive integration

You need to understand that in most practical learning situations, one type of software generally doesn't stand alone as *the* solution. That is, full integration may mean that you use data management *and* other software such as Web development, spreadsheets, and word processing. For this Workout:

1. Read through the lesson plan you designed within the previous Workout.
2. Identify how your suggestions for the integration of data management may be enhanced by the use of other software (e.g., Web development, presentation software).
3. Describe the benefits and the problems that may be associated with the integration of other software within the same project.
4. Describe how additional technology standards (e.g., NETS*T II.A.: " . . . design developmentally appropriate learning opportunities that apply technology-enhanced instructional strategies to support the diverse needs of learners") can be addressed by the integration of various types of applications software.

Further ideas on using data management as a learning tool

Note: These ideas are to help you generate your own ideas of what could be done. Don't let it bother you if they are not the right content or grade level; use the idea and adapt it to be helpful within your own situation. These are meant to be stimuli for additional ideas.

Here are a few ideas that may help you perceive how a database might be beneficial:

1. Give the students a table to investigate and fill out. The table might include comparative fields of information about countries, people, places, and so on. Help the students see trends in the data by sorting or filtering based on specific criteria. For example, have them collect data on weather patterns for various geographic regions around the world. Based on a comparison of average temperatures, what could the students predict about the type of agriculture that can be produced in those regions?

2. Have the students collect data within a specific experiment. For example, using different degrees of acid-based water for plants, measure the growth rate of different types of plants. Using the database, compare various acid levels and predict what the impact of acid rain would be on plant life given certain concentrations of acid within the rain.

3. Have the students create a database of the world's most recognized scientists during the 17th, 18th, 19th, and 20th centuries. Have them categorize the type of discoveries made and the country of origin. Have the students examine, sort, and filter the data to see from which parts of the world the most notable discoveries came and if there are specific trends based on location, century, and so forth.

4. Have the students create a reference database of research articles (including author, title, full publication information, key words, and short annotated bibliography) and then merge the information into the reference section of a research paper you have assigned.

5. Using the above reference list database, have students cooperatively create a database of articles about a specific topic (e.g., cyber ethics) and combine their efforts into a single large database for students to use on a related research project.

6. Have the students develop a database about their favorite animal (or state, or national park, or relative). Have them list the salient features of their animal (name, what it looks like, color) and then have them all combine their efforts into a single database of information. Have the students then search and sort based on specific characteristics and note the common elements of the different selected animals.

7. Have the students identify different symptoms of various ailments or conditions. Also have them include the name of the ailment and potential prescriptions to overcome the problem. Give the students specific scenarios that require them to filter their database based symptoms and determine possible prescriptions for solutions.

8. Develop databases about different types of governments from countries of the world. Include information about population, average income, religious affiliations, and so on. Filter to compare the type of government expected given specific affiliations, such as religions, of the respective country's population.

Additional ideas for using data management as an assistant	1. **Organizer.** For the classroom teacher, databases are frequently used to help organize information. For example, if you have a personal book collection, it would be wise to have a database that lists the relevant information about the books, their locations, and so forth. You can even get fancy and indicate which of the books has been borrowed and by whom. This is a great way to avoid buying multiple copies of the same book and to know where they are all located.

2. **Label maker.** Create all kinds of folder labels. In your filing cabinets you have all kinds of folders with different lesson plans, activities, and so on. A database of these titles with the ability to mail merge labels allows you to quickly print off labels for those folders.

3. **Label maker II.** On the first day of class (or when you are going on a field trip, dividing kids into special activity groups, for example), create name tags via a label mail merge with your student info database.

4. **Mailing lists.** Create info sheets of all of your students, parents, and possibly others. You can keep specific information about each of your students and use that to sort, filter, or merge within personalized letters.

5. **Lesson plans.** List all of your lesson plans based, for instance, on content, type of learner, instructional methods, or media.

6. **Electronic portfolios.** Create a database that allows you to know what is in each of your students' portfolios, assessment information, location of the pieces, and so forth. With electronic means, you can even save and duplicate versions of the students' work when needed.

7. **Examples.** Use a database to list all your examples of past students' work, what lesson plan the project relates to, key words about it, and where it is located so that you can find it again to show other students.

Data Management References

Teachers using data management

Online tutorials and Web sites *are not always reliably available* (that is, they come and go); therefore, going to a search engine (e.g., www.google.com) and then using productive search terms is very important. Here are some search terms that can be helpful in finding lesson plans for school topics that involve using database management systems:

- Database lesson plans

  Examples of such sites include the following:

  www.askeric.org/Virtual/Lessons/

  AskERIC is a Web resource with thousands of lesson plans. Once at this site, enter the word *database* in the search feature and select the age group you desire. Appropriate examples of lesson plans should be quickly retrieved.

  http://www.teach-nology.com/teachers/lesson_plans/computing/

  The lesson plans found at this site focus on the use of the computer. As you look through the list, several pertaining to spreadsheet and database should be easily identified.

  www.essdack.org/tips/page1.htm

  Look on this page for some sensible ideas on how to use the spreadsheet (and other application programs) within practical classroom lessons.

Tutorials and other references

Search terms for learning how to use databases and other useful tips:

- Database tutorials
- Database tips

Within this text we have emphasized that for most teachers a spreadsheet with the power of Excel can be used in the place of a full-blown database (e.g., Microsoft's Access). Additional Web sites for studying various features of Excel are listed at the conclusion of chapter 3.

Additional example tutorial sites that should prove helpful with other databases include the following:

  www.microsoft.com/education

  This site has select tutorials and other instructional materials for all Microsoft products across various grade levels and subject areas.

  www.techtutorials.com/Applications/Microsoft_Office/MS_Access

  Various links to a wide variety of database explanation pages and tutorials can be found here. This site also provides a short description of the sites it lists, as well as a rating on how useful individuals have found the sites to be.

  www.microsoft.com/office/previous/tips/access2000.asp

  Here is Microsoft's "Tips and Tricks" for using Access 2000. Great ideas submitted by individuals using Access.

Chapter 5

PRESENTATION SOFTWARE

MS PowerPoint: The Basics of Creating Presentations, Handouts, and Much, Much More

Introduction

What should you know about presentation software?	Presentation software (e.g., Microsoft's PowerPoint) is designed to help you get your message across to others and look good in the process. This software can become one of the most interesting, enjoyable, and fruitful for a teacher to learn. Within this introduction, we want you to discover

- what a presentation program is, what it can do, and how it can help in teaching and learning;
- how to justify the use of the presentation program as an effective tool—by knowing when and why it should or shouldn't be used.

Words to know	*slide*	*normal view*	*action button*
	slide sorter view	*slide show view*	*master slide*
	animation		

What is "presentation software" and what does it do?	Presentation software is a computer application that allows you to do just what the name implies—create and deliver presentations. As a teacher and/or student, a great deal of learning focuses on presentations of some kind—thus this application is one that should become a regular in your learning arsenal.

Review Figure 5.1 and note the three slides that have been created as part of a presentation about computer hardware. With relative ease, you can build individual slides and then sequence them together into a full slide show. On each slide you can put text, pictures, Internet links, audio clips, animations—the list goes on and on. Plus you can instruct this program to create handouts and run itself automatically if you want the "no-hands" approach.

With all of these benefits, it's also a great tool to have students use as they design and create their own presentations.

What are some commonly known presentation-type software?	- Microsoft's PowerPoint - Adobe's Persuasion - Lotus's Freelance Graphics - Corel's WordPerfect Presentations - Gold Disc's Astound - Sun Microsystems' StarOffice Impress

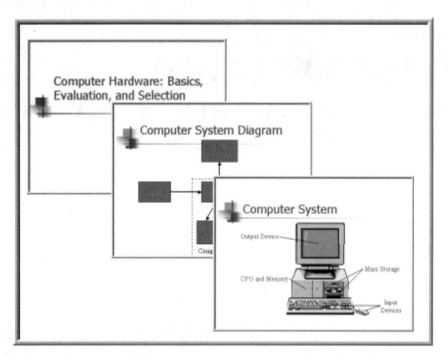

Figure 5.1 Three individual slides or screens in a PowerPoint presentation

Note: We focus on MS PowerPoint (PPT). However, **what we present can be done in most of these other presentation programs listed.** So if you don't have access to MS PPT at home, don't be alarmed—you can still complete the projects and learn the basic skills.

Why bother learning how to use PowerPoint or other forms of presentation software?

- **Quality shows.** PPT allows you to create presentations that will pleasantly surprise you. Suddenly your work can look better and your message cleaner and clearer for your audience.
- **It's fast.** Because many of the processes within this program are automated, you can develop presentations in very quick order. You can brainstorm using an outlining function within the program and immediately turn the outline into a basic set of presentation slides. This helps when time is important (and when is time *not* important?).
- **It's easy to adapt.** Once you have the basics of a presentation completed, you can easily adapt it for a new audience. It also works well with other programs. If you have a graph in Excel and want it included—PPT can do that. Or if you have a poem in a word-processed file, a simple cut and paste and it's now in your presentation.
- **Ease of adding multimedia.** Sometimes a picture can say a thousand words—so here's the chance to use visuals, audio, video clips, additional Web sites, and so forth to enhance your presentation. All can be added with relative ease and speed.
- **Two (or three) things at once.** Guess what? As you work to develop your presentation slides, PPT automatically creates handouts you can print, copy, and have ready to distribute. Likewise, as you finish your presentation, if you want to "put it on the Web"—it is ready to go. Such features allow you to seem as if you put in more effort than actually needed.
- **Helps with learning.** Often we hear "the teacher actually learns the most." You can use this to the benefit of your students by having them develop presentations.
- **It's not just for oral presentations any more.** PPT can be a very effective and efficient way to create individualized instruction. For example, PPT can be used to create

learning centers that allow learners to select the sequence of information, give responses, and receive feedback on their efforts.

- **Creates its own backup system.** Suppose you go to a convention to deliver your presentation and your needed computer setup isn't available. You can simply print your slide and copy it as a transparency to be used on a normal overhead machine. Also, the handouts can be useful if the bulb in the overhead burns out.

How are presentation programs used at school?	By the teacher:	By the student:
	• Lectures and presentations • Individual tutorials • Parent–teacher nights • Classroom handouts • Staff development	• Student-made presentations • Oral reports • Electronic portfolios • Group projects • Science experiments

Workout

Think back to the last two days. How many presentations (formal and informal) have you been exposed to? Perhaps several took place within a classroom or training setting. Others may have occurred while you were waiting in line at the bank, the store, or at the gas station. You may have viewed other presentations while watching the news, listening to your teenager explain why he needs his own car, or even listening to how the new basketball coach runs his plays differently than what you are accustomed to. As you ponder the numerous presentations constantly hounding you, think about the following:

1. How could this presentation have been improved by added media (e.g., visuals, audio, Internet access)?
2. Would I have benefited from a *handout*?
3. How could the presentations have made more of an impact?

Orientation

What's the workspace look like?

Figure 5.2 shows the common workspace used to create presentations using MS PPT. This figure shows an example of a presentation currently being developed. Note the use of the outline area to quickly add content, and the note area used to add notes for the speaker.

What tools can be used?

The Standard and Formatting toolbars have many of the main tools that you will use to create and edit most PPT slides. However, there are many other features that can be used when needed. To find other tools, look for the Toolbar menu (**View>>>Toolbars**) and you will find tools to work with pictures, forms, tables, drawing, and so on.

Workout: Explore the territory

Turn on your computer and launch PPT.

1. Create a new PPT presentation with a blank first slide.
2. Look around and review the different toolbars displayed, and make sure the Standard, Formatting, and Drawing toolbars are up and running (see **View Menu >>> Toolbars >>> *Select the one you desire***).
3. Try adding some words to the outline portion and then attempt the same on the slide portion of the normal view.
4. Play with the toolbars, and note the similarities and differences of other software products you have used.

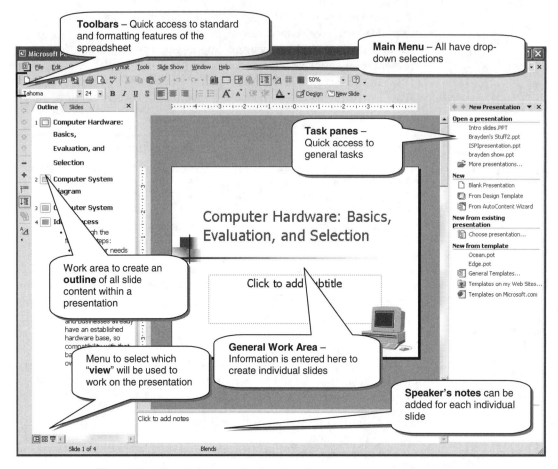

Figure 5.2 Normal view workspace used to create PPT presentations

Key features: The Views

To work effectively within PPT, there are different ways that you can view your workspace. To select one of these views, **View>>>Normal** (or **Slide Sorter** or **Slide Show**), or click on the View bar generally located in the lower left portion of the PPT screen (see Figure 5.2). It looks like

Normal View.

Note that you can view and work in the outline on the left, the slide itself (upper right), and enter in any speaker notes directly below the slide. This is generally the view used to complete most work. Figure 5.2 is a larger version of this.

> **Note:** When you are creating a number of slides and entering a large amount of text, *or* even when you are brainstorming a potential presentation, click on the Outline tab and work in that view. You can expand this view to a majority of the workspace and it is very similar to working in MS Word outline. This can facilitate the development of your presentation.

Slide Sorter View.

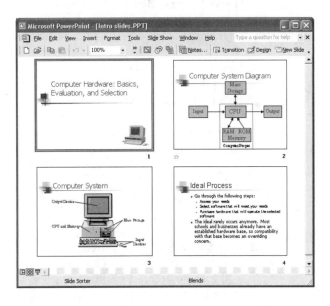

When you have a number of slides created, it often becomes difficult to change their order, to quickly see where a new slide needs to be inserted, or to delete a slide no longer needed. This is where the Slide Sorter view comes to the rescue. This view allows you to see all of your slides in a smaller version that can easily be grabbed and moved, deleted, added, and sequenced to your specifications. You will also find that this is a good view to use if you are adding transitions between slides.

Slide Show View.

This is the view that you use to present your slide program. Within this view, the slide takes up the full screen, and no toolbars or other features are displayed. You should also note that within this view all of the animations and action buttons (more on those later) are executed when selected to do so.

Workout: Further explorations of the territory

While in PPT, try the following:

1. Create a new presentation (**File>>>New**).
2. Slide 1 of the new presentation should appear and you should be viewing it within the Normal view. The task pane on the right-hand side of the view should indicate the type of text layout selected and give you alternatives if you wish to change it. Don't worry about this—we deal more with slide layouts soon.
3. Create several blank slides within this new presentation (to create a new slide: **Insert>>>New Slide**).
4. Click on the Outline tab and add text to each of your new slides. Note what happens on the graphic of the slide as you type the information into the outline. You also can directly enter the text onto the slide graphic. Try both ways and see which you prefer.
5. Switch to Slide Sorter using the View bar. Try changing the position of the slides in your presentation. For example, click and hold the first slide, and drag it to the last slide position and release the button.
6. Play around with the different views. Think about and compare the advantages of one view over another for different times when you will be using PPT and creating presentations.

Key features: The Masters

What is a "Master" slide?   A "Master" is a background that repeats on all slides, notes, or handouts of a presentation. It can contain text, graphics, automatic slide numbers, action buttons, and so forth.

Why use Masters?   Masters are fantastic time savers. In many cases, you will want some element of a slide to be consistently presented on all slides of a presentation (e.g., the same colored background, the school logo, a set of action buttons). The Master allows you to create it *once*, and it automatically appears on all slides in the presentation (you also can indicate those you don't want it to appear on if need be).

Are there different kinds of Masters?   Yes, besides the Slide Master (see Figure 5.3 for an example), there is also a Handout Master and a Notes Master. This way you can control how the pages for your handouts and/or the speaker's notes appear.

How do you access the Masters?   Simple—go to the **View menu >>> Master >>> Slide** (or **Handout** or **Notes**) **Master**.

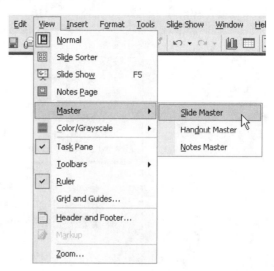

Figure 5.3 Master Slide.

How do you use the Masters?   Review Figure 5.3. This is a Master slide that has some suggestions already. By simply clicking in the different elements, you can adjust and add to this Master just as you would to any other PPT slide. You can adjust what's already present (e.g., change the style, size, font of the heading), and this is automatically applied to all slides currently in your presentation or that are later added to your presentation. If you don't like what you did, you can always change it back—nothing's permanent.

Key features: The time savers

Several elements can be highlighted in this section. PPT has a number of nice features that allow you to create, alter, and produce, saving you time and energy. We only look at a few of the most common.

1. Slide Layouts   PPT has a number of different "pre-made" layouts that may match what you need for the slide you are about to create. If one of these matches, it can be quickly selected, and then information can be automatically formatted to meet the specifications of your selected layout. You "point and click," and let PPT do the work instead of having to create the layout yourself. This is an excellent time saver!

If you don't like the way it looks once you have used a layout, you can adapt it directly, or even select a different auto layout and have it reformatted automatically.

How do you access the slide layouts?   Make sure the task panes are revealed (**View>>>Task Panes**) and that you have selected to work within the Normal view.

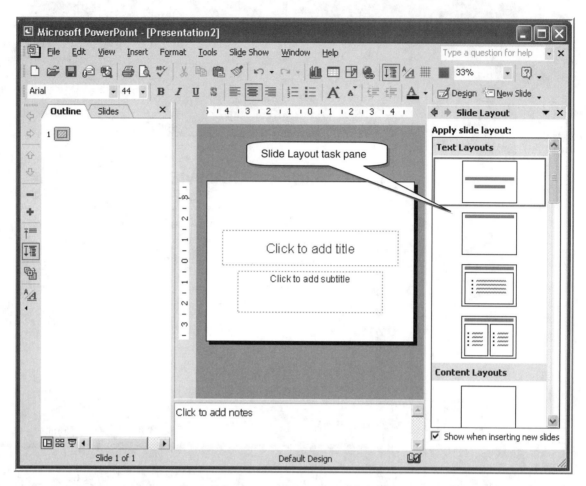

Figure 5.4 New slide with Slide Layout task pane exposed

Whenever you begin a "new slide," the Apply Slide Layout task pane should appear on the right side of your normal PPT view (see Figure 5.4).

MAC USERS

Whenever a new slide is created, the "Slide Layout" window appears. You can make a selection of the layout at that point. If you desire to change the layout at any time, **Format>>>Slide Layout. . .** brings back the Slide Layout window.

How does the slide layout work?   First, you select the layout of your choice (scroll to a preferred layout and click your selection). The new slide is immediately adapted to the type of layout you have selected (instructions to "Click here . . ." within dashed line boxes indicate the layout). As you insert content or pictures in your slide, you simply click the area where you want to work. All spacing, fonts, and formatting have been done for you. Figure 5.5 is an example of a new slide with a slide layout that has been set up to allow for a title, bulleted list of items, and other forms of media to be quickly inserted. Again, this is a great way to speed the process along.

2. Design Templates   What is a design template? Design templates are already completed Master slides that can be selected and applied to your presentation to give it a professional design. PPT comes with a large variety of professionally designed templates.

Why use templates?   These templates were developed by professionals who have considered the color combinations, font styles, and background graphics to give a presentation an overall polished look. By merely selecting and choosing one of the templates, that look can be incorporated within your presentation without further effort.

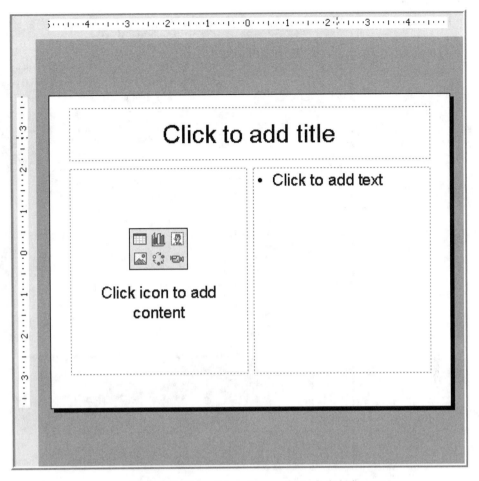

Figure 5.5 New slide with a selected slide layout

This allows you to concentrate on your content for the presentation and not worry about making it perfect.

How do you select and apply a template? Simply click **Format>>>Slide Design....** The Slide Design task pane (see Figure 5.6) appears, and you can preview and select from the list of the various designs. Simply click on your selected design and it is applied to the slides in your presentation.

If you ever desire to change this design, repeat the process and select a new template. Once applied, it automatically replaces the previously selected template.

To apply the Slide Design—**Format>>>Apply Slide Design,** and a window appears that helps you select and apply the design. Likewise, if a change is needed, this procedure makes the slide design changes.

Workout:
Explore the key
features

While in PPT:

1. Create or select two or more slides.
2. Select and apply a slide design to your slide show.
3. Add a new slide; select a layout from the Slide Layout task pane. Note how your selected slide design is automatically applied to the newly added slide.
4. Open the Master slide and alter some feature on the Master (e.g., add your name to the bottom of the Master slide).
5. Return to your slides and note the changes made on all slides using the same Master.

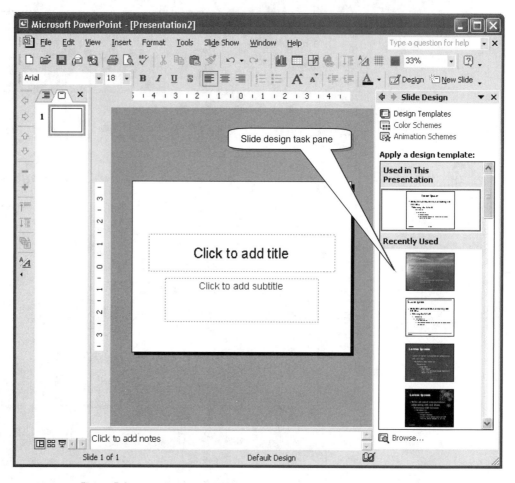

Figure 5.6 New slide with Slide Design task pane exposed

LEVEL 1: Designing, Creating, and Producing Presentations

What should you be able to do?

Given specific guidelines and step-by-step procedures, you will be able to use various tools and techniques of an electronic presentation program (specifically PPT) to design, create, and deliver a presentation.

The situation . . .

Janice, another eighth-grade teacher and one who is viewed as the computer "expert" in the school, comes to you with a request. She has been asked by the principal to give a series of short in-service lessons on integrating technology in the classroom. This week's lesson is designed to focus on how technology can address individual student differences. She explains that she needs your help in reviewing the common differences of students faced by teachers, and then she will follow with what can be done with technology to address those issues.

Even though you feel that this is another addition to your long "to-do list," you quickly remember all the times Janice has rescued you in the computer lab with her suggestions and practical help. So you smile and hear yourself enthusiastically reply, "Sure, I'd be happy to."

After a day or two of thought (and a little research), you develop the following short outline and send an e-mail to Janice to get her thoughts and approval:

I. Introduction: How students differ
   A. Begin with a story about how two students differ on how they approach a problem.

II. Highlight how students differ:
    A. Developmental level
    B. Intelligence
    C. Learning style
    D. Gender
    E. Culture
    F. Socioeconomic status
    G. Special needs
    H. Motivation
    I. Existing knowledge and skills

Later that day, she sends you an e-mail reply with two attached PPT slides (see Figures 5.7a and 5.7b).

The plan

- Take a close look at Figures 5.7a and 5.7b. These figures highlight what has been done to the PPT slides so they look like a finished product. Pay attention to the numbered callout bubbles.

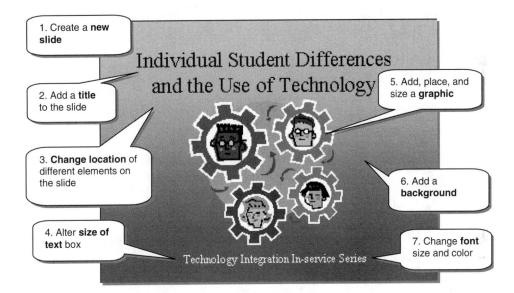

Figure 5.7a

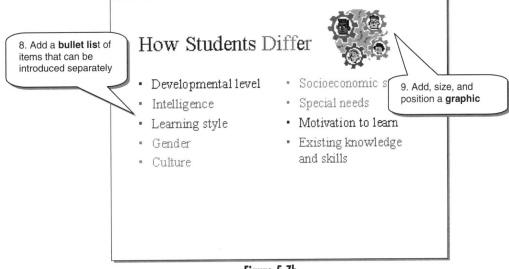

Figure 5.7b

- Follow the step-by-step procedures outlined by the numbered callout bubbles and create two similar slides. They don't have to be exact replicas—just demonstrate that you can carry out the highlighted functions.

Workout:
By the numbers . . .

1. Launch your presentation program (e.g., Microsoft PowerPoint).
2. Open the existing unformatted version of the document on the CD [**File >> Open ...,** and then navigate to the CD, view the CD contents, open chp5_PPT folder, launch (double-click) the "differ1" file], or if you like, you can open a new presentation and create the slides for yourself. Figures 5.7a and 5.7b represent the slides that you should view from the CD.
3. If you have opened the "differ1" program, click on the Slide Show view and go through the different slides.
4. Review Figures 5.7a and 5.7b, and note the numbered callouts. Those numbers correspond with the table below and what you will be doing to create such a presentation.
5. For simplicity, we finish the presentation by the numbers. Those numbers correspond with the instruction table.

No.	What We Are Working on	How You Go About Getting It Done
1.	**Create a new slide**	**Goal:** Create a new slide and select the proper slide layout. **Steps:** 1. Start PPT and create a new presentation (**File>>>New**). 2. Make sure the task panes are revealed (**View>>>task panes**). 3. On the Slide Layout task pane, select a layout for your new slide. For this demonstration, we have selected the one that looks like
2.	**Add a slide title**	**Goal:** Add text to the slide layout template. **Steps:** 1. Click the area in the new slide designated for the title. Type in the title of this slide (e.g., "Individual Student Differences . . ."). 2. Click the subtitle area of the slide and type in the subtitle (e.g., "Technology Integration . . ."). Note how the Slide Layout feature controls the location, font type, and size.
3.	**Change location of slide layout elements**	**Goal:** Move elements of the slide layout to different positions on the slide. **Steps:** 1. To move any element on a slide, click once on the item to be moved, and "handles" (little boxes) with a line around the item appear. 2. Move your cursor directly over the line and it turns into a four-way arrow. 3. Click, hold, and drag the item to the new location on the slide and then release the button.

No.	What We Are Working on	How You Go About Getting It Done
4.	**Alter text box size**	**Goal:** Change the size of the text box to get more or less words on a specific line. **Steps:** 1. Click once on the text box and the handles appear. 2. Move the cursor over one of the handles and it changes into a double-headed arrow. 3. Click, hold, and drag, and the size of the box changes in the direction you are dragging. Play with the different handles and see their different effects on the size of the box. 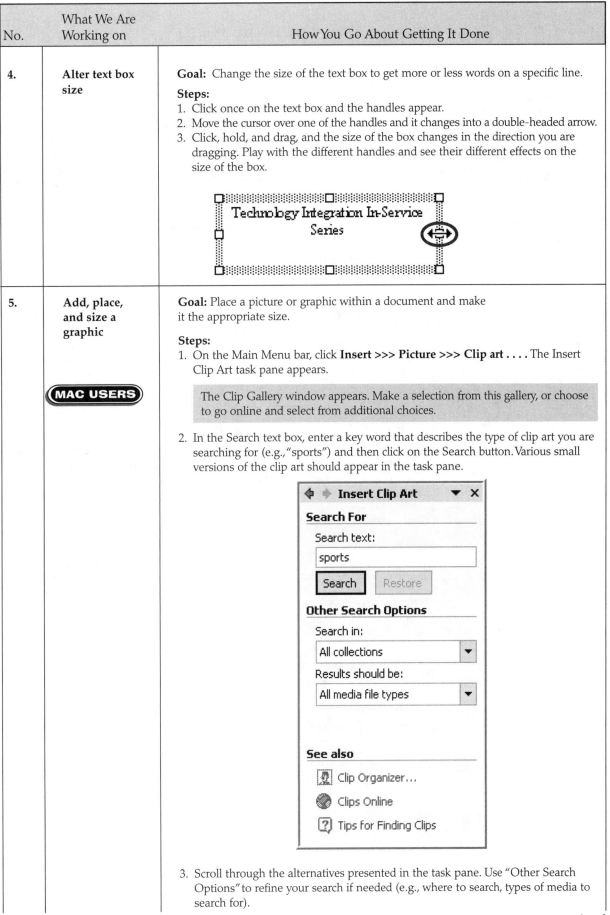
5.	**Add, place, and size a graphic** (MAC USERS)	**Goal:** Place a picture or graphic within a document and make it the appropriate size. **Steps:** 1. On the Main Menu bar, click **Insert >>> Picture >>> Clip art . . . .** The Insert Clip Art task pane appears. The Clip Gallery window appears. Make a selection from this gallery, or choose to go online and select from additional choices. 2. In the Search text box, enter a key word that describes the type of clip art you are searching for (e.g., "sports") and then click on the Search button. Various small versions of the clip art should appear in the task pane. 3. Scroll through the alternatives presented in the task pane. Use "Other Search Options" to refine your search if needed (e.g., where to search, types of media to search for).

continued

No.	What We Are Working on	How You Go About Getting It Done
	 Selected clip art with handles.	4. Click your selected clip art and the picture is automatically inserted within your document. **Note:** Some of your selected pictures may not be stored on your hard drive or server. In that case a window appears and states that your selection was not found. To solve this dilemma, you can do one of several things. Find the CD-ROM that contains the library of clip art and insert it. Retry the insertion process and the clip art should be retrieved from the CD. Another option is to go directly to the Microsoft "Clips Online" site. There should be a direct link located at the bottom of the Insert Clip Art task pane. Once you arrive at that site, follow the directions for selecting and using its clip art. 5. If your inserted clip art is the perfect size for your document—great, leave it as is. However, in many cases, the size is not perfect. So point your mouse at the picture and left click once. You should note that a box is drawn around the picture and handles are placed at each of the corners and in the middle of each of the sides. You can grab a handle by putting your mouse pointer on the handle (note that your pointer changes into a double-headed arrow), left click, and hold it. Dragging a handle causes the picture to be altered. Try different handles, and see what happens to the shape and size of the picture. 6. Once your picture is inserted and sized appropriately, you can move it to a different location on the slide by clicking, holding, and dragging it to the new location. **Note:** Working with clip art and other graphic files may take a bit of practice. You will find that some don't look that nice when their size is changed to a drastic degree—others work great. You will also find that access to the Internet gives you an endless supply of various clip art, pictures, and so forth that you may want to use and insert within your documents.
6.	**Add (or delete) a** *background* **to a slide**	**Goal:** Alter a background on any given slide. **Steps:** 1. On the Main Menu bar, click on **Format >>> Background** . . . . 2. The Background window appears. This window shows you the color scheme currently in place. If you desire to change it, you can select the drop-down menu in the Background fill area and make your selection for colors or other fill effects. These effects include adding gradients, textures, patterns, or pictures to your background.

No.	What We Are Working on	How You Go About Getting It Done

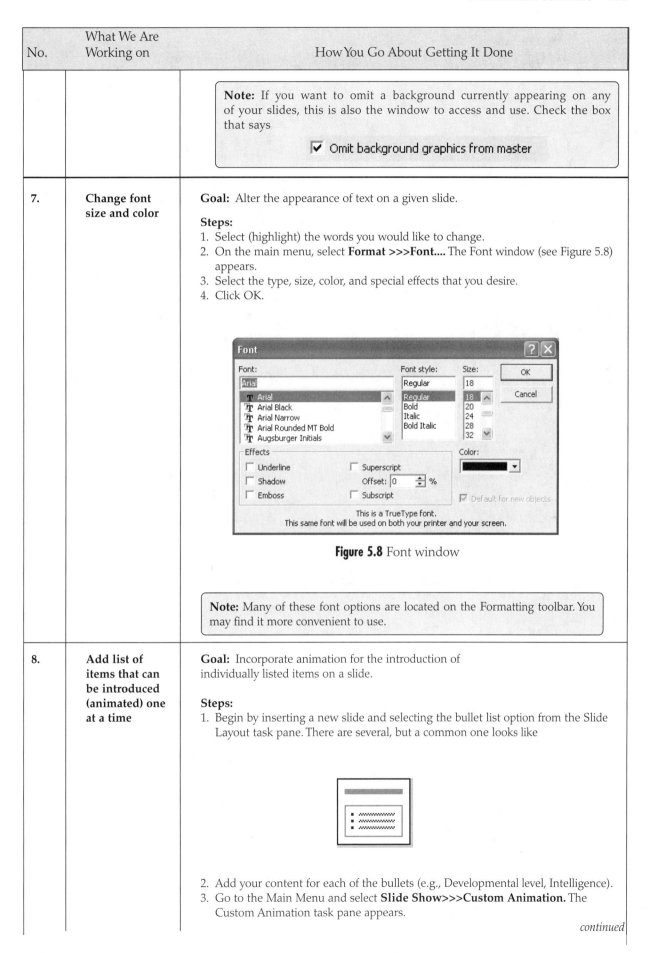

Note: If you want to omit a background currently appearing on any of your slides, this is also the window to access and use. Check the box that says

☑ Omit background graphics from master

7. | **Change font size and color**

Goal: Alter the appearance of text on a given slide.

Steps:
1. Select (highlight) the words you would like to change.
2. On the main menu, select **Format >>>Font....** The Font window (see Figure 5.8) appears.
3. Select the type, size, color, and special effects that you desire.
4. Click OK.

Figure 5.8 Font window

Note: Many of these font options are located on the Formatting toolbar. You may find it more convenient to use.

8. | **Add list of items that can be introduced (animated) one at a time**

Goal: Incorporate animation for the introduction of individually listed items on a slide.

Steps:
1. Begin by inserting a new slide and selecting the bullet list option from the Slide Layout task pane. There are several, but a common one looks like

2. Add your content for each of the bullets (e.g., Developmental level, Intelligence).
3. Go to the Main Menu and select **Slide Show>>>Custom Animation.** The Custom Animation task pane appears.

continued

No.	What We Are Working on	How You Go About Getting It Done
		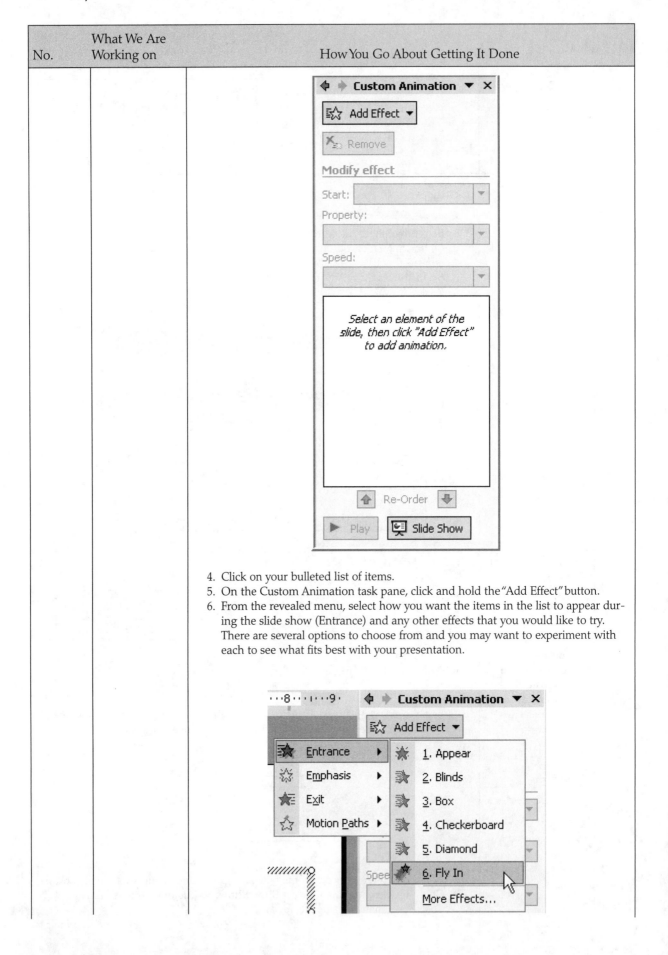

4. Click on your bulleted list of items.
5. On the Custom Animation task pane, click and hold the "Add Effect" button.
6. From the revealed menu, select how you want the items in the list to appear during the slide show (Entrance) and any other effects that you would like to try. There are several options to choose from and you may want to experiment with each to see what fits best with your presentation.

No.	What We Are Working on	How You Go About Getting It Done
		7. You may also make a selection based on whether your list of items should be emphasized in any way, on how you want them to exit the slide, and/or if you want them to move across the slide and show motion in some way. All of these effects are selected within this Add Effect area. 8. Each of the effects can be modified (when to occur, to what degree, and so forth) within the Modify effect area of the task pane. 9. Once you have selected one or more effects, view what the effects will look like by clicking on the Play button. If alterations are needed, return to the Modify effect selections. 10. To remove an effect, simply select the element (e.g., the list) and click on the Remove button. **Note:** Not only can you do these custom animation effects with bulleted and numbered lists of items, it also works for any element (e.g., clip art, words, word art) that you select on the slide. By selecting the elements, you can determine the sequence and the timing for the animation. Lots of fun stuff to play with.
	MAC USERS	Although you don't use task panes, the procedures for custom animations (and the results) are very similar. Use the **Slide Show>>>Animations>>>Custom...** menus, and the custom animation window will appear. Make your selection for the type of effect, as well as the order and timing.
9.	Add, size, and position a graphic	This is basically a repeat of what we learned in Step 5. Notice how you can use a graphic in a smaller version as a logo or theme within other PPT slides.

Level 2: Templates, Animations, and More

What should you be able to do?

In this section we want you to create, edit, and format several original presentations and sets of individualized instructional materials using advanced PPT features. In addition, you should learn to effectively use the Help feature of the software.

A little story . . .

Getting ready for the school Science Fair offers a number of challenges. One of the biggest is persuading parents to buy into the project. For Roberta Andrews, educating the parents of her students about the different elements of the project hadn't always been consistent and hadn't produced reliable results in the past. One key element that had often led to confusion—but always critical to the projects—is "The Scientific Method."

This year, Roberta decided to do something different. Early within the school year—in fact, during her school's "Meet the Teacher Night"—she decided to introduce the topic to the parents. To do this effectively, she thought of using a PPT presentation. This would allow her to present the material in a professional manner and efficiently create handouts that the parents could take home and discuss with their kids. Later, she might actually reuse the presentation as an introduction to the Science Fair projects for her students and give them the handouts to take home to remind the parents of what they had heard during her presentation.

Getting some Help

Similar to **Help** in Windows, there is also **Help** in MS PPT and most other sophisticated presentation software. To use **Help**, click the **Help menu>>>Microsoft PowerPoint Help.** A **Help** window opens, and by clicking on the Answer Wizard tab you can type in your question and **Help** responds with a variety of potential answers. To get a general overview of what **Help** has to offer, click on the Contents tab.

Help generally *does not* have all of the answers—but it will have a lot of them. Make sure you get a good feel for how it works and how often it can be of assistance.

> **Note**: Check out "Getting and Using **Help**," Crib Note, 6 in appendix A, for more information and insights on using the **Help** feature.

Explore: "The Scientific Method"

Within Level 2 of this software application, an open house presentation has been created.

Look closely at Figure 5.9 and note the salient features included in the printout of these PPT slides. Also, go to the CD, open the chp5_PPT folder, and launch (double-click) the "SciMethod" slide show.

Within Figure 5.9 specific items have been highlighted for your attention.

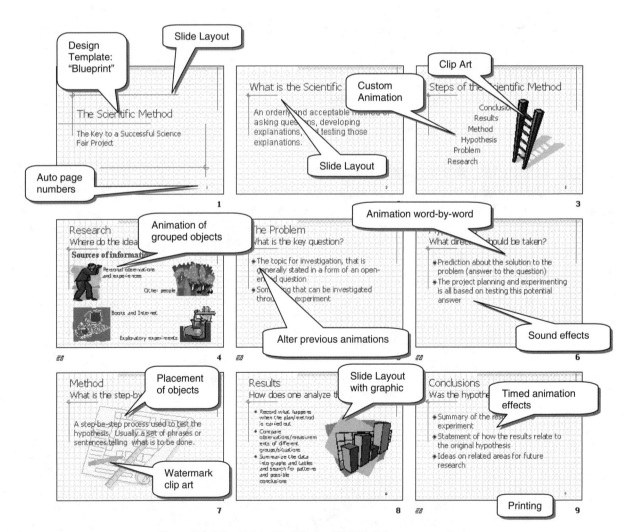

Figure 5.9 "The Scientific Method" PPT slide presentation

Workout: Stretching with a little Help . . .

After reviewing the SciMethod slide show and all of the features included in Figure 5.9, it's time for you to create your own PPT presentation. Using similar functions (e.g., action buttons, templates), create an original presentation that can be given to an audience of your selection.

Our purpose here is not to explain every step (as in the Level 1 version) on how to complete this; however, we do supply you with the example of what the various features are and some critical questions you can think about and investigate (via Help/Office Assistant) to find the needed procedures and solutions. After a short time period, incorporating these various techniques will become second nature to you. You should also quickly realize that you don't have to remember everything—you just have to recall the software's capabilities and how to ask Help for guidance.

This is actually quite fun. With a few easy steps you can be creating presentations that look as if you have spent hours working on them. If you want to "show off"—PPT is a good way to do it.

Feature	Ask the Office Assistant (Help)
Create a new PPT presentation	• **How do you create a new presentation?** Click on the section about creating a presentation.
Change slide layout	• **How do you change the layout of a slide?** Click on the "Apply a slide layout" alternative.
Insert auto slide numbers	• **How do you add slide numbers?** Click on the section about "Headers and Footers."
Use design templates	• **What is a design template?** Look for a subheading that discusses "About design templates." • **How do you change templates?** Click on the section about applying a design template.
Adding and altering custom animation	• **What is custom animation?** Click on the section about animating text and objects. This also walks you through the steps to get this done.
Inserting clip art	• **How do you insert a picture?** By asking for the "picture," you are given a selection of alternatives for inserting clip art, imported pictures, and even scanned pictures
Grouping objects and text	• **How do you group objects?** Look for the alternative that explains "Group objects." There is good information in this section about how to group objects, how to align and distribute objects, and even how to rotate and flip objects.
Animation of grouped objects	• **How do you use animation effects?** Look for the section on "About animating text and objects." Click on the section "Animate text and objects" to find of the steps involved.
Altering animations that have already been presented	• **How do you use animation effects?** Look for the section on "Change the color of text after an animation." **Note:** This is a good technique to use during a presentation to help the audience know which point you are discussing. That is, it helps the audience focus their attention.
Introducing animations word-by-word (or letter-by-letter)	• **How do you use animation effects?** Look closely at the explanation given in the topic "Animate text by letter, word, or paragraph."

continued

Feature	Ask the Office Assistant (Help)
	Note: There are times when letter-by-letter or word-by-word presentations may be effective. However, use this effect sparingly—it becomes boring for the fast reader who has to wait for the letters or words to appear individually.
Adding sound effects to slide animations	• **How do you add sounds to slide animations?** Click on the topic about "Add a sound to an animation." **Note:** Take a look at the option "About music and sounds," and you will find all kinds of additional information on inserting music, videos, sounds, and even animated GIF pictures.
Placing objects on the slide	• **How do you move an object on a slide?** Click the "Move an object" alternative. Make sure you note the Tips given about constraining objects to move only horizontally or vertically, or in moving objects very short distances.
Using washed out clip art	• **How do you alter the clip art contrast in a slide?** Click on the section about "Change the contrast or brightness of a picture."
Slide layouts with graphics	• **How do you change the layout of a slide?** This is addressed within the Level 1 section of this chapter.
Timing the animation effects	• **How do you animate text and objects?** Look for a selection that deals with animating text and objects. Within that section there is a procedure explaining order and timing.
Creating and printing handouts	• **How do you create handouts?** Look for the section "About handouts." This explains how to create the handout and how to print it with a selected amount of slides appearing on each handout page.
Printing options	• **What can you print?** Several options are revealed (e.g., print handouts, print slides, print an outline). Select the most relevant topic and it lists the steps involved to achieve what is desired.

"The Scientific Method" repurposed as individualized instruction

CD ACTIVITY

After successfully using "The Scientific Method" presentation at "Meet the Teacher Night," Roberta Rena now has other ideas. Using this presentation for the basic content, she quickly adapts it into a self-instructional program that can be used in her classroom as a key part of the Science Fair project. Review the program on the CD, in the chp5_PPT folder, by launching (double-clicking) the "SciMeth2" PPT presentation.

In this case, she wants the program to be used by individual students, who can control which portions of the presentation they see and can be quizzed on what they have read.

Note how the active buttons are used to navigate throughout the program and how they can be used to set up review questions with specific feedback.

Here are some key features that have been added within the SciMeth2 version of the Scientific Method presentation. Make sure you examine it first on the CD—then these features and questions will make sense.

Feature	Ask the Office Assistant (Help)
Action buttons	• **What is an action button?** Look for the section "About action buttons."
Inserting action buttons	• **How do you insert action buttons?** Check the section on inserting action buttons.
Making action buttons transparent	• Inserting a normal action button and then changing its fill color to "no fill" and its line color to "no line" can create invisible or transparent buttons. The button (and its associated action) are still present; however, you can now lay it over the top of a picture, graphic, word, and so forth, and it appears as if the action button does not exist. However, clicking on the item with the transparent button overlay produces the associated button action (that is, the button still works).
Placement of action buttons	• Note how action buttons that need to appear on every slide of the presentation can be inserted on the Master slide. These show up and work on every slide in which the Master is used.
Inserting hyperlinks	• **How do you insert hyperlinks?** Click on the section "About hyperlinks and action buttons." Information is presented about using hyperlinks in various ways within a presentation.
Adding a common logo or object to each slide	• **How do you add an object to each slide of a presentation?** Refer to the section, "Add a picture throughout a presentation."

Workout: Create your own presentation

Now you try it.

1. Review your calendar, school lesson plan, or day planner to see when your next presentation is. Select one that is coming up in the near future. It can be anything (e.g., class discussion on worm segments, proper swimming strokes, visit to the local art museum).
2. Jot down some important notes and an outline of what you would want others to see and hear during your presentation.
3. Start PPT and create some simple slides that cover the major concepts that should be in your presentation.
4. Add backgrounds, clip art, action buttons, and custom animations to your presentation.
5. Add speaker notes to the presentation and print out a copy of the handout with notes included.
6. Give your presentation to another student, friend, spouse, or relative. See what the reaction is and ask how the presentation can be enhanced.
7. Make any changes and try a test run one more time.

Level 3: Integration and Application

What should you be able to do?

Here is where you use this software to help yourself and your students. This section helps you see all the applications possible with using PPT (or similar software). You can use these examples as a springboard to launch ideas on ways to improve levels of student learning and your personal productivity.

Introduction

The examples given in Levels 1 and 2 coupled with your own development efforts should put you in a good position to perceive the possibilities for this type of presentation program.

Now we want you to expand your use of this program and think of what you could show and demonstrate to others. Here we give you different ideas, some that you may or may not find helpful, but we hope they are ideas that you can expand upon to make them relevant to your work and those with whom you work.

Presentation software integration

Creating the enhanced learning experience: A partial lesson plan

Topic: A study of the people, places, and culture of an African country.

Overview: Mr. Carpenter, an eighth-grade social studies teacher at Lowell Middle School, is continuing to search for ways for his students to "explore" Zimbabwe to find out about this African country and its people. Moreover, he wants his students to discover that much can be learned about the people of today by exploring their history and ancestors. With the help of one of his former students, Jonathon Rogers (who now is a university graduate student going to Zimbabwe on an internship with an international health and education organization), Mr. Carpenter hopes to guide his students as they discover the past of this fascinating country.

Through the use of e-mail, regular mail, digital photography, and audio recordings, Jonathon should be able to explore several historically significant sites within the borders of Zimbabwe and then share those with the Lowell social studies classes of Mr. Carpenter.

Specific Learning Task: To explore the history of the people of Zimbabwe, the students in Mr. Carpenter's social studies classes are to investigate the ancient city known as the "Great Zimbabwe." Each class is divided into smaller cooperative groups who are asked to address one of the following sets of questions:

- What was the "Great Zimbabwe"? Who were the people that built it? What did the city look like when it was populated? What caused it to decline and decay?
- If one lived in the Great Zimbabwe, what was life like? What did people do, what did they wear, what did they eat, how did they travel from place to place, what did they believe in, and how did they communicate and conduct business? What were some interesting aspects about living in this city?
- How were the ruins of the Great Zimbabwe discovered? Who made those discoveries? What was done to the ruins after they were discovered? What is the role of the archeologist in uncovering and understanding a people who no longer are alive? What does the Great Zimbabwe look like today?

Sample Learning Objectives: Students will be able to do the following:

1. Identify and describe important elements and events about life during the time of the Great Zimbabwe and how people lived within that society.
2. Examine and explain potential reasons for the rise and fall of great societies such as those who lived within the Great Zimbabwe.
3. Explain the role of archeologists in the discovery of places and people of the past.

Procedure:

1. Break into the groups, examine the assigned questions for study, and brainstorm methods to investigate.
2. Examine Web sites and other reference materials for information about the Great Zimbabwe. For example:

- Great Zimbabwe Ruins
  http://www.worldheritagesite.org/sites/site364.html
- Great Zimbabwe 500-1600 A.D.
  http://campus.northpark.edu/history/WebChron/Africa/GreatZimbabwe.html
- Riddle of the Great Zimbabwe
  http://www.archaeology.org/9807/abstracts/africa.html
- Mystery of the Great Zimbabwe
  http://www.pbs.org/wgbh/nova/israel/zimbabwe.html

3. Contact Jonathon to see if he has visited this archeological site and/or if he has heard anything about it. Ask for further information if he can find it from individuals who live in the country. If he does visit, have him write his impressions of what it was like and send pictures of what he found.
4. Using the assigned questions as a starting point, create a group presentation about the Great Zimbabwe.

Questions About the Integration of Presentation Software

This lesson could be completed in a number of ways, including simple oral reports, reenactments or role plays, or video or live presentations by subject matter experts such as archeologists. In addition, the use of presentation software, such as PPT, can be used to create overhead slides and handouts to accompany an oral presentation. Use the following reflective questions to explore the value of potentially integrating PPT or another form of presentation software within such a lesson as outlined by Mr. Carpenter.

- How will the small research groups cooperatively brainstorm and plan the presentation? Can presentation software be used to facilitate the planning process?
- Can the development of specific sets of information (e.g., tables or lists of information, charts, and maps) increase the level of understanding for the individual group members?
- Will the presentation involve the use of audio, visual graphics, and/or video clips of some kind? Will these items need to be presented in such a way that a large (more than ten people) group of people can see and hear?
- During and/or following the presentation, can learning be enhanced by the production and distribution of a handout of the presented information? Would such a handout facilitate a group discussion on the topic?
- Will there be a need for the presentation to be stored for later use by other classes, individual students, or interested parents, faculty, and so on?

Workout: Integrating PowerPoint

1. Read each of the following situations. Imagine being directly involved in the planning for each of these projects. Select one (or more if you wish) for further consideration.

School Days

The lives of children throughout the world vary based on many different factors. One common element for most is that they go to some kind of formal school. But how similar are the experiences that the students have? How does a typical school day in various places of the world compare? What kinds of subjects are studied, how much time is spent on each subject, how much variety is given between the different subjects? How do kids get to school, how long do they stay there, how much homework do they have? How is the learning of the students assessed? After examining all these different ways of "doing school," what would be an appropriate method to examine and evaluate the similarities and differences between the various school systems? If asked to suggest a plan for the "best" school system, how would the proposal be created and presented?

Pet Care

Third-grade students were learning about pets. In separate groups they focused on different common family pets. They studied the types of food needed, the care needed, the living space, and even the amount of play and exercise that the animal needed. Together they decided to create a program that would help other students learn about the care of family pets. They desired to assemble all of their information and produce a resource for other students to use when they had a question about a pet they might own or might be thinking about owning.

Invention Evolution

Over time, good ideas have a tendency to evolve. Transportation, for example, has evolved from riding animals to riding in spaceships. As inventions have been used and evaluated, changes naturally occur. In what ways have some of our common tools (such as the dishwasher, vacuum cleaner, computer, light bulb, television) evolved over time?

Marketing a business

A new start-up business has come to your company and asked you to make a presentation about marketing one of its new products. The product is a new form of software that companies use to monitor and report all Web activity by their employees. It helps companies make sure employees are properly using the Internet during office hours. How can the new company be convinced that you have the knowledge and capabilities to market their new software?

2. Based on your selected project, consider the following questions that concern the integration of presentation software such as PPT. Mark your response to each question.

Integration assessment questionnaire (IAQ)

Will using **PRESENTATION** software as a part of the project:			
Broaden the learners' perspective on potential solution paths and/or answers?	_____ Yes	_____ No	_____ Maybe
Increase the level of involvement and investment of personal effort by the learners?	_____ Yes	_____ No	_____ Maybe
Increase the level of learner motivation (e.g., increase the relevance of the to-be-learned task, the confidence of dealing with the task, and/or the overall appeal of the task)?	_____ Yes	_____ No	_____ Maybe
Decrease the time needed to generate potential solutions?	_____ Yes	_____ No	_____ Maybe
Increase the quality and/or quantity of learner practice working on this and similar projects?	_____ Yes	_____ No	_____ Maybe
Increase the quality and/or quantity of feedback given to the learner?	_____ Yes	_____ No	_____ Maybe
Enhance the ability of the student to solve novel, but similar, projects, tasks, and problems in the future?	_____ Yes	_____ No	_____ Maybe

3. If you have responded "Yes" to one or more of the questions, you should consider the use of PPT to enhance the student's potential learning experience.
4. Develop a lesson plan based on this project. Within the plan, indicate how and when the learner will use PPT. Additionally, list potential benefits and challenges that may occur when involving this software within the lesson.

Workout: Exploring the NETS Standard connection

Developing and executing a lesson plan that integrates the use of presentation software such as Microsoft's PPT directly addresses several of the NETS Standards for both teachers (NETS*T) and students (NETS*S). See appendix B for a full listing of the standards.

Part A: Generally, the main purpose for learning and using application software is to increase your level of production—that is, to do things faster, better, or both. NETS standards (NETS*T Standard V and NETS*S Standard 3) help you focus on these productivity objectives for both teachers and students. There are other technology standards, however, that may also be potentially addressed through your knowledge and use of presentation software. Reflect on the following questions and consider the potential impact of the integration of such software (refer to appendix B to review the full sets of standards):

- When designing a presentation, how can the use of the outlining feature within PPT (and similar presentation programs) increase brainstorming for creative thinking? Can this feature also be used to increase collaborative planning between groups of individuals during the planning process? (NETS*T III.B. and III.C.; NETS*S 3 and 6)
- In what ways can the use of linked graphics, as well as video and audio clips, be integrated to increase levels of learning for diverse audiences? (NETS*T VI B. and VI.C; NETS*S 4)
- By using action buttons to produce individualized instructional materials, in what ways could the use of linked activities, Web sites, and other information be used to manage the students' learning environment? (NETS*T II.E.)
- Presentation software was created to help disseminate information. How could the use of such software improve the communication skills developed by both teachers and students (NETS*T V.D.; NETS*S 4)

Part B: Go to the ISTE Web site http://cnets.iste.org. Within that site, select to review either the student or the teacher NETS Standards. Once you have selected the standards to review, select either the student or teacher profiles, and look for the corresponding scenarios. Review the scenarios and determine how presentation software can be used within several of those situations.

While visiting the ISTE Web site and exploring the scenarios, go to the lesson plan search area and select different lesson plans of interest. Review those and determine the role (if any) of presentation software within the development, implementation, and assessment of the lesson. Note this from both the perspective of the teacher developing the lesson and from the perspective of the student participating in the implemented lesson.

Workout: Comprehensive integration

You need to understand that in most practical learning situations, one type of software generally doesn't stand alone as *the* solution. That is, full integration may mean that you use PPT *and* other software such as Web development, spreadsheets, and data management. For this Workout:

1. Read through the lesson plan you designed within the previous Workout.
2. Identify how your suggestions for the integration of presentation software may be enhanced by the use of other software (e.g., Web development, word processing).
3. Describe the benefits and the problems that may be associated with the integration of other software within the same project.
4. Describe how additional technology standards (e.g., NETS*T II.A.: ". . . design developmentally appropriate learning opportunities that apply technology-enhanced instructional strategies to support the diverse needs of learners") can be addressed by the integration of various types of applications software.

Further ideas on using PowerPoint as a learning tool

When using presentation software such as PPT, people often think immediately about using it merely for verbal presentations. The first few examples are ideas based on such presentations—but then look beyond to see other possibilities for this software and how individuals can adapt and use it to learn.

> **Note:** These ideas are to help you generate your own ideas of what could be done. Don't let it bother you if they are not the right content or grade level; use the idea and adapt it to be helpful within your own situation. These are meant to be a stimulus for additional ideas.

1. Classroom demonstrations: With the use of scanned pictures, imported videos, sound, and other media, you can readily demonstrate concepts, procedures, and so on to a group of individuals.
2. Have students create their own reports and practice verbal skills by making presentations to the class (e.g., book reports).
3. Have the students create and deliver a group project where the presentation is the central product they create. For example, have groups of students create science fair oral presentations about their group projects.
4. Develop a debate between two or more groups of students. Each "side" could develop their own key points and present those to a panel of judges via presentation software.
5. Use the outlining feature within PPT to have groups of students brainstorm certain concepts and how they would be presented for logical explanations.
6. Using action buttons, have the students create interactive presentations that link with the Internet and specific Web sites for additional information, media, and activities.
7. Create a preview or review quiz or test for students that allows them to make a selection and receive feedback on their performances.
8. Create an interactive calendar that allows students to click on the day and receive information on what will occur, homework assignments, links to various activities, student jobs, and so on.
9. Create an interactive book club where students can click on any book (active button) listed and learn about the book, read student critiques about the book, and perhaps even send questions via e-mail to the author.
10. Create a map of the city (or of the world, or of the human body, and so forth), and have transparent action buttons that allow students to click on a certain section so that further information will be given about that section.
11. Create a flier for advertising some product or an announcement—for example, simple fliers using graphics to promote a school dance, someone's birthday, or a special award.
12. Develop a comparison table that lists the pros and cons of a specific issue (e.g., building a new power plant in a nearby location). Each cell can be hyperlinked to other slides explaining the pros and cons of the issue in more detail.
13. Create an interactive time line based on some period in history. Along the time line have action buttons that activate relevant graphics, videos, text, or audio media revealing important elements of that point in history.
14. Have students create a presentation on a proposal for a major course project. Perhaps this can be a presentation about a future science fair project, a major English, history, and math integrated project, and so on. Have them create handouts of their work, and defend their ideas and overall proposal.
15. Create a *WebQuest* (see http://webquest.sdsu.edu/webquest.html) using PPT and hyperlinks as the software instead of a Web development editor.
16. Have students create a self-instructional, automatic presentation. Have the program play music in the background as it demonstrates and explains the steps

involved in some type of procedure (e.g., how a paleontologist outlines and evaluates a potential dig site, how a farmer tills the ground, the processes used to refine petroleum, how potatoes are processed into potato chips).

17. For a geography, social studies, or history lesson, have each student in a class create a slide about a specific place, people, or time period. Put all of the slides together to form one slide show. Each of the students can then discuss his or her contribution.

Additional ideas on using PowerPoint as an assistant

1. **Handouts.** Several of the key slides can be printed as handouts for the students. These can then be used while the presentation is being made so that students can concentrate on what is being said versus trying to write down key concepts of the presentation. These also serve as very good advance organizers and as reviews following the presentation.

2. **Notes pages.** Often presentations are given on several occasions or for different classes. With the notes page, it is possible to create a version of the presentation that also has your notes of what you should say and an explanation for each of the slides presented. These notes can also be helpful to students who missed the presentation or who may not have caught everything said at the time of the presentation.

3. **Templates.** Many individuals find that a good presentation can be readily "repurposed" and adapted for another audience. By using the saved presentation as a template, a few changes can be made and a "new" presentation created.

4. **Storage places.** This is slightly different, but individuals have been known to use certain presentations on specific topics as a good place to "hold" important Web sites, pictures, ideas, and so on. For example, within a specific science presentation, an individual may find it convenient to create a resource page or slide of other related Web site addresses that can readily be found and used if a later need on this topic is uncovered or when an update of the presentation is required. This same idea may hold for specific pictures, graphics, ideas, or sound clips.

5. **Graphics.** Use the draw function in this program to create all kinds of charts, procedures, and other learning aids that students can see and follow. A seating chart or even an organizational chart, for example, can be created quickly. A job aid (simple procedure to follow) can be created in a matter of seconds (e.g., fire drill procedures, steps to follow to check out a library book, steps to completing a proper serve in tennis).

6. **Awards.** Create certificates for extra effort and merit.

Presentation Software References

Teachers using PowerPoint

Online tutorials and web sites *are not always reliably available* (that is, they come and go); therefore, going to a search engine (e.g., www.google.com) and then using productive search terms is very important. Here are some search terms that can be helpful in finding lesson plans and other examples for school topics that involve using PPT:

- **PowerPoint lesson plans**
- **Teachers using PowerPoint**

Examples of such sites include the following:

http://www.teach-nology.com

Link to the "Lesson Plan Center" and select the option for "Computing." Lesson plans are found at this site that focus on the use of the computer. As you look through the list, those that focus on PPT are easily identified.

http://www.lessonplanspage.com

This is a site devoted to lesson plans for teachers. There is a section that identifies and links to lesson plans specifically for computers and the Internet, and you can select lesson plans based on grade level.

http://www.teachers.net

This is a teacher resource site that contains hundreds of lesson plans. Click on the "Lessons" section and then search for "PowerPoint." Several examples of lessons (identified by content and by age group) can be retrieved with direct links to access those plans.

http://www.internet4classrooms.com

One of the most comprehensive sites for teachers. In particular, there are "On-Line Practice Modules" that can be accessed from this home page. Specific models for all types of PPT lesson plans and tutorials are linked. Additionally, within the "Links for K-12 Teachers" section, lesson plans involving PPT can be quickly accessed.

Tutorials and other resources

Search terms for learning how to use PPT and other useful tips:

- **PowerPoint tutorials**
- **PowerPoint tips**

http://www.internet4classrooms.com/on-line2.htm

Click on the section for PowerPoint and find a number of quickly accessible tutorials covering all types and versions of this presentation software.

http://www.microsoft.com/education

This site has select tutorials and other instructional materials for all Microsoft products across various grade levels and subject areas.

http://www.actden.com/pp/

A highly interactive and entertaining Web-based tutorial about using PPT in the classroom.

	Desired task to accomplish	Reference menu or toolbar*
Basic Tools	Create a new presentation	**File>>>New . . .**
	Access toolbars	**View>>>Toolbars**
	Access task panes	**View>>>Task Pane**
	Change view of workspace	**View>>>[Normal, Slide Sorter, *or* Slide Show]**
	Insert new slide	**Insert>>>New Slide**
	Insert picture or clip art	**Insert>>>Picture**
	Insert table	**Insert>>>Table . . .**
	Insert chart	**Insert>>>Chart . . .**
	Select slide layout	**Format>>>Slide Layout . . .**
	Access notes page	**View>>>Notes page**
	Create action button	**Slide Show>>>Action Buttons**
	Print slides, notes, handouts	**File>>>Print . . .**

	Desired task to accomplish	Reference menu or toolbar*
Additional Features	Text (font type, color, size effect)	**Format>>>Font**
	Text alignment	**Format>>>Alignment**
	Text box	**Insert>>>Text Box**
	Slide master	**View>>>Master>>>Slide Master**
	Notes master	**View>>>Master>>>Notes Master**
	Handout master	**View>>>Master>>>Handout Master**
	Slide layout	**Format>>>Slide Layout . . .**
	Slide design	**Format>>>Slide Design . . .**
	Background	**Format>>>Background**
	Picture (text alignment, contrast, color, size)	**View>>>Toolbars>>>Picture**
	Slide numbers	**Insert>>>Slide Number**
Formatting Features	Headers and footers	**View>>>Header and Footer . . .**
	Grids and/or guides	**View>>>Grid and Guides . . .**
	Altering color schemes	**Format>>>Slide Design . . .>>>task pane: color scheme**
	Inserting movies and sounds	**Insert>>>Movies and Sounds**
	Transitions between slides	**Slide Show>>>Slide Transition . . .**
	Animations—inserting on-demand *also* slide elements	**Slide Show>>>Animation Schemes . . .** **Slide Show>>>Custom Animation . . .**
	Action settings	**Slide Show>>>Action Settings . . .**
	Hyperlinks to other slides, presentations, Internet	**Slide Show>>>Action Settings . . .**
	Comments	**Insert>>>Comment**
	AutoShapes	**Insert>>>Picture>>>AutoShapes**
	WordArt	**Insert>>>Picture>>>WordArt**
	Create duplicate slide	**Insert>>>Duplicate Slide**

*NOTE: The first item listed is the Main Menu or toolbar. As explained earlier in chapter 1, the >>> indicates the selection to be made once a drop-down menu has been revealed. For example, **View>>>Task Panes** means to click on the View option of the Main Menu bar. This exposes a drop-down menu, and from that menu click the "Task Pane" option. This activates the relevant Task Pane window.

Chapter 6
WEB EDITOR
MS FrontPage: The Basics of Web Page Development

Introduction

What should you know about Web editors?

Web editing software allows you to create materials that can be distributed on the World Wide Web (WWW). In this opening section, we want you to know

- what a Web editor is, what it can do, and how it can help in teaching and learning;
- how to justify the use of the Web editor as an effective tool—by knowing when and why it should or shouldn't be used.

Terms to know

HTML	*links*	*WWW*
Web page or site	*browser*	*Web editor*

What is a Web editor and what does it do?

Web editors are tools used to efficiently and effectively design and develop *Web pages*. They allow you to insert and manipulate text, graphics, sound, movies, and so on, as well as to create links to other Web page elements and other sites on the WWW. For most of us, using a Web editor is very similar to using a word processing program. You can point and click to have items inserted, formatted, highlighted, or sized. In the case of the word processor, the end product generally is printed as hard copy—but with the Web editor, the end result can be effectively displayed by a Web browser on the Web.

For Web browsers (such as Internet Explorer or Netscape Navigator) to understand what to display, specific HTML (*Hypertext Markup Language*) codes need to be inserted in the documents you create. You can learn these codes and insert them yourself, *or* you can have a Web editor do it for you. For most of us, using the editor is faster, does a more sophisticated job, and creates less mistakes (and headaches).

What are some common Web editors?

- Microsoft's *FrontPage*
- Macromedia's *Dreamweaver*
- Adobe's *GoLive*
- Claris's *HomePage*

> **Note:** We focus on MS FrontPage in this text. However, **what we present can be done in any of the other Web editors listed.** So if you don't have access to MS FrontPage, don't be alarmed—you can still complete the projects and learn the basic skills.

> **Note:** Many of today's word processing programs (and other desktop publishing programs) have an option that allows you to save your documents as HTML. This is simple and easy; however, these programs are not designed specifically for Web page development and they may not be as easy to work with when dealing with advanced features and the editing of Web pages.

Why bother learning how to use a Web editor?

- **It's faster than learning and using HTML.** The editor does the tedious coding for you, and thus you can concentrate on the content of your creation.
- **It allows you to use what you already know.** If you know how to use a word processor, many of the same features (e.g., creating a table, inserting a picture, formatting words) will be very familiar to you.
- **It can enhance communication.** Developing Web pages and displaying them on the Web can be a simple way to provide consistent information to students, parents, colleagues, and administrators.
- **It can lead to greater learning experiences.** Using the editor may allow you to develop learning experiences that can draw on the depth of information found on the Web and thus impact student learning to a greater degree.
- **It allows for creative expression.** Whether working on something for class or developing a personal page for a hobby, the tools within the Web editor allow you to be creative in the design and presentation of your information.
- **It's fun.** Learning the basic features of the Web editor is not difficult or time-consuming. You can quickly find projects that are enjoyable to construct and immediately rewarding in their appearance and impact.

How can Web editors be used at school? A brief list of ideas

By the teacher:
- Ancillary information sites for students to visit and use
- Information boards
- Class or school Web site
- Unit or topical projects
- Virtual field trips

By the student:
- School digital newspaper or magazine
- Publish student projects
- Electronic portfolio
- Develop WebQuest-type projects
- Cooperative group designed projects

Workout

The use of Web pages is becoming more and more of a "normal" instructional practice. WebQuests, for example, are one such activity that teachers are finding available for their use and are finding ways to develop on their own. Get on the Internet and visit one or more of the following Web sites and explore the WebQuests available. These should help you see one special way teachers and students can develop Web projects to enhance teaching and learning that go beyond the normal pursuits allowed by common textbooks.

http://webquest.sdsu.edu/webquest.html

> This is the original WebQuest page from Bernie Dodge at San Diego State University. You will find links to an overview of WebQuests, training materials, and many example WebQuests.

http://school.discovery.com/schrockguide/webquest/webquest.html

> This is Kathy Schrock's "Guide for Educators" site at DiscoverySchool. You will find all kinds of very teacher-relevant materials about WebQuests, as well as some directions on how to develop them and examples to explore.

For other sites, go to your search engine (e.g., www.google.com) and type in the keyword **WebQuest.**

Once the sites have been visited, reflect on the following:

- How can you develop an activity similar to these for one of the topics that you teach?
- How would your students receive such a project?
- Would there be an advantage to your students if they developed such projects for themselves?

Orientation

What's the workspace look like?

Figure 6.1 is an example of the workspace of a common Web editor (MS FrontPage). Note where you can enter in your information and some of the common toolbars, buttons, and menus placed around the workspace.

> **Note:** The toolbars and Main Menu have several new tools that are designed specifically for Web page development and editing. However, there should be an "air of familiarity" about many of the tools that appear on these toolbars and menus. Yes, many work here as they do in other applications such as word processing and spreadsheets. That should help you start working on this even faster.

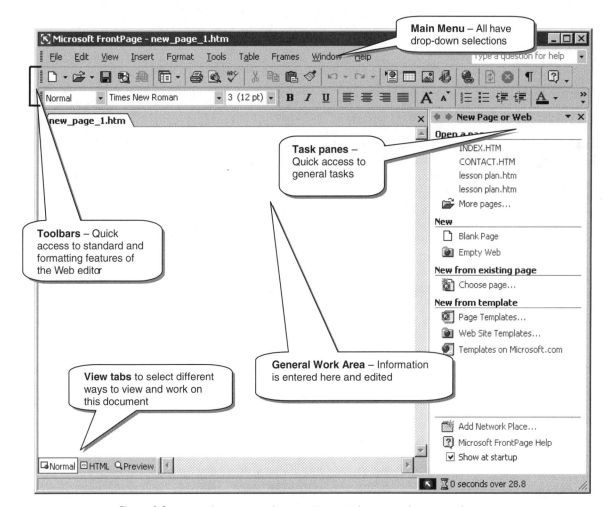

Figure 6.1 View of a Microsoft FrontPage Web page editing work area

> **Note:** Once you have FrontPage up and running and have entered in a sentence or two, it might be interesting for you to click on the HTML View tab in the bottom left corner of the workspace. This should give you a better appreciation for what the Web editor is doing for you. Without the editor, you would be entering in many of the <b> , <p> type codes to tell the browser how to handle this page when it's encountered on the Web.

What is a "browser"?

 Internet Explorer

 Netscape Navigator

A browser is a computer application program used to access Web pages on the WWW. The two most common browsers are **Internet Explorer** and **Netscape Navigator.** These programs allow the user to view and explore pages and sites found on the Web (they do this by accessing and interpreting the HTML code).

What are the key elements of a Web page?

When you look at some of the fancy things being done on Web sites, often it is easy to get the feeling that "I'll never be able to do that!" Actually, there are three basics that you should learn in order to do almost everything a teacher needs to create an instructional site. You need to know how to create and display

1. *Text*
2. *Images*
3. *Links*

On a difficulty scale of 1–5 (1 being simple, 5 being difficult), each of these skills falls right around a 1 or 2 (simple, fun, easy to grasp).

What are "links"?

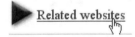

One of the most powerful features about Web pages is their ability to jump from one section of a Web page or site to another section of that same page or site, or even to another totally independent site on the WWW. *Links* tell the browser where to go. For example, you can mention on your Web page that some interesting activities can be completed on a different Web site and create a link to that site. Those viewing your page can click on the link and immediately jump to that location that your link has sent them to. Links are generally designated by the linked words highlighted in a different color (e.g., blue) and underlined. When the browser's mouse pointer passes over an active link, it changes into a "pointed finger," which indicates a click on the mouse button activates the link.

A nice advantage of such links is that if the individual using the browser doesn't want to visit the link, he or she can skip it. If more information is desired, the user is in control of what is seen and experienced.

You can imagine that this may also cause some confusion if too many links are provided and the user gets "lost," or if the user skips some important information because he or she chose not to explore a specific connection.

What kind of prep work is needed before building a Web page or site?

1. Plan what your Web site is about. Think about its purpose, the audience who may be viewing it, and the content that you are developing.
2. For a Web site to work properly, you need to have the proper folder structure so that all content is ordered and saved correctly. Here is what you should do:

a. Create a new folder on the desktop of your computer. Call this folder something that you'll remember as the Web folder for this particular content. Something like "dino1__web" will work nicely if you were developing a Web site about dinosaurs.

b. Open that new "dino1__web" folder and create another new folder inside it. Name this new folder "images." This is the folder that stores all the pictures you acquire and use in your Web site. To help you recall how to create a folder inside a folder, review the Level 1 Workout: By the Numbers, found in chapter 1.

> **Note:** By keeping everything inside one "dino1__web" folder, as you move the folder to different disks, computers, and elsewhere, all the contents are also successfully transported. Likewise, by keeping all the images in one folder ("images") inside of the "dino1__web" folder, access to the pictures will always be completed correctly.
>
> Also note that it is fine for you to create other folders inside the "dino1__web" folder and inside the "images" folder. These can be used to help keep things organized as you build your Web site.

> **Note:** It is generally wise when developing Web pages to limit the names of your folders and Web pages to eight lowercase characters or less with no spaces or special characters, other than the underscore (__).

Workout: Explore the territory

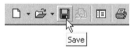

Turn on the computer and launch your Web-editing program. Once it's displayed on the screen, try the following:

1. Examine the Main Menu. Click on each Menu title (e.g., File, Edit) and note the various selections available under each. You won't need all, but it's a good idea to know where to find them. Pay special attention to where the Help menu is located.

2. Look over the toolbars available (**View Menu >>> Toolbars. . .**). Make sure the Standard and Formatting toolbars are checked.

3. Note that the tools located on the toolbars show icons representing what the tool is for. If you lay the mouse pointer over any specific tool (don't click), the name of the tool appears. Use of the toolbars is a fast way of accessing commonly used tools.

4. Try entering in a line or two of text on the workspace of the Web editor. Highlight one or two words, and then click on various tool icons on the Formatting toolbar. Note how your highlighted words change based on the tool that you have selected. (See Crib Note 2a, Selecting More Stuff . . ., in appendix A if you need help selecting words.)

5. Also try to save your Web page by using either a drop-down menu (**File >>>Save As. . .**) or the Save icon on the standard toolbar.

6. Try out several different functions to see what happens. For example, try making a bulleted or numbered list of a lesson plan, change the font style, size, and color of one or more words, and then create a table. Try opening the Font Format window (**Format >>> Font**) and reviewing what can be done in the Web editor to the fonts that you want to work with.

7. Now, before doing anything else, go back to the section on the prep work and do that. Set up a folder on the desktop (e.g., "dino1__web" folder) that has another folder inside of it (e.g., "images" folder).

Level 1: Designing, Creating, and Producing a Course Web Site

What should you be able to do?

Within Level 1, you should be focused on developing skills using the basic tools of simple Web page and site development. At the conclusion of this level, you should be able to create several Web pages, insert text and graphics, and use links effectively by following specific guidelines and step-by-step procedures.

The situation. . .

Helen Smith's second-grade unit on dinosaurs has always been a fun learning experience for her students. This year, Helen decided to expand it by adding a simple Web site that students could access from home and from the school's computer lab. She has started with some simple pages and plans over the next few weeks to add other pages to her site.

The plan

Take a close look at Figure 6.2. This is a composite picture of Mrs. Smith's course Web site that includes three Web pages. Follow the step-by-step procedures and produce a Web site with similar key features. It doesn't have to be exactly the same—just demonstrate that you can carry out the highlighted functions.

Workout: By the numbers. . .

1. First, examine the real Web site. Launch your browser (either Netscape Navigator or Internet Explorer) and open the file on the CD (**File>>>Open**). Navigate to the CD, then locate the folder "chp6__FP." Inside of that folder should be the folder "dino1__ web." Open the "dino1__web" folder and locate the page named "index." Double-click on the "index" page and the browser should begin to display Mrs. Smith's Web site.
2. Go through the site and note text, formatting, and links.
3. Launch your Web page editor application program (e.g., Microsoft FrontPage).
4. Now look over Figures 6.4–6.6. These are the same Web site pages, but what is salient has been identified. Additionally, Figure 6.3 is a beginning or template page constructed to help with the common elements found in each of the Web site pages. Those highlights correspond with the table on p. 136 and what you will be doing to achieve the finished product.

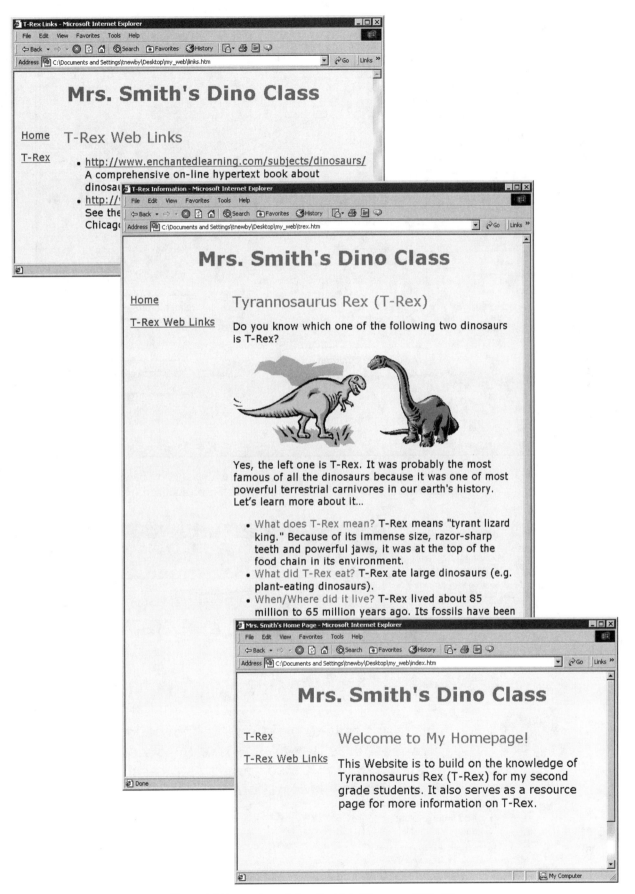

Figure 6.2 Pages from Mrs. Smith's Dinosaur Web Site

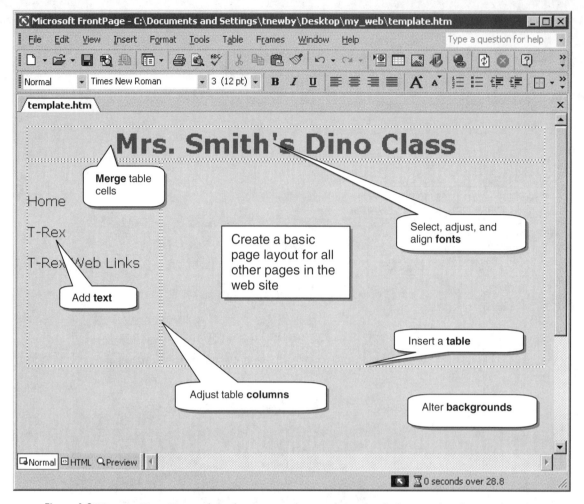

Figure 6.3 View in FrontPage of the basic page layout (template) designed to be used as the starting point for all other Web pages within Mrs. Smith's Web site

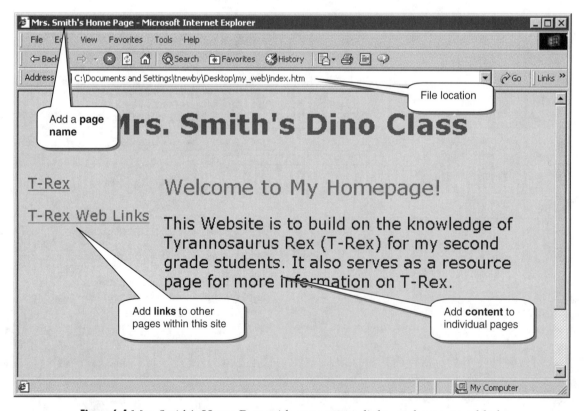

Figure 6.4 Mrs. Smith's Home Page with page name, links, and content added.

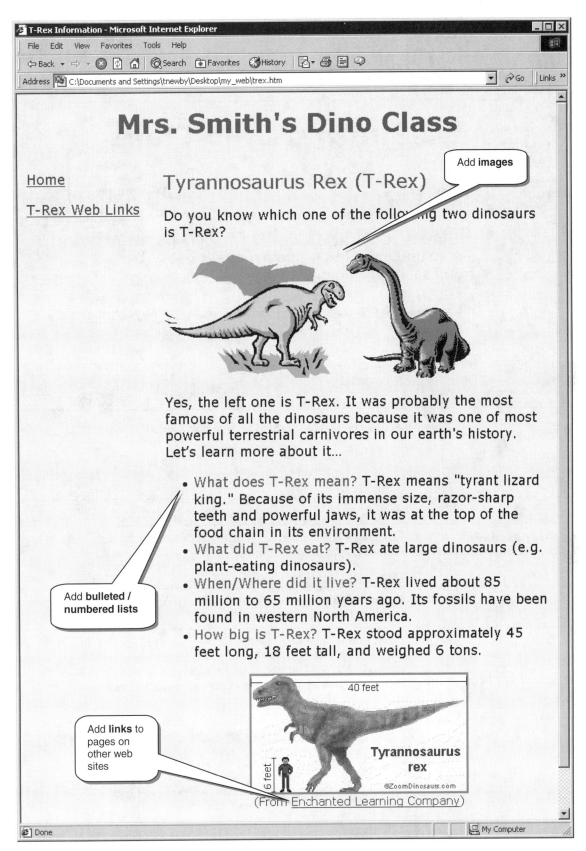

Figure 6.5 T-Rex information page with images and links added
Copyright EnchantedLearning.com. Used by permission.

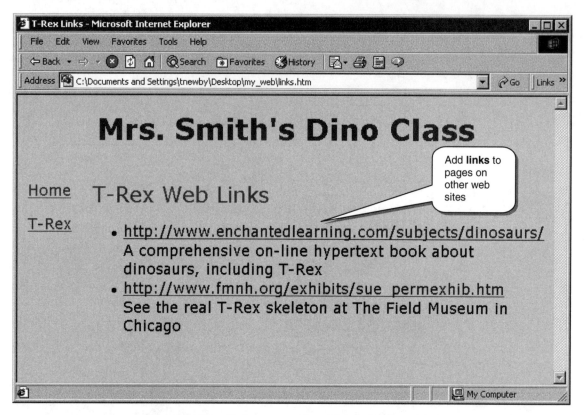

Figure 6.6 T-Rex links page with additional links added

No.	To Do	How to Get It Done
1.	**Create a consistent page layout (Figure 6.3)**	**Goal:** Create a simple page design that can be copied as the basic template page for each of the Web pages to be constructed.
		Steps:
	Launch	1. **Open MS FrontPage** (or your Web editor). With the normal view tab selected you should see a page similar to Figure 6.1.
	Tables	2. **Insert a table.** Tables are essential for organizing and keeping items where they belong on the Web page. For this template page, we begin by inserting a 2 × 2 (2 rows and 2 columns) table. Figure 6.7 shows how to insert such a table and Figure 6.8 shows what one looks like once it has been created.

Figure 6.7 Creating a table in FrontPage

No.	To Do	How to Get It Done

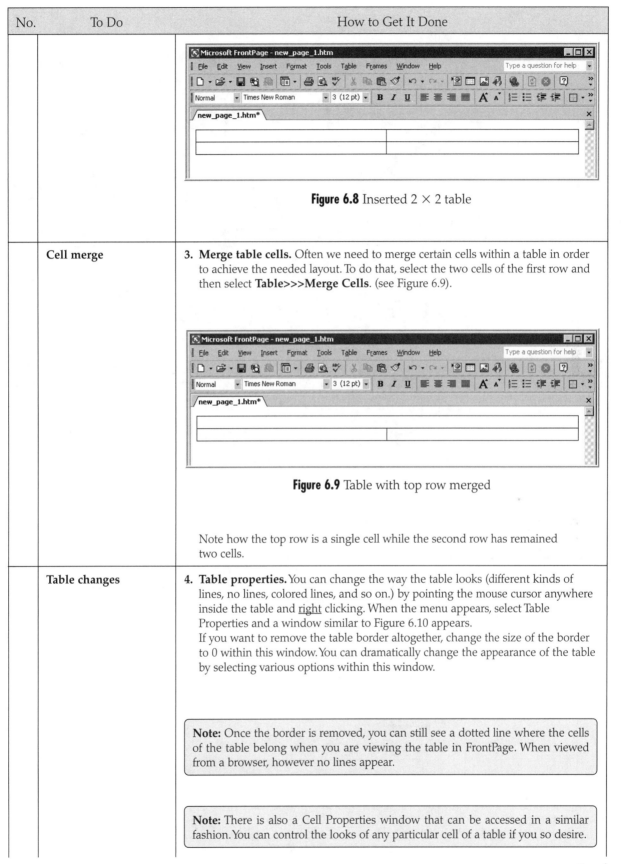

Figure 6.8 Inserted 2 × 2 table

| | Cell merge | 3. **Merge table cells.** Often we need to merge certain cells within a table in order to achieve the needed layout. To do that, select the two cells of the first row and then select **Table>>>Merge Cells**. (see Figure 6.9). |

Figure 6.9 Table with top row merged

Note how the top row is a single cell while the second row has remained two cells.

| | Table changes | 4. **Table properties.** You can change the way the table looks (different kinds of lines, no lines, colored lines, and so on.) by pointing the mouse cursor anywhere inside the table and <u>right</u> clicking. When the menu appears, select Table Properties and a window similar to Figure 6.10 appears. |

If you want to remove the table border altogether, change the size of the border to 0 within this window. You can dramatically change the appearance of the table by selecting various options within this window.

> **Note:** Once the border is removed, you can still see a dotted line where the cells of the table belong when you are viewing the table in FrontPage. When viewed from a browser, however no lines appear.

> **Note:** There is also a Cell Properties window that can be accessed in a similar fashion. You can control the looks of any particular cell of a table if you so desire.

continued

No.	To Do	How to Get It Done

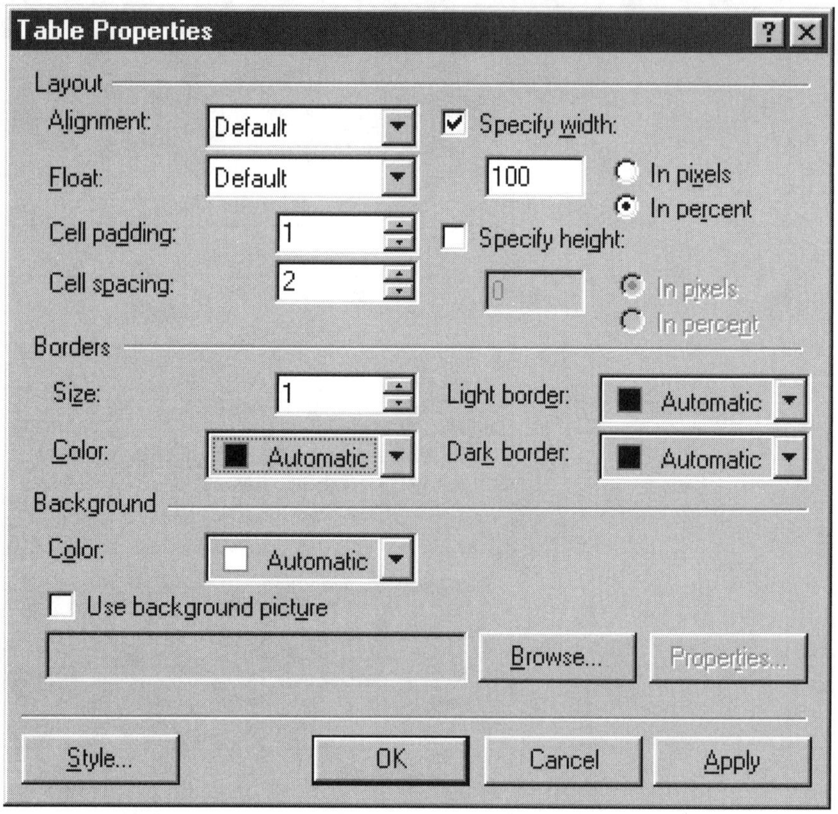

Figure 6.10 Table Properties window

| | Text | 5. **Insert template text information.** Type in the information that should appear on each of the Web pages within the Web site. For Mrs. Smith's Web site, Figure 6.11 shows the consistent information found on every page within the site.

Figure 6.11 Inserting text |
| | Fonts | 6. **Adjust fonts, text size, style, color, and alignment.** Use the Formatting toolbar to make the needed changes to selected words. For example (see Figure 6.12), highlight "Mrs. Smith's Home Page" and then select the proper tools on the Formatting toolbar to achieve the desired effect. |

No.	To Do	How to Get It Done
		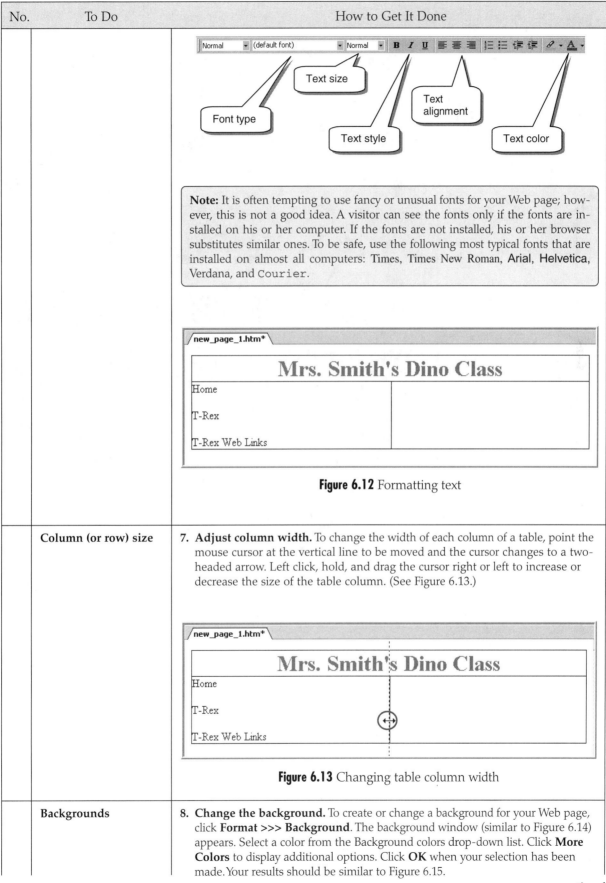
	Column (or row) size	7. **Adjust column width.** To change the width of each column of a table, point the mouse cursor at the vertical line to be moved and the cursor changes to a two-headed arrow. Left click, hold, and drag the cursor right or left to increase or decrease the size of the table column. (See Figure 6.13.)
	Backgrounds	8. **Change the background.** To create or change a background for your Web page, click **Format >>> Background**. The background window (similar to Figure 6.14) appears. Select a color from the Background colors drop-down list. Click **More Colors** to display additional options. Click **OK** when your selection has been made. Your results should be similar to Figure 6.15.

Note: It is often tempting to use fancy or unusual fonts for your Web page; however, this is not a good idea. A visitor can see the fonts only if the fonts are installed on his or her computer. If the fonts are not installed, his or her browser substitutes similar ones. To be safe, use the following most typical fonts that are installed on almost all computers: Times, Times New Roman, Arial, Helvetica, Verdana, and Courier.

Figure 6.12 Formatting text

Figure 6.13 Changing table column width

continued

No.	To Do	How to Get It Done
		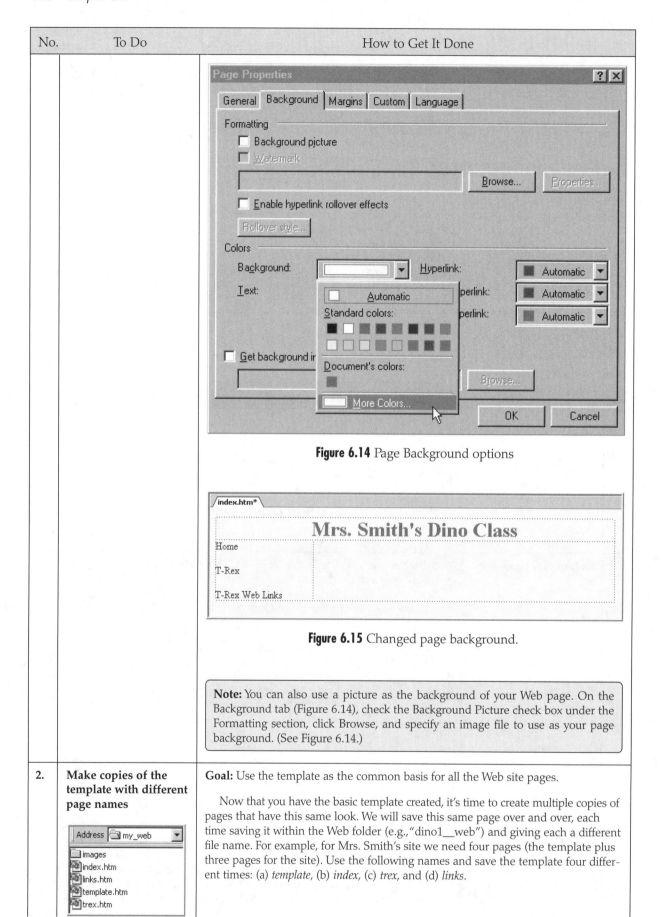

Figure 6.14 Page Background options

Figure 6.15 Changed page background.

> **Note:** You can also use a picture as the background of your Web page. On the Background tab (Figure 6.14), check the Background Picture check box under the Formatting section, click Browse, and specify an image file to use as your page background. (See Figure 6.14.)

No.	To Do	How to Get It Done
2.	**Make copies of the template with different page names**	**Goal:** Use the template as the common basis for all the Web site pages. Now that you have the basic template created, it's time to create multiple copies of pages that have this same look. We will save this same page over and over, each time saving it within the Web folder (e.g., "dino1__web") and giving each a different file name. For example, for Mrs. Smith's site we need four pages (the template plus three pages for the site). Use the following names and save the template four different times: (a) *template*, (b) *index*, (c) *trex*, and (d) *links*.

No.	To Do	How to Get It Done
		Note: In most cases, the home page (main page) of the site is referred to as the *index* page. Thus the home page is generally saved under the name *index*.

3.	**Add content to individual pages**	**Goal:** Insert the specific content for each individual page of the Web site.
		
		Steps:
		1. Add textual content
		  a. Open the *index* page of the Web site. Type in the text content for that page (see Figure 6.16).
		  b. Alter any font style, size, or color for needed emphasis.
		
		Figure 6.16 Example *index* page with inserted content
		
		  c. Spell check your work and save your page.
		  d. Add content for each of the other content pages (e.g., *trex* and *links*), and save each of those pages.

	Images	**2. Add figures, pictures, and images**
		
		Important Info: Web pages handle images differently than other software such as word processors. Instead of sticking the image directly into the document so that it becomes a part of the document, the Web editor inserts a reference that tells the browser where to go to find the image and then how to display it. So when working with images and pictures, it is wise to have an *"images"* folder inside of your *dino1__web* folder. This is the location that all of your Web site images will be stored. If the *dino1__web* folder is moved to another disk or computer, the nested *images* folder and all of the needed pictures will also travel safely with the Web site.
		
		Here are some simple steps for adding images to your Web page:
		
		  a. Locate the images you wish to incorporate and save them directly into the *images* folder within your Web site folder. Use Crib Note 9, Obtaining and Saving Images from the Web found in appendix A to guide you through the process of locating and pulling images from other Web sites.
		  b. On your Web page, place the cursor where you want the image to be inserted.
		  c. Click **Insert>>>Picture>>> From File. . .** A "Select File" window appears. Navigate to your *images* folder where you have saved the to-be-inserted image. Click on the title of your image and click OK.
		  d. The image should now appear at the cursor's position in your Web page.

continued

No.	To Do	How to Get It Done
	Clip art	**Note:** If you choose to use FrontPage's clip art, the procedures are very similar—with slight modifications. a. Click **Insert>>>Picture>>>Clip Art. . . .** b. A clip art window appears and you can select from those pictures that are available. c. After inserting your clip art picture, you need to save your Web page. When you attempt to do that, a new window (Save Embedded Files window) appears indicating that any clip art that you have inserted within your Web page must now be saved into a new folder (basically it is saying you need to put the clip art picture into your *images* folder for your specific Web site). Click the "Change folder" button and navigate to your *images* folder and click OK. The image should now be a separate image within your *images* folder.
	Image edits Selected clip art with handles	**3. Adapting images** Frequently, the inserted image may not be the correct size. If you need to alter the size: a. Point your mouse at the picture and left click once. Note that a box is drawn around the picture and small dark squares are placed at each of the corners and in the middle of each of the sides. These are called **handles**. You can grab a handle by putting your mouse pointer on the handle (note that your pointer changes into a double-headed arrow), left click, and hold it. Dragging a handle causes the picture to be altered. Try different handles, and notice what happens to the shape and size of the picture. b. Once your picture is inserted and sized appropriately, you can align it by clicking it once (the handles should appear), and then selecting from the alignment icons on the Formatting toolbar. **Note:** Pictures and images come in a variety of formats; however, Web browsers only support those known as GIF and JPG. The GIF format works best for images such as clip art, whereas the JPG format works best for photographic images. If your image is in a different format from GIF or JPG, it will either have to be converted or it will have to be replaced. **Note:** It's often helpful to use tables to place images. Think about inserting a table and then placing the images strategically within specific cells of the tables.
	Lists Bullet list Numbered list	**4. Adding bulleted or numbered lists** Bullet points or numbers are often used to highlight a list of items. This is easily accomplished on a Web page as follows: a. Enter all of the items that are to be included in the list. b. Select all of the items. c. Click **Format>>>Bullets and Numbering. . .** and select from the given options. It is also possible to click on the bullet or numbered list icon on the Formatting toolbar.

No.	To Do	How to Get It Done
4.	**Web page names**	**Goal:** Name a Web page. **Steps:** 1. The title of a Web page is the actual name of the page, not the page's file name. When a browser displays the page, its name shows in the browser's title bar. This is helpful for those cruising Web sites and helps some Web search engines find materials. 2. To create or change the name of a Web page, right click anywhere on the page, and choose Page Properties from the pop-up menu. As shown in Figure 6.17, click the General tab and enter the title of the page in the Title section. In our example, we titled the index page "Mrs. Smith's Home Page." Click OK. **Figure 6.17** Using the Page Properties window to title a Web page 3. Figure 6.4 shows how a browser displays the page name, as well as the page's file location.
5.	**Hyperlinks**	**Goal:** Create a simple electronic connection between text or graphics so that with a simple mouse click, the "linked" information is immediately accessed.
	Link the pages of your web site together Hyperlink button Explore local button 	As shown in Figure 6.4, links have been created between that Web page and others within Mrs. Smith's Dino Class (e.g., the T-Rex page). Here are the steps to complete a similar process for your work. **Steps:** 1. Select (highlight) the words of text that you want to serve as a link to another page within your Web site (e.g., "T-Rex"). 2. Click **Insert>>>Hyperlink** (you can also click on the Hyperlink button on the Standard toolbar). 3. The Create Hyperlink window (see Figure 6.18) appears. 4. If you see the desired Web page listed in this window (e.g., T-Rex Information) that you want to link to, click on that title and then click OK. If you don't see it in this list, you can explore your computer files by clicking on the Explore button, then navigating to the appropriate page and clicking OK. 5. Once you click OK, the link is established and your selected text changes to indicate it now consists of a link [generally, this means that the selected words are underlined with a changed font color (generally it is blue).] 6. Link all of the pages in your Web site together using this method. Through the use of such links, individuals can navigate in, out, and through your site.

continued

No.	To Do	How to Get It Done
		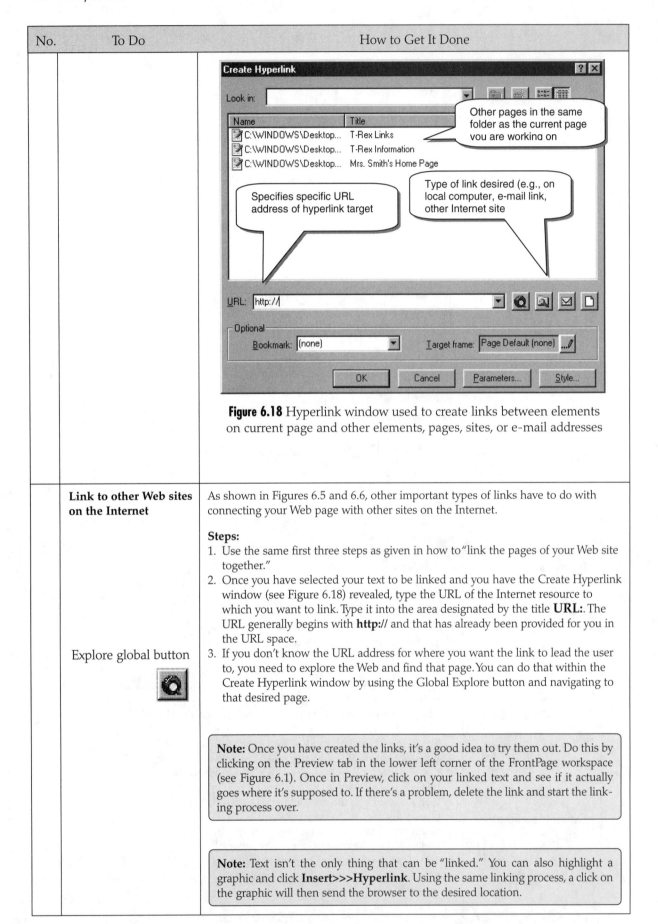 **Figure 6.18** Hyperlink window used to create links between elements on current page and other elements, pages, sites, or e-mail addresses
	Link to other Web sites on the Internet Explore global button	As shown in Figures 6.5 and 6.6, other important types of links have to do with connecting your Web page with other sites on the Internet. **Steps:** 1. Use the same first three steps as given in how to "link the pages of your Web site together." 2. Once you have selected your text to be linked and you have the Create Hyperlink window (see Figure 6.18) revealed, type the URL of the Internet resource to which you want to link. Type it into the area designated by the title **URL:**. The URL generally begins with **http://** and that has already been provided for you in the URL space. 3. If you don't know the URL address for where you want the link to lead the user to, you need to explore the Web and find that page. You can do that within the Create Hyperlink window by using the Global Explore button and navigating to that desired page. **Note:** Once you have created the links, it's a good idea to try them out. Do this by clicking on the Preview tab in the lower left corner of the FrontPage workspace (see Figure 6.1). Once in Preview, click on your linked text and see if it actually goes where it's supposed to. If there's a problem, delete the link and start the linking process over. **Note:** Text isn't the only thing that can be "linked." You can also highlight a graphic and click **Insert>>>Hyperlink**. Using the same linking process, a click on the graphic will then send the browser to the desired location.

Level 2: Links, Bookmarks, and Buttons

What should you be able to do?

The use of a Web editor to develop Web pages can be a very helpful tool. The goal in this level is for you to expand your skills with several additional features of the Web editor; however, the most important goal is for you to develop a skill of working with the Help feature to gain the guidance you need to find solutions to future questions and problems.

A little story. . .

Everyone at Helen Smith's school knew she was constantly on the lookout for dinosaur paraphernalia for her students to experience. Occasionally she would receive e-mail messages from other teachers who would send her a favorite Web site that Helen might find helpful. On one occasion she received a Web address (URL) that accessed a simple Web site of a lesson plan that intrigued her in a number of ways. First, she liked the content and she thought she might be able to adapt it for her students. Second, she thought the idea of putting up important items (such as lesson plans) for others to access and use was a good one. She thought she should place those on her "Dino" Web site. And finally, this particular Web site had a few other features that she wanted to try on her own site.

Let's take a look at a printout of a simple Web site that Mrs. Smith has created based on a lesson plan given to her by one of her colleagues. You can actually explore it for yourself by launching your Internet browser (either Internet Explorer or Netscape Navigator), opening the "index" page in the "dino__lplan" folder, found within the chp6__FP folder on the CD.

Use of Help in FrontPage

Similar to Help in Windows and MS Word, there is also Help in MS FrontPage and most other sophisticated Web page composer software. To use Help, simply go to the Help menu on the Main Menu bar and select "Microsoft FrontPage Help." A Help window appears as in Figure 6.19.

The Contents tab of the Help window organizes topics into categories that are represented by book icons. By clicking its plus sign, you can display a category's topics. By clicking a topic (designated by a question mark icon), you can display its information in the right pane of the Help window.

The Answer Wizard tab of the Help window allows you to type in your question in plain language and it responds with a variety of potential answers for you to investigate. Type your question in the edit box, and click Search.

The Index tab allows you to type a key word in the edit box. The list below scrolls to display topics beginning with the letters you type. Click the Search button. Now you can select a topic from the "Choose a topic" list to display the information that you need.

You can't expect Help to offer all solutions; however, it does contain most of what you need—as long as you can come up with a good descriptor of what you need to investigate.

> **Note:** If your screen is large enough, you can expose the Help window at the same time that you work on your document. In this way you can read the suggestions and complete the task at the same time.

Explore: "A Sample Web Lesson Plan"

Within Level 2 of this software application, the content of "A Sample Web Lesson Plan" isn't all that important—what *is important* are the formatting features presented within this lesson plan and the idea that you can use such features in your own work.

Look closely at Figures 6.20–6.22, and note the key items we have included: hover buttons, links to bookmarks, horizontal lines, hyperlinks to an Office document, and

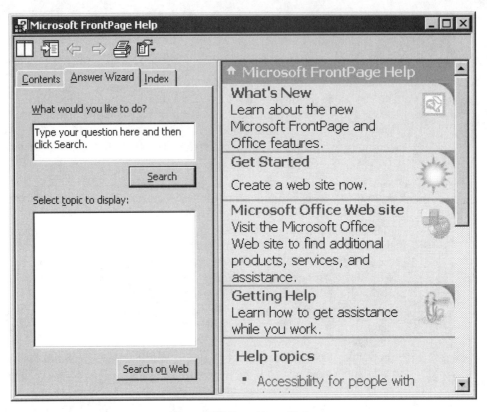

Figure 6.19 FrontPage Help

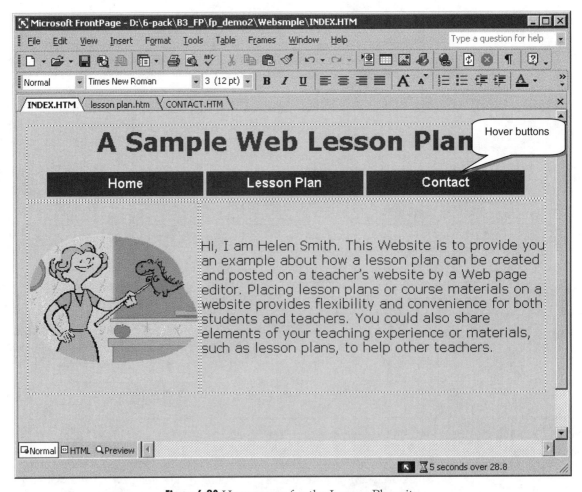

Figure 6.20 Home page for the Lesson Plan site

shading in a table. These features help you organize your documents and make them more readable. That is important for your students.

Implement

You may already have a favorite lesson plan that you can use at this point—or you may want to create a lesson plan about a topic that you haven't had the needed motivation or time to get to—until now. Either way, select a topic and create something of value to you and your teaching (or future teaching).

Use Figure 6.21 as a template for your plan. As you include your content, make sure you have a good idea of the following formatting features. We don't explain exactly how to do each, but we do give you an example of the feature and critical questions you can think about and investigate (via Microsoft FrontPage Help) to find the needed answers. (Note: Content for this lesson plan was adapted from http://school.discovery.com/lessonplans/programs/tle-dinosaurs/)

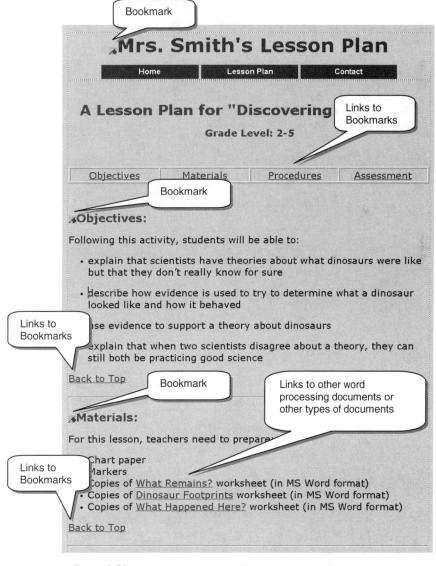

Figure 6.21 Main content page for the Lesson Plan site

continued

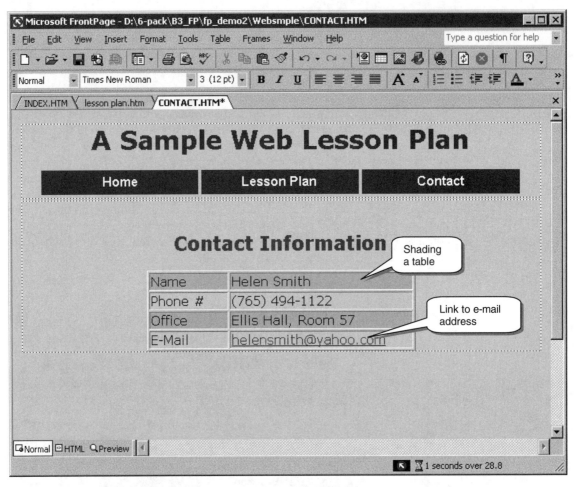

Figure 6.22 Contact information page for the Lesson Plan site

Feature	Ask the Office Assistant (Help)
Hover Button	• **What is a hover button?** Check out the section "About hover button." This button can be created with FrontPage, and is helpful when you need an animated button with hyperlinks. • **How do you set properties for a hover button?** Look at the option "Set properties for a hover button" under the section "About hover button." This provides ideas on how to modify the text label, default hyperlink, effects, colors, and size of a hover button. • **Also investigate:** Click **Insert>>>Component>>>Hover Button.** **Note:** Occasionally, there are specific features that can be constructed within FrontPage that only work on Microsoft-based servers. That is, the feature of hover buttons works fine as long as it is stored on a MS server. If this Web site is saved on another type of server, there are possibilities that this (and similar) type features may not work properly.
Links to Bookmarks	• **What is a bookmark?** A bookmark is a set of one or more characters on a page that serves as the target of a link. A bookmark is very handy especially when a Web page is long

Feature:	Ask the Office Assistant (Help):

	because a bookmark provides a means for jumping from one location to another within the same page (or even in another page). Look for the option "About bookmarks" and check out how a bookmark is created and other related matters.
	• **How to create a hyperlink to a bookmark.** Look again at the option "About bookmarks." Scan through the information, look for a category "Create a hyperlink," and then select the topic specific to "Create a hyperlink to a bookmark."
	• **Also investigate:**
	  a. Click **Insert>>>Bookmark . . ..**
	  b. Click **Insert>>>Hyperlink . . ..**

Horizontal line	• **What is a horizontal line?** Look for the option. "About horizontal line." Using horizontal lines on a page is a great way to separate sections, topics, or other elements. • **Also investigate:** Click **Insert>>>Horizontal Line.**
Hyperlink to an Office document	• **How do you create a hyperlink to an Office document, such as a MS Word document**? Check out the section "About hyperlinks" and look for the topic related specifically to "create a hyperlink to an Office document." This provides you with the basic information about how a desired document is opened when a visitor clicks the hyperlink you've created. • **Also investigate:** Click **Insert>>>Hyperlink . . ..**
Shading in a table	• **Why use shading in a table?** You can shade specific columns or rows (or the entire table) to add emphasis, or to make them more attractive and easy to read. Look at the option "About shading." Scan through the information and look for topics related specifically to setting the background color in a table. • **Also investigate:** Click **Format>>>Borders and Shading....**
Link to an e-mail address	• **How do you create a hyperlink to an e-mail address?** Click on the section "Create a hyperlink" and then click on the section "Create a hyperlink to an e-mail address." • **Also investigate:** Click **Insert>>>Hyperlink . . ..**

Practice: Your Web lesson plan

With this information and example, create a lesson plan that you can use later or find a lesson plan from some helpful (online) resources, such as Discovery School's lesson plans library at http://school.discovery.com/lessonplans/index.html, to practice the above features.

Adapt the lesson plan to meet your needs. Besides the formatting features we showed you in Levels 1 and 2, you can also explore and add new features (e.g., "frames page," which divides the browser window into different areas called frames, each of which can display a different page) that you may find valuable and eliminate those that you feel are not helpful. If questions arise, use the Help function to find some guidance and answers.

Finally, don't forget the Rules to Live By (see Introduction).

RULES TO LIVE BY:

1. Save your work frequently.
2. Work on the content first, then worry about making it "pretty."
3. Always look for the simple way—don't worry about a lot of bells and whistles.
4. Watch for other examples that show you good ideas you can use.
5. Develop a good example and use it as a template for other similar projects.

Publishing the Web site	Once you have completed creating a Web site, it doesn't naturally "appear" on the WWW. You must go through a process of "publishing." To learn how this is accomplished, go to the FrontPage **Help** and ask, "Tell me something about publishing." Read the section "about publishing" to understand what is needed. There are other procedures to follow in order to get your Web site up and running successfully. In many cases within school corporations, you need to get in contact with the school's technology coordinator in order to publish on the school or district's Web server.

Level 3: Integration and Application

What should you be able to do?	Here is where you use this software to help yourself and your students. In this section you begin to see all the possibilities once you understand the basics of building Web pages. You can use these examples as a springboard to launch ideas on ways to improve levels of student learning and your personal productivity.
Introduction	Accessing information and activities on the Internet has proven very beneficial for both students and teachers. Early within the school experience search strategies are learned in order to utilize effectively the benefits of the information on the Web. The ability to create and publish materials on the Internet adds a whole new set of benefits for both teachers and students. Examine the following lesson plan. We think you'll find this example can help you envision how effective Web development experiences might enhance student learning, as well as enhance the capabilities of teachers and the effectiveness of their lessons.

Web site development integration: An example lesson plan	**Creating the enhanced learning experience: A partial lesson plan** **Topic:** A study of the people, places, and culture of an African country. **Overview:** One of the goals for Mr. Carpenter, the eighth-grade social studies teacher at Lowell Middle School, was to have his students come to view the world from a more global perspective. He wanted his students to examine and compare other cultures, lifestyles, and people in order to grasp the benefits and challenges of a very complex, diverse world. By exploring the differences, as well as the similarities, the Lowell students might be more open to attempting new experiences, be more willing to broaden their perception of people and potential friends, be more able to see areas where their service now or in the future may have a dramatic impact on other individuals, and perhaps be more able to solve some common problems. Jonathon Rogers, a past student of Mr. Carpenter, is now working on a college internship with an international health and education organization in the country of Zimbabwe. Through his help and other reference materials, the students in Mr. Carpenter's classes are able to explore this different culture, make some comparisons, and gain insights. **Specific Learning Task:** To further their study of Zimbabwe, Mr. Carpenter's students are to examine specific aspects of life within this country. Individually, they are to select from one of the questions below and then attempt to answer it by referencing materials on the Web and other sources. Students are encouraged to find or obtain firsthand accounts (with Jonathon's possible help) to confirm their research.

Questions:

- On any given day, what is it like to live in Harare (or any other major city), Zimbabwe?
- On any given day, what is it like to live in rural Zimbabwe away from the big cities?
- What do people do in Zimbabwe for entertainment (e.g., music, movies, sports)?
- What special occasions do people celebrate and how are those occasions celebrated?
- Are people religious? What do they believe and how do they show their beliefs?

Once completed, the class as a whole will develop a Web site to assemble and link all of the pieces. Students will work as designers, developers, and evaluators of the Web site to be sure it works and the information is correct.

Sample Learning Objectives: Students will be able to do the following:

1. Explain and describe lifestyles of the common people within Zimbabwe.
2. Identify and describe the different forms of entertainment that Zimbabweans enjoy, as well as the special occasions that they celebrate.
3. Describe the religions of Zimbabwe and how individuals of that country worship.
4. Describe the process of gathering research information on the Web and the process needed in order to develop and evaluate a Web site.

Procedure:

1. Have the students select a question they wish to investigate.
2. Research answers for the questions by using the Web and other library resources. Contact Jonathon to see if he has contact with individuals who could give additional insights into some of these questions.
3. Divide the class into Web designers or developers and Web evaluators. Have them work interactively to develop the plans for the Web site, and to evaluate and give feedback on those ideas. Depending on the ideas, it may be best to divide the class and create more than one Web site.
4. Create and confirm the initial Web plan. Have Jonathon review and find places where additional information could be added by him and his contacts.
5. Develop and evaluate the remaining portions of the Web site. Add the needed graphics, audio, and video as available.
6. Post the site live on the WWW, and if possible, have Jonathon get feedback from several classes of students in Zimbabwe. Get some suggestions from them and rework the site based upon those suggestions.
7. Make the final changes to the site.

Questions about Web Development Integration

Most of the lesson objectives identified for this lesson plan could be accomplished without the development of a specific Web site. However, reflect on the following questions and think about the potential value that the integration of the Web site development may add to what is learned.

- In what ways can the Web environment facilitate the access and use of additional sources of information to support knowledge and understanding of the Zimbabwe people and culture?
- How can the planning, development, and evaluation processes involved in the Web site production impact the students creating the site? If access were possible, can students in Zimbabwe be used to help develop and/or evaluate the site in some way? What advantage would this add to the overall production process for Mr. Carpenter's students?
- Can the site be used to expand the understanding of students in other middle schools?

- How can the Web site be used to focus the efforts of all students working on the collaborative project? What additional interpersonal and communication skills could they learn from the collaborative Web development effort?
- Can the use of graphics, and/or audio and video clips within the hyperlinked environment of the Web increase what students gain from developing and using the site?
- How can this Web site and its development be used to bring together students from different areas of the globe to work together and communicate to a greater degree? What value is there in students from diverse areas and cultures cooperatively working on projects?
- What potential problems or pitfalls should one be wary of when attempting to create such a class Web site?

Workout: Integrating Web development

Once you have had a chance to review the lesson plan—and examine and ponder the questions concerning integration—it's time for you to develop your own plan. Complete the following steps to this Workout.

1. Read each of the following situations. Imagine being directly involved in the planning for each of these projects. Select one (or more if you wish) for further consideration.

Creating a sister site

Students in Mt. Pleasant Junior High School have had an ongoing pen pal relationship with students in their sister city of Hof, Germany. In fact, some students from each city have occasionally traveled to the sister city for a short visit. Students have been challenged at both schools to think of ways to expand on these cultural exchanges in order for others to experience the similarities and differences between the schools, towns, and individuals from the different countries.

Living in another time

If you were allowed to be a commoner (i.e., a normal person) from the past, discuss your life and what you have discovered as you have ventured through it. Explain what life is like, show pictures of your surroundings, indicate what your goals would be, and tell about interesting people you have met or have heard about that lived during your time. For example, be a newspaper delivery boy during the days of Jesse James and explain what life was like then. Be a young girl who travels by wagon train with your family from Ohio to a gold rush town in California in the late 1840s. Explain what it was like to be recruited to march and fight for England during the Crusades. What would it have been like to be a young black man in South Africa during the heated days of Apartheid? What would it have been like to be a young white person in the same place and time? Is there a way to compare those experiences with what we experience today?

Professional insights

Wouldn't it be nice to sit down and discuss various occupations with individuals who are currently involved in that line of work? What would it be like to be a scientist, or a judge, or a traffic patrolman, or an oceanographer, or even a dance instructor? Is it possible to create a job site that helps individuals investigate different professions and what those who are currently in those jobs have to say about them?

National Debt WebQuest

In a high school current issues class, a group of students converge together for a special project investigating issues concerning the national debt. Although a huge amount of information can be accessed via the Internet, organizing that information into a coherent unit is a challenging problem. One student suggests they attempt to select materials to help teach other students in their class about the key issues involved in their topic and another member mentions that a WebQuest may be a possible way of accomplishing this task.

2. Based on your selected project, consider the following questions that concern the integration of Web editing. Mark your response to each question.

Integration assessment questionnaire (IAQ)

Will using **WEB DEVELOPMENT** software as a part of the project			
Broaden the learners' perspective on potential solution paths and/or answers?	___ Yes	___ No	___ Maybe
Increase the level of involvement and investment of personal effort by the learners?	___ Yes	___ No	___ Maybe
Increase the level of learner motivation (e.g., increase the relevance of the to-be-learned task, the confidence of dealing with the task, and/or the overall appeal of the task)?	___ Yes	___ No	___ Maybe
Decrease the time needed to generate potential solutions?	___ Yes	___ No	___ Maybe
Increase the quality and/or quantity of learner practice working on this and similar projects?	___ Yes	___ No	___ Maybe
Increase the quality and/or quantity of feedback given to the learner?	___ Yes	___ No	___ Maybe
Enhance the ability of the student to solve novel, but similar, projects, tasks, and problems in the future?	___ Yes	___ No	___ Maybe

3. If you have responded "Yes" to one or more of the IAQ questions, you should consider the use of Web editing software to enhance the student's potential learning experience.
4. Using the example lesson plan, develop a lesson plan based on this project. Within the plan, indicate how and when the learner will develop Web-based materials. Additionally, list potential benefits and challenges that may occur when involving this software within the lesson.

Workout: Exploring the NETS Standard Connection

Developing and executing a lesson plan that integrates the use of Web editors and Web site development directly addresses several of the NETS Standards for both teachers (NETS*T) and students (NETS*S). See appendix B for a full listing of the standards.

Part A: Generally, the main purpose for learning and using application software is to increase your level of production. That is, to do things faster, better, or both. NETS Standards (NETS*T Standard V and NETS*S Standard 3) help you focus on these productivity objectives for both teachers and students. There are other technology standards, however, that may also be potentially addressed through your knowledge and use of Web editing software. Reflect on the following questions and consider the potential impact of Web editor integration (refer to appendix B to review the full sets of standards):

- How can the use of Web editing software help develop students' higher order skills and creativity? Is there something about the development of a Web site that promotes organization, writing, analysis, research, as well as message design skills? In what ways can the development of a collaborative Web site be used to increase communication, leadership, and decision-making skills of both students and teachers? (NETS*T III.C.; NETS*S 3)
- In what ways can Web editing software and the development of a Web page or site be used to facilitate the communication and collaboration between teachers, students, parents, and subject matter experts on specific projects that ultimately

impact student learning? Are there alternative means of communicating information that would allow for diverse audiences to better grasp the meaning of the information? (NETS*T V.D. and VI.B.; NETS*S 4)

- How can the development of WebQuests, Web Scavenger Hunts, and so on be used to successfully manage learning activities designed for a specific student audience? (NETS*T II.D.)
- In what positive ways can the knowledge that student work would be published on the Web impact the quality of work that is produced? (NETS*S 2 and 4)

Part B: Go to the ISTE Web site http://cnets.iste.org. Within that site, select to review either the student or the teacher NETS Standards. Once you have selected the standards to review, select either the student or teacher profiles, and look for the corresponding scenarios. Review the scenarios and determine how Web editors can be used within several of those situations.

While visiting the ISTE Web site and exploring the scenarios, go to the lesson plan search area and select a number of different lesson plans of interest. Review those and determine the role (if any) of Web editors within the development, implementation, and assessment of the lesson. Note this from both the perspective of the teacher developing the lesson and from the perspective of the student participating in the implemented lesson.

Workout: Comprehensive integration

You need to understand that in most practical learning situations, one type of software generally doesn't stand alone as *the* solution. That is, full integration may mean that you use Web development *and* other software such as the word processing, spreadsheets, and data management. For this Workout:

1. Read through the lesson plan you designed within the previous Workout.
2. Identify how your suggestions for the integration of Web development may be enhanced by the use of other software (e.g., word processing, presentation software).
3. Describe the benefits and the problems that may be associated with the integration of other software within the same project.
4. Describe how additional technology standards (e.g., NETS*T II.A.: ". . . design developmentally appropriate learning opportunities that apply technology-enhanced instructional strategies to support the diverse needs of learners") can be addressed by the integration of various types of applications software.

Further ideas using a Web editor as a learning tool

- Have students research content and develop Web sites about specific topics or subject matter.
- Have the students research and locate various information Web sites, and then construct a Web site that links and references these information sites.
- Have students develop WebQuests, Scavenger Hunts, and ThinkQuests.
- Have students develop a site that incorporates and demonstrates proper visual design.
- Have students create a cooperative group project that involves the research, design, and development of a comprehensive Web site about a selected topic of interest.
- Have the students develop a site that compares viewpoints and/or materials. For example, have them compare the educational philosophies of various secondary level schools across the country or across several different countries. Likewise, have them compare the governments of different countries and link important sites that explain the pros and cons of each type.
- Develop sites that incorporate the use of various activities from applications programs such as presentation programs (e.g., PowerPoint) and word processing (e.g., Word).
- Develop data collection instruments (e.g., surveys) that can be sent out via a published Web site and collect data for various Web projects.

- Have the students develop Web sites about specific areas of interest (e.g., favorite pet, favorite class in school, special place to visit with one's family).

Additional ideas on using a Web editor as an assistant	- A site can be created for basic administrative information and information exchange. This can be a Web site that students, parents, and administrators can go to to receive specific information (e.g., class information). - Use the Web editor to develop a specific course or class Web site. This site can include the syllabus, activities, explanations, linked information and sites, and important information and announcements that students need constant access to. - In terms of support material for classroom activities, ancillary Web sites can be created to hold things such as class notes (overheads) and even additional media (audio and visual) presentations. - To present additional viewpoints of a specific concept, idea, or philosophy, develop a Web site that links additional, expanded, or different viewpoints to give the students wider perspectives on what is being learned. - Develop a portion of a course Web site that contains a question and answer section. This can be as complex as a searchable database that stores key questions and responses to important class questions. Students (or parents, administrators, and so forth) can submit questions that are then posted with a response. Other students can then review the different questions and responses that have been posted.

Web Editor and FrontPage References

Teachers using Web editors	Online tutorials and Web sites *are not always reliably available*; therefore, going to a search engine (e.g., www.google.com) and then using productive search terms is very important. Search terms for finding sites that have lesson plans for school topics that involve using FrontPage include: - **Teachers using FrontPage** Examples of such sites include the following: **http://home.socal.rr.com/exworthy/building.htm** Here are links to sites that help design and construct a school or class Web site, plus links to visit various examples of school or classroom sites. **http://www.minot.k12.nd.us/html/** This is another site with links to school-oriented Web sites. Ideas such as including forms, adding calendars, or surveys to Web sites can be found here. **http://www.siec.k12.in.us/%7Ewest/online/** This site has tips on developing school Web pages. There is a link on the home page to see projects that have been created by the staff at an elementary school. Example elementary school sites that give some insights into what can be done by a teacher for a class Web site: **http://www.dentonisd.org/rayzor/lattaya/index.htm** **http://mizgomez.com**
Tutorials and other resources	Search terms for learning how to use Web editors and other useful tips: - **FrontPage tutorials** - **Frontpage tips**

Example tutorial sites that should prove helpful:

http://www.actden.com/fp2000/java/index.htm

A well-designed site that walks you through the development of Web pages using FrontPage 2000.

http://www.actden.com/fp/index.htm

This is FrontPage in the Classroom—a wonderful tutorial that even works for a younger audience.

http://www.microsoft.com/education

This site has select tutorials and other instructional materials for Microsoft products across various grade levels and subject areas.

http://www.trainingtools.com/online/FrontPage2000/index.htm

This site provides a basic overview of FrontPage 2000 by TrainingTools.com.

http://nt.watauga.k12.nc.us/br/front_page_2000.htm

A site that provides another basic overview of FrontPage 2000 for teachers. This was created by teachers for teachers within a specific school district. Don't let that bother you—you can still discover interesting tips and insights from their explanations.

http://www.jegsworks.com/Lessons/web/index.html

A general tutorial on HTML and other basics of the Web can be found here. This one doesn't directly discuss how to use FrontPage, but it is well designed and gives you good straightforward information that is teacher and student friendly.

	Desired Task to Accomplish	**Reference Menu or Toolbar**[*]
Basic Tools	Create a new web page	**File>>>New . . .**
	Access toolbars	**View>>>Toolbars**
	Access task panes	**View>>>Task Pane**
	Insert text	**Click on workspace, begin typing**
	Insert picture	**Insert>>>Picture**
	Insert table	**Table>>>Insert>>>Table**
	Insert hyperlink	**Insert>>>Hyperlink . . .**
Formatting Features	Text (font type, color, size, effect)	**Format>>>Font . . .**
	Paragraph (alignment, indention, line spacing)	**Format>>>Paragraph . . .**
	Picture (text alignment, contrast, color, size)	**View>>>Toolbars>>>Picture**
	Tables (alter rows and columns)	**Table>>>Insert>>>Rows or Columns . . .**
	Tables (alignment, borders, background)	**Table>>>Table Properties . . . >>>Table**
	Cells within a table (layout, borders, background)	**Table>>>Table Properties . . . >>>Cell**

Desired Task to Accomplish	Reference Menu or Toolbar[*]
Cells within a table (merging)	**Table>>>Merge Cells**
Cell padding and spacing	**Table>>>Table Properties>>>Table**
Lists	**Format>>>Bullets and Numbering . . .**
Borders	**Format>>>Border and Shading . . . >>> tab: Borders**
Shading	**Format>>>Border and Shading . . . >>> tab: Shading**
Themes	**Format>>>Theme . . .**
Symbols	**Insert>>>Symbol . . .**
Thesaurus	**Tools>>>Language>>>Thesaurus**
Comments	**Insert>>>Comment**
AutoShapes	**Insert>>>Picture>>>AutoShapes**
WordArt	**Insert>>>Picture>>>WordArt**
Horizontal line	**Insert>>>Horizontal line**
Bookmark	**Insert>>>Bookmark . . .**
Positioning an element on a page	**Format>>>Position . . .**
Hover Buttons	**Insert>>>Web Component . . . >>> Component type: Dynamic Effects>>> effect: Hover buttons**
Page transitions	**Format>>>Page Transition . . .**

(The rows from "Themes" through "Page transitions" are grouped under the vertical label "Additional Features".)

*NOTE: The first item listed is the Main Menu or toolbar. As explained earlier in chapter 1, the >>> indicates the selection to be made once a drop-down menu has been revealed. For example, **View>>>Task Panes** means to click on the View option of the Main Menu bar. This exposes a drop-down menu, and from that menu click the "Task Pane" option. This activates the relevant Task Pane window.

Appendix A
CRIB NOTE PROCEDURES

Crib Note Index:

Crib Note 1: Mouse Clicking

Purpose	There are multiple uses for the "mouse clicking" procedure, as well as several ways in which the mouse click can be completed. In all cases, the click is combined with a placement of the cursor or mouse pointer, and indicates an action that is desired or to gain access to menus of information and procedures.
Procedure	1. Place the mouse pointer or cursor in the desired position (e.g., directly over a main menu selection). 2. Quickly depress and release the mouse button.
Types	There are a variety of clicks that can be used by software developers that produce various results. The most common types of clicks include • Single left click • Double (and triple) left clicks • Single right click
What to watch out for	Whenever you are attempting a double or triple click, you need to make sure that you don't move the mouse between the clicks. This may be interpreted by the computer as two separate single clicks and the end result is not what you desired. Those who are "mouse challenged" often find that with a little practice double and triple clicking soon becomes a natural talent.

Crib Note 2: Selecting a File

Purpose	Identify for the computer which file or folder you want to work with or edit in some way.
Procedure	1. Place the mouse pointer directly over the target file or folder. 2. Single left click and the file should turn a shaded color. This indicates that the file has been *selected*. soccer.doc Nonselected file Selected file
Multiple selections	• If you desire to select a number of different files or folders, you can click on the first item, hold down the **Control** key on the keyboard, and then click the second file. Now both files should be selected simultaneously. • Another version is to select multiple files at one time. To do this, select the first item, hold down the **Shift** key on the keyboard, and then click on another file. All files between the first and second selected files are now selected at the same time.

Crib Note 2a: Selecting More Stuff: Words, Sentences, Paragraphs, and Full Documents

Purpose	Identify for the computer which words, sentences, paragraphs, or full documents need to be edited or worked on in some way.
Procedure	To select a single **word:** 1. Place the mouse pointer directly over the target word. 2. Double left click and the word should become shaded. This indicates that the word has been *selected*. the word should become shaded To select a sentence in a **paragraph:** 1. Place the mouse pointer directly over the target sentence. 2. Hold down the **Control** key and then single left click. The full target sentence should be *selected*. To select a full document: 1. Single-click anywhere within the document. 2. From the Main Menu select **Edit >>> Select All.** The full document should be *selected*.
Multiple selections	• If you desire to select a number of different words, paragraphs, and so forth at a single time, put the cursor in front of the first word to be selected (single left click). Move the mouse pointer to behind the last word to be selected, hold down the **Shift** key, and single left click. All words between

	the original cursor position and the position of the mouse pointer should now be selected. This procedure works for multiple words, sentences, paragraphs, and so on.

Crib Note 3: Dragging a File

Purpose	Move a file from one location on the screen (or from one folder) to another.
Procedure	1. Select the file that is to be moved. 2. Single left click and hold down the mouse button. 3. With the mouse button continually held down, drag the file (move the mouse) to the new location on the screen. 4. Once it's in the correct position, release the button.
Placing a file in a new folder or the recycle bin	Often you may want the file to be inserted within a folder or the Recycle Bin. To do this, just drag the file over the top of the target folder or Recycle Bin. When you see the target folder or Recycle Bin become selected (it changes color or shade), release the button. The file disappears (that means it's now inside of the target folder or recycle bin). To check if it's there, double left click the folder and it opens so that you can check its content. Your deposited file should now be listed as one of the contents.

Crib Note 4: Copying, Cutting, and Pasting

Purpose	When working with items such as files, folders, and specific text, it's often nice to be able to either cut an item from its current location, cut it and later paste it in a new location, or even copy it (leaving the original in the current position) and pasting the copy in another location.
Procedure: Copy and Paste	1. Select the item you wish to copy. 2. **Edit>>>Copy.** 3. Move the mouse pointer (cursor) to the location in which you want the copy to appear and paste the copy into that position (**Edit >>> Paste**).
Procedure: Cut and Paste	1. Select the item you wish to cut. 2. **Edit>>>Cut** and the item now is gone. 3. If you wish to paste the cut item in a new location, place the cursor or mouse pointer where you want the item to be pasted and select **Edit >>> Paste.**
Alternate Procedures	There are a number of different ways to copy, cut, and paste. For example, after selecting the item, right click and immediately a menu appears and you can select from the given copy, cut, and paste options. There are also *hot keys* that you can learn that allow you to accomplish these procedures without lifting your fingers from the keyboard. Those hot keys are listed below (hold both down together): **Cut . . . Control key + x** **Copy . . . Control key + c** **Paste . . . Control key + v**

Crib Note 5: Launching an Application Program

Purpose	Start a software program that allows you to work with the computer in a specific way (e.g., launch MS Word so that you can use the computer as a word processor).
Procedure	1. Locate the program icon on your computer's hard drive. 2. Double left click on the program icon. If the program is correctly installed, it should load and begin working.
Alternative procedure	Another way of launching a program is to locate the program and then right click with the mouse pointer directly on top of the icon. A menu appears and you select the Open option.

Crib Note 6: Getting and Using Help

Purpose	Today's software is getting very comprehensive and complex. For most of us it's impossible to remember every feature and function available. To help us understand and access all these features, most software publishers now include some type of built-in **Help** within their programs. **Help** offers assistance to the software user by answering questions and giving needed directions.
Procedure	1. Access **Help** by clicking on Main Menu **Help >>> Microsoft Help.** **Note:** Many individuals are accustomed to accessing and using the Microsoft Office Assistant **(Help >>> Show Office Assistant)**; however, the search results are often not quite as complete as using the full **Microsoft Help** version. Both are easy to use—but we prefer the full **Help** versus the Office Assistant version. **Another note:** For quick assistance, look in the upper right side of the Main Menu bar. Office XP programs have a place to "Type a question for help." Insert your question or key word, and Help immediately comes up with a list of potential solutions. 2. Review Figure A1 and note the **Help** tabs for Content, Answer Wizard, and Index. In most cases, you will want to select the Answer Wizard. There may be times, however, that a review of the contents accessed via the Content tab will be very beneficial. Don't forget to look it over occasionally. 3. With the Answer Wizard tab selected, enter a question into the box that asks, "What would you like to do?" 4. Review the topics displayed below your original question. 5. Click on a topic that may contain your desired answer. The suggested answer or procedure is displayed in the right-hand column of the **Help** window. 6. Follow that procedure or select a new topic to review and consider.

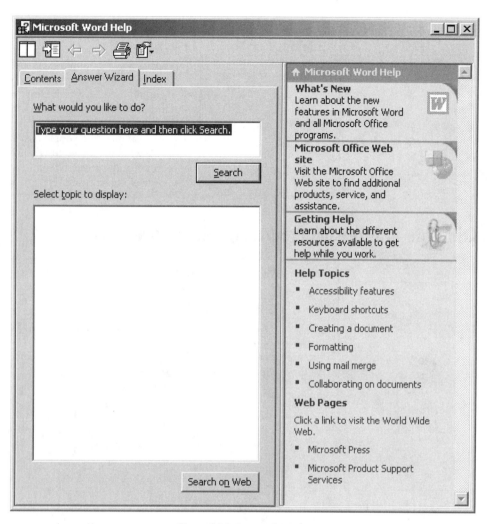

Figure A1 Microsoft Help

	Note: Finding the correct procedure is often not a perfect science. That is, you may not know the needed key word, or the needed procedure may not be exactly as you had envisioned it. In either case, be open to the different alternatives and review several of them so that you can select the most appropriate. At times it may also help to go to the Index tab and try different key words to see what can be found and to help you recognize the needed key word to search and find the appropriate information.
Some thoughts about using **Help**	• Using **Help** isn't cheating. There's too much in these programs to retain in your memory. It's nice to know that something exists that you can access to find out important information. • Use **Help** even when you don't need it. It could be that there are other ways of solving a problem—you may know one way, but **Help** may offer another way that proves more efficient or effective for you now or in the future.

continued

- It may not get you what you need—but generally **Help** gets you close. There are times when **Help** just won't help. However, in most cases, it's because you don't know the proper key word or phrase. At such times, you may need to try different alternatives to figure out what works best for you.
- Spend time investigating **Help.** Even in times when you may not need specific help, you may want to look through the contents and see what information is given. In many cases, you may find yourself saying, "I didn't know that" or "I've always wondered how you did that." Look over the contents and see the different topics discussed within this feature of the software.

Crib Note 7: Accessing Programs, Folders, and Files

Purpose	Frequently you will need to access specific programs, folders, and/or files located somewhere on your computer's hard drive, and or on the floppy disk drive, CD ROM, or other peripheral storage device. This procedure helps you navigate to the proper location to access the needed files.
Procedure: Using Windows Explorer	1. Left click on the Start Menu and launch the Windows Explorer option. 2. On the address bar, click the down arrow to make the selection of where you want to look for the folder or file (that is, if you want to access the computer's hard drive, a zip drive, a CD ROM drive, and so on.). See Figure A2. 3. Click on the drive you want to examine (see Figure A3).

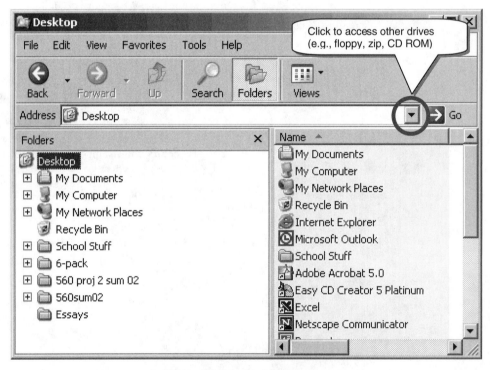

Figure A2 Windows Explorer

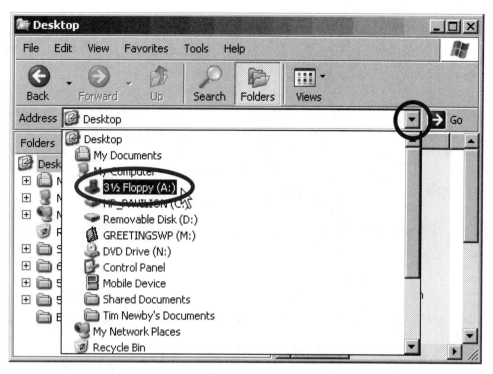

Figure A3 Windows Explorer with the Floppy drive selected for access

	4. In the left column, examine folders, files, and programs (see Figure A2) listed on that drive. Click on the target folder if you wish to see the contents of any given folder (this is revealed in the right-hand column of the Explorer window). 5. Identify the file you wish to open and double-click it.
Procedure: Accessing and opening files from within a specific application program	Once you have launched a specific application (e.g., MS Word), you often may want to open a file stored on the hard drive or other storage device (e.g., floppy, zip, CD ROM). To do this, most applications use the following procedure: On the Main Menu bar, select **File>>>Open...**. A window appears that allows you to either select a file from those that are shown or you can navigate to the proper location to access the needed file (see Figure A4). In some application programs there will be a need to locate a file or separate program. Generally, these programs allow you to browse (navigate) your folders and files to find the correct item you are looking for. The **Browse** windows work in the same way as the **Open...** window as depicted in Figure A4.

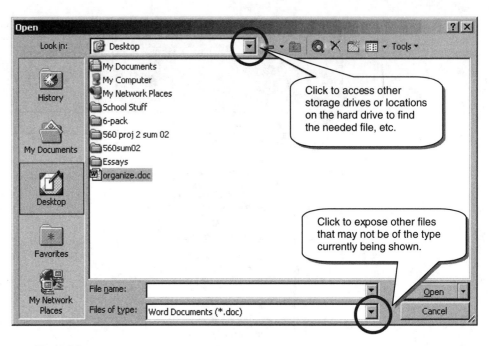

Figure A4 Typical window used to navigate to and open documents within an application program

Crib Note 8: Charting Excel Data

Purpose	Utilize the Chart Wizard to create a chart using data from an Excel spreadsheet. *Note*: The Wizard walks you through four basic steps. Each step is important to successfully complete the chart.
Procedure: **Preparing for the chart**	1. Enter your data within the Excel spreadsheet worksheet. 2. Select the data that you want included within the chart (see Figure A5).
	Note: To select separate columns of data (e.g., columns A, E, F, and G in Figure A5), hold down the *Control* key as you select each desired column of data. **Note:** Make sure you include the column headings on your selected data worksheet; otherwise you will need to add them during Step 2 of the Chart Wizard.
Procedure: Chart Wizard Step 1—Selecting your chart type	3. Click the Chart Wizard button ▥ or use the Main Menu option (**Insert >>> Chart . . .**). 4. From the Step 1 window (see Figure A6), select a chart type. Once selected, several chart subtypes appear and you can select a specific subtype if you desire. 5. View a sample of what your data looks like when charted based on your selection. 6. Try several different chart types. **Note:** If you need to customize your chart type, select the **Custom Types** tab. However, in most cases, the **Standard Types** will be sufficient.

	A	B	C	D	E	F	G
1				Science - 3rd Period			
2							
3	Last Name	First Name	Assign 1	Assign 2	Quiz 1	Quiz 2	Final
4	Barrymore	Cade	15	12	24	29	85
5	DeFore	Alexis	15	15	29	30	97
6	Drury	Landon	9	8	22	20	65
7	Jeski	Robert	10	11	22	25	78
8	Moreno	Elizabeth	11	12	20	28	82
9	Packard	Dale	12	14	27	25	90
10	Polk	Madison	13	14	26	27	88
11	Saterwaite	Kimberly	13	10	26	26	80
12	Smith	Fiona	15	14	27	28	92
13	Washington	Violet	6	12	18	26	73

Figure A5 Sample spreadsheet with data selected to be included in a data chart

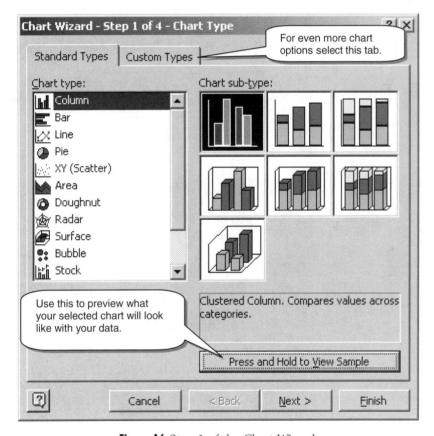

Figure A6 Step 1 of the Chart Wizard.

Procedure:
Chart Wizard
Step 2—Labeling key elements and defining the data ranges

7. When satisfied, click the **Next>** button.
8. The Wizard's Step 2 window now appears displaying a miniature version of your charted data (see Figure A7). Both X- and Y-axes of the chart are now labeled and a legend has been inserted.
9. If you desire to modify the data ranges and/or the series labels, select the Series tab (see Figure A8).

continued

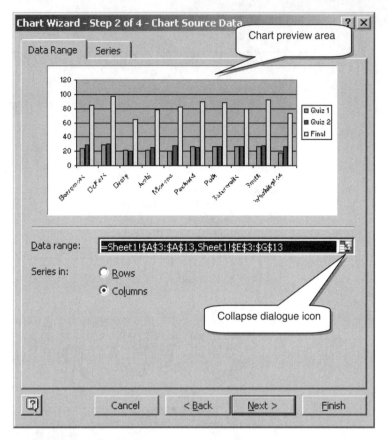

Figure A7 Step 2 of the Chart Wizard

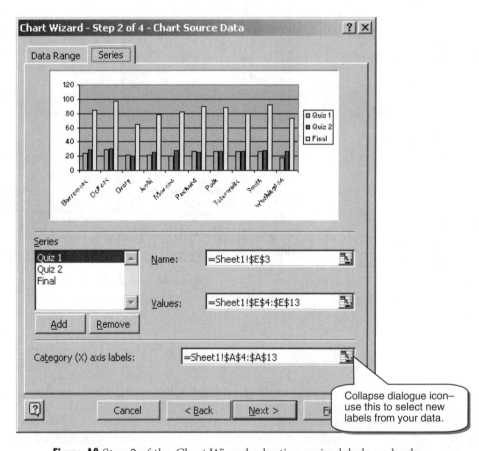

Figure A8 Step 2 of the Chart Wizard adapting series labels and values

Note: In many cases, this area of the Chart Wizard is needed to make sure you have everything labeled correctly. For example, if you want to change the X-axis labels from the last name of each of the students to the first name—this is the place to do that. To accomplish it:

a. Click on the Series tab of Step 2 of the Chart Wizard (see Figure A7).

b. On the section titled "Category (X) axis labels," click on the Collapse Dialogue icon.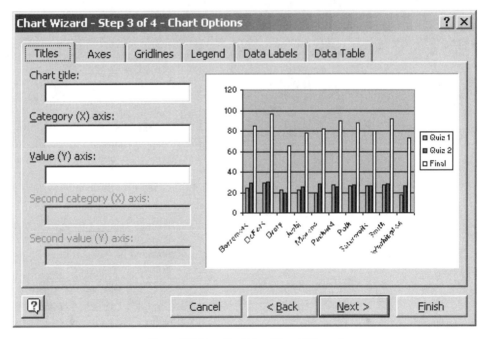

c. The Step 2 window is collapsed; now highlight all students' first names (B4–B13) and then click on the Collapse Dialogue icon again.

In the Step 2 preview area, you should now see that the students' last names have been replaced by their first names.

Using this same procedure, try adding a different series (a new column of data) to your chart. Click on the **Add** button and then use the associated Collapse Dialogue icons to select the name for your new series and the values.

Note: At times, this step can be somewhat confusing. Our suggestion is for you to set up a small spreadsheet (three or so columns of data) and practice changing the labels for the series and the axis, or even adding a different series to the chart. Using the Collapse Dialogue icon soon becomes second nature and it will improve the output that you get from this portion of the Wizard.

Procedure:
Chart Wizard
Step 3—Labels, Lines, and Legends

10. When you are satisfied with the appearance of your chart, click the **Next>** button.

11. As shown in Figure A9, you can add titles, gridlines, data labels, and so on. Additionally, you can position the legend. Select each of the tabs within this step of the Wizard and fill in the relevant information.

Figure A9 Step 3 of the Chart Wizard

continued

> **Note:** Here again we suggest that you go through each of the tabs and try various options. Always note the changes and see which are most appropriate. You can always turn off any changes that don't prove beneficial.

Procedure:
Chart Wizard
Step 4—Placing
the chart

12. Check the results in the preview area. When satisfied, click **Next>**.
13. Determine if you want your newly created chart to be a part of the current worksheet (included with all of your data) or if you want it to be on its own separate worksheet.
14. Make the selection (see Figure A10) and click **Finish.**
15. Evaluate what you have created. Are changes needed? If you need to adapt the chart, see the next procedure (Adapting the Results of the Chart Wizard); otherwise, smile at your creation and think of other ways that your new charting capabilities may be useful!

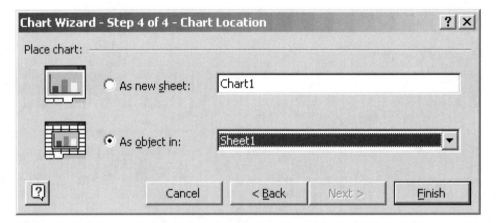

Figure A10 Step 4 of the Chart Wizard

Procedure:
Adapting the
results of the
Chart Wizard

Once you have created your chart, you may notice that various adaptations may be needed. It's relatively simple to make such changes (really!). Here's a simple way to make the needed changes:

1. Determine what change you would like to make.
2. Double left click on that portion of the chart where the modification needs to occur. For example, if you want to make a change to the X-axis (something about the labels bugs you), double-click on that portion of the chart.
3. A relevant Format window appears. There are several varieties of these windows. Each appears based on where you click on the chart. These Format windows include

   Format Axis
   Format Chart title
   Format Gridlines
   Format Plot Area
   Format Legend

An example of a Format window is given in Figure A11. Notice that there are several tabs that can be selected for further alternatives from which to select your adaptations.

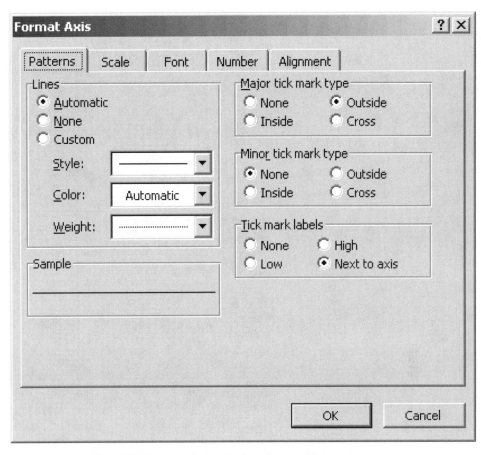

Figure A11 Format Axis window for modifying chart axes

Crib Note 9: Obtaining and Saving Images from the Web

Purpose of the procedure	Within many software programs you have the option of inserting pictures. In some cases, the best options for such graphics, images, and pictures are located on the Web. (*Note:* You must consider copyright issues and make sure you get the proper copyright permissions before using and publishing the work of others.) The purpose of this procedure is to show you how to copy pictures from the Web and store them so they can be incorporated into your materials.
Procedure	1. Access the Internet and locate a picture or graphic that you would like to save. 2. Point your mouse pointer directly over the target picture and single right click your mouse button. 3. From the menu that appears (see Figure A12) select the option **Save Picture As . . . .** 4. A window appears that allows you to navigate to your desired folder (see Figure A13). Additionally, you save the picture under a name you create and you can see in this window the type of file that you are saving (e.g., .gif, .jpg, .png). 5. Click **Save** and the picture is now saved in your selected location.

Figure A12 Save Picture As . . . menu

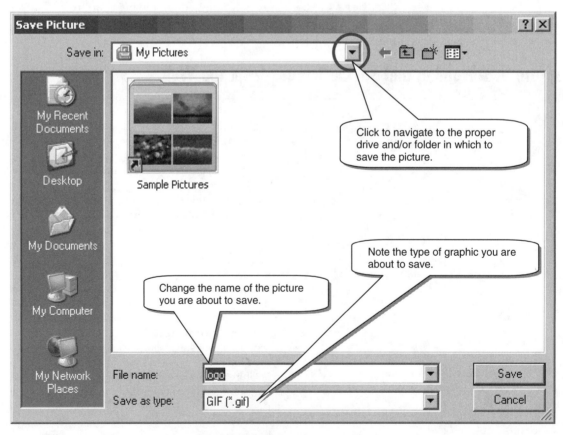

Figure A13 Save Picture window

Crib Note 10: Simple Web Search Procedures

Purpose	Efficiently search and identify relevant information on the World Wide Web.

Procedure	1. Know where you are going. That is, identify the important target concepts of your search.
	2. From the concepts, select key words that effectively describe the target concepts. Don't forget about synonyms, related terms, or variations of the key words that may also be effectively used as key words. Your selected key words should be as specific and concise as possible.
	3. Select an initial search engine or directory to do the work (see relevant information on search engines at www.searchenginewatch.com). There are literally hundreds to choose from—some, however, are better than others. Highly rated search engines include the following:
	  • Google (www.google.com)
	  • AltaVista (www.altavista.com)
	  • Fast (www.alltheweb.com)
	Note: Just because one search engine doesn't produce the desired results, you may want to try a different one. They use different ways to locate Web pages and a different engine may produce different results.
	4. After accessing the search engine, read the information it provides on how to conduct a search (look for "Help," "Advanced Search," or "Frequently Asked Questions" to get specific information. Most search engines have a certain way to enter key words and phrases, and they generally explain that in brief but important instructions located on their Web site.
	5. Incorporate search techniques to help include or exclude pages. For example:
	  • Use of Boolean operators (words like *and, or, not*). Some search engines use "+" and "−" signs to achieve the same effect. The features chart at www.searchengineshowdown.com/features identifies the terms supported by the different engines.
	  • Use quotation marks (" ") around groups of words so that they are treated as a single term and not as individual search terms. That is, "Robin Hood" will access Web sites dealing with the leader of the band of merry men while not accessing references to a type of bird or a piece of clothing that keeps rain from falling on one's head.
	6. Create a search expression and give it an initial try.
	7. Evaluate your results. Review the different types of Web sites that were located and see if your target information was obtained. Select and scan several of the identified sites. Ask yourself, "Are the results relevant?" "Did I obtain enough information?" "Is the amount of information too overwhelming to get through?"
	8. If additional changes are needed, begin by reviewing the search expression to see if it can be revised in some fashion. Think about additional search techniques to include (e.g., use of quotation marks). Attempt another search and note the differences produced by the adapted search expression.
	9. Continue to evaluate your results and adapt the search expression.
	10. If after several attempted searches less than adequate results are obtained, try a different search engine.

Appendix B

NATIONAL EDUCATIONAL TECHNOLOGY STANDARDS

National Educational Technology Standards for All Teachers (NETS-T)*

I. Technology Operations and Concepts	Teachers demonstrate a sound understanding of technology operations and concepts. Teachers:
	A. demonstrate introductory knowledge, skills, and understanding of concepts related to technology (as described in the ISTE National Education Technology Standards for Students).
	B. demonstrate continual growth in technology knowledge and skills to stay abreast of current and emerging technologies.

II. Planning and Designing Learning Environment and Experiences	Teachers plan and design effective learning environments and experiences supported by technology. Teachers:
	A. design developmentally appropriate learning opportunities that apply technology-enhanced instructional strategies to support the diverse needs of learners.
	B. apply current research on teaching and learning with technology when planning learning environments and experiences.
	C. identify and locate technology resources and evaluate them for accuracy and suitability.
	D. plan for the management of technology resources within the context of learning activities.
	E. plan strategies to manage student learning in a technology-enhanced environment.

III. Teaching, Learning, and the Curriculum	Teachers implement curriculum plans, that include methods and strategies for applying technology to maximize student learning. Teachers:
	A. facilitate technology-enhanced experiences that address content standards and student technology standards.
	B. use technology to support learner-centered strategies that address the diverse needs of students.
	C. apply technology to develop students' higher order skills and creativity.
	D. manage student learning activities in a technology-enhanced environment.

---

*From National Educational Technology Standards for Teachers, 2002. ISTE: Eugene, OR. Copyright, 2000, ISTE 800-336-5191, iste @ iste.org, www.iste.org. All Rights Reserved. Reprinted with permission. Reprint permission does not constitute endorsement by ISTE.

IV. Assessment and Evaluation	Teachers apply technology to facilitate a variety of effective assessment and evaluation strategies. Teachers:

IV. **Assessment and Evaluation**

Teachers apply technology to facilitate a variety of effective assessment and evaluation strategies. Teachers:

A. apply technology in assessing student learning of subject matter using a variety of assessment techniques.
B. use technology resources to collect and analyze data, interpret results, and communicate findings to improve instructional practice and maximize student learning.
C. apply multiple methods of evaluation to determine students' appropriate use of technology resources for learning, communication, and productivity.

V. **Productivity and Professional Practice**

Teachers use technology to enhance their productivity and professional practice. Teachers:

A. use technology resources to engage in ongoing professional development and life-long learning.
B. continually evaluate and reflect on professional practice to make informed decisions regarding the use of technology in support of student learning.
C. apply technology to increase productivity.
D. use technology to communicate and collaborate with peers, parents, and the larger community in order to nurture student learning.

VI. **Social, Ethical, Legal, and Human Issues**

Teachers understand the social, ethical, legal, and human issues surrounding the use of technology in PK-12 schools and apply those principles in practice. Teachers:

A. model and teach legal and ethical practice related to technology use.
B. apply technology resources to enable and empower learners with diverse backgrounds, characteristics, and abilities.
C. identify and use technology resources that affirm diversity.
D. promote safe and healthy use of technology resources.
E. facilitate equitable access to technology resources for all students.

National Educational Technology Standards for Students (NETS-S)*

1. **Basic Operations and Concepts**

- Students demonstrate a sound understanding of the nature and operation of technology systems.
- Students are proficient in the use of technology.

2. **Social, Ethical, and Human Issues**

- Students understand the ethical, cultural, and societal issues related to technology.
- Students practice responsible use of technology systems, information, and software.
- Students develop positive attitudes toward technology uses that support lifelong learning, collaboration, personal pursuits, and productivity.

3. **Technology Productivity Tools**

- Students use technology tools to enhance learning, increase productivity, and promote creativity.
- Students use productivity tools to collaborate in constructing technology-enhanced models, prepare publications, and produce other creative works.

*From National Educational Technology Standards for Students, 2000. ISTE: Eugene, OR. Copyright, 2000, ISTE 800-336-5191, iste@iste.org, www.iste.org. All Rights Reserved. Reprinted with permission. Reprint permission does not constitute endorsement by ISTE.

4. Technology Communications Tools	• Students use telecommunications to collaborate, publish, and interact with peers, experts, and other audiences. • Students use a variety of media and formats to communicate information and ideas effectively to multiple audiences.
5. Technology Research Tools	• Students use technology to locate, evaluate, and collect information from a variety of sources. • Students use technology tools to process data and report results. • Students evaluate and select new information resources and technological innovations based on the appropriateness for specific tasks.
6. Technology Problem-Solving and Decision-Making Tools	• Students use technology resources for solving problems and making informed decisions. • Students employ technology in the development of strategies for solving problems in the real world.

GLOSSARY

action button   In MS PowerPoint, a ready-made button that can be created, inserted, and hyperlinked within a presentation. By clicking the button, the hyperlinked activity is carried out. See also *button.*

active window   Describes the window currently selected or being used.

alignment   How text is positioned on a screen, page, or specific portion of a page or screen. Left alignment lines all text flush on the left margin. Right alignment creates flush text on the right margin. Center alignment creates text centered in the middle of the page and full alignment creates flush margins on both right and left margins.

animation   A special visual or sound effect added to an object or text. For example, in PowerPoint having bulleted lists of items enter and leave a presentation at specific times or based on specific actions.

applications software   Programs used by the computer to assist in specific tasks (e.g., word processing, desktop publishing, presentation development). See also *computer applications.*

audio clips   Sound and music files that can be hyperlinked, accessed, and played within Web pages and other electronic files.

background   Pictures or text that are placed on a screen, slide, or within a text document to appear behind other elements. Backgrounds are generally used to add color and interest to the screen, slide, and so forth.

bookmark   Identifies a specific reference location in a Web document that can be referred or linked to. For example, the top of a long Web document can be bookmarked and later accessed when a link to the top of the document bookmark is clicked or activated.

border   Lines around cells, tables, or pages that add emphasis, interest, and/or organizational clarity.

browser   Computer applications, such as Netscape Navigator or Internet Explorer, used for accessing the World Wide Web.

bulleted list   Dots or other symbols placed immediately before each item within a list. This design feature adds emphasis and facilitates organization of materials. See also *numbered list.*

button   A specific location on a computer screen that triggers an action when clicked.

cell   A single block in a spreadsheet grid, formed by the intersection of a row and a column.

cell reference   Identifies a cell or a range of cells in a spreadsheet program (e.g., cell reference "D5" identifies the cell where column D and row 5 intersect).

chart   A graphic representation of a data set of numbers. Charts can add visual appeal and facilitate comparisons, patterns, and trends in data. Charts are also referred to as graphs.

click   To press a button on a computer mouse.

click and hold   To depress the computer mouse button and keep it depressed until a specific action has occurred or been completed.

click, hold, and drag   Used to move an item (e.g., icon) on the computer desktop. Completed by pointing the mouse pointer at the item to be moved, depressing the mouse button, holding the mouse button down, and then moving the mouse to the new location and releasing the button.

clip art   Previously prepared graphics that can be accessed, selected, and inserted within files such as word processed documents, presentation programs, or Web pages.

clipboard   Temporary storage in the computer's memory.

columns   A vertical arrangement of cells in a table or spreadsheet. In most common spreadsheets the columns are initially designated by letters (e.g., column D, column F).

computer applications   Computer programs designed to perform tasks such as word processing, desktop publishing, mathematical/statistical calculations, and so on. See also *applications software.*

custom animation   A sound or visual effect that has been added to an object or text within a PowerPoint presentation. See also *animation.*

database   An organized collection of information, often stored on a computer.

design templates   A prepared layout designed to ease the process of creating a product in certain computer applications, such as, a slide design and color scheme for presentation software or a standard Web page layout.

desktop   A description of the screen that appears after the computer has been turned on. The computer screen is commonly compared to the top of a desk that contains folders, files, and various tools for working.

DOS   Disk Operating System. The computer system that controls how the computer operates and runs applications software. Microsoft's DOS was the common operating system used in most non-Macintosh computers.

drag   To move a selected item/icon/text on a computer screen, point the mouse pointer at the target item, click and hold the mouse button, and move the mouse. The selected item follows the mouse movement until the mouse button is released.

field   Each individual category of information recorded in a database (e.g., a student's first name).

file   Any data saved onto a hard disk or other storage device (e.g., a word document file, a spreadsheet file). Also within a database, this refers to a group of related database records.

fill   A spreadsheet feature that allows one to automatically continue a series of numbers, number/text combinations, dates, or time periods based on an established pattern. Commonly used in a spreadsheet program to automatically allow a specific equation/ function to be applied to additional rows or columns of data.

fill handle   A small box in the lower right corner of an active spreadsheet cell. It can be used to complete a fill. See also *fill.*

filter   A means to select a subset of records/data in a table or worksheet based upon certain selected criteria.

folder   An icon that represents where applications, documents, and other folders are located. It is considered an organizational device that serves a similar purpose to a file folder found inside an office filing cabinet.

font   The appearance (typeface and size) of text on the computer screen and/or in printed form. Typefaces include Times New Roman, Arial, Courier, and so on.

footers   Information that appears in an area at the bottom of a document page (e.g., page number, title of document, date, logo). Footers can be set to appear at the bottom of all or selected pages of multiple page documents. See also *headers.*

format   To design how a document will look (e.g., type of font, selection of borders, use of color). Also used to describe the preparation/initialization of a disk to receive computer files.

formula   A mathematical expression (equation) that directs an electronic spreadsheet to perform various kinds of calculations on the numbers entered in it. See also *function.*

function   Predefined formulas used in spreadsheets or databases that perform calculations. See also *formula.*

grammar check   Ancillary feature of word processors that identifies a range of grammatical and format errors such as improper capitalization, lack of subject–verb agreement, split infinitives, and so forth. Suggestions on corrections to the errors may also be provided by the check.

graphic   Any pictorial representation of information such as charts, graphs, animated figures, or photographic reproductions. Frequently referred to (especially within Web page development) as *images.*

handles   Small squares that appear around a selected object that can be dragged to alter the size and shape of the object.

handout   A version of a PowerPoint presentation that can be printed. The handout page can be constructed to include various numbers of slides per page and space for notes to be written.

headers   Information that appears in an area at the top of a document page (e.g., page number, title of document, date, logo). Headers can be set to appear at the top of all or selected pages of multiple page documents. See also *footers.*

Help   Built-in resource within most applications programs that supplies practical advice, tutorials, and/or demonstrations on the use of the software and its various features.

hold   Depressing a mouse button and not releasing it until some task is completed (e.g., depressing until a specific menu appears on the screen or until the dragging of an icon has been completed). See also *click and hold; click, hold, and drag.*

HTML   See *Hypertext Markup Language.*

hyperlinks   Connections between items/elements (e.g., text, objects) within a hyperenvironment. For example, an action such as the playing of a sound clip is executed when a connected (i.e., hyperlinked) icon is clicked. Hyperlink is frequently referred to simply as *link.*

Hypertext Markup Language (HTML)   The authoring "language" used to define Web pages.

icon   A small pictorial or graphical representation of a computer hardware function or component.

images   See *graphics.*

integration   Within a classroom setting, the use of the computer in ways that facilitate the learning of subject matter/content (e.g., accessing additional information, incorporation of graphics, calculation and charting of data).

Internet   A network of computer networks that links computers worldwide.

keyboard   The most common computer peripheral device used for inputting information. Keyboards can vary in size, shape, type, and arrangement of keys to input data.

links   See *hyperlinks.*

mail merge   Inserting data from applications programs such as databases or spreadsheets into a form letter or document.

margins   Blank space outside the boundaries of the text and/or images on a document page. Margins can also pertain to specific blank areas within table or spreadsheet cells.

master slide   A template that stores information concerning font styles, placeholder sizes and positions, background design, and color schemes for a presentation program such as PowerPoint.

menu   On-screen list of available options (e.g., File menu consists of options to open a new document, save the current document, close the current document.)

Microsoft FrontPage   Software created by Microsoft Corporation for the purpose of developing and editing Web pages.

Microsoft Office   A set of applications softwares developed by Microsoft Corporation that typically includes programs such as MS Word (word processing), MS PowerPoint (presentation software), MS Access (database management), MS Excel (spreadsheet), and MS Outlook (planning and calendaring).

mouse   A pointing device used to select and move information on the computer display screen. As the mouse is physically moved, a pointer on the computer screen moves in a similar fashion. The mouse typically has one to three buttons that may be used for selecting or entering information.

Microsoft Excel   Spreadsheet software created by Microsoft Corporation to organize, analyze, calculate, and present data such as budgets and grades.

Microsoft PowerPoint   Presentation software created by Microsoft Corporation to plan, organize, design, and deliver professional presentations.

Microsoft Word   Word processing software created by Microsoft Corporation to plan, organize, and produce professionally looking text documents (e.g., letters, papers, reports).

normal view   In MS PowerPoint, normal view is the main editing view used to write and design presentations.

notes page   In MS PowerPoint, each notes page shows a small version of the slide and the notes that go with the slide. This can be used as an easy way to create speaker's notes to accompany the presentation.

numbered list   Sequential numbers or letters placed immediately before each item within a list. This design feature adds emphasis and facilitates organization of materials. See *bulleted list.*

page border   Various types of line styles, graphics, and colors that can be added to the edge of a document page to increase interest and emphasis.

page setup   Option on the File menu that allows for the selection of page margins, orientation, layout, and paper size.

point   Manipulation of a mouse (or trackball, touchpad, and so on) to select a specific word, graphic, or location on a computer screen.

presentation software   Computer software designed for the production and display of computer text and images, intended to replace the functions typically associated with the slide and overhead projectors.

record   A collection of related fields within a database of information. See also *fields* and *database.*

recycle bin   The location where deleted files are stored. Deleted files can be recovered from this storage location or can be permanently deleted by emptying the recycle bin.

row   A horizontal arrangement of cells in a table or spreadsheet. In most common spreadsheets the rows are initially designated by numbers (e.g., row 2, row 232).

ruler   A bar displayed across the top of the document window that is marked in units of measurement (e.g., inches). Margins, tabs, column widths, for example, can be set through the use of the ruler.

search   A common feature within application programs to find words, numbers, and/or characters within a file. Additionally, operating systems can use searches to locate specific files, folders, programs, and so on.

section break   A mark used to show the end of a section.

sections   The layout of a document can be altered by dividing it into sections. Each section can be formatted in a different manner (e.g., one section with two column format and another section with single column format) and divided by the section break.

select   To indicate that a text or object will be used or worked with by the program. To select, point the mouse pointer click, hold and drag across the text or object. Once "selected," the text or object will be highlighted in some fashion (e.g., color change). To remove the selection, a mouse click on anything other than the selected item will remove the selected status.

shading   A darkening or coloring of the background behind text or graphics. It is used to add emphasis and interest to a table, paragraph, cell, page, and so forth.

slide   The fundamental unit within a presentation (e.g., PowerPoint). It can contain graphics, text, sounds, movies, and action buttons.

slide layout   The manner in which elements (headings, text, lists, graphics) on a slide are arranged. In MS PowerPoint, for example, templates can be selected from the slide layout menu and used to automatically arrange slide elements.

slide show view   In MS PowerPoint, slide show view shows how the presentation will look when given to an audience. The full screen is used and all animations, graphics, links are activated.

slide sorter view   In MS PowerPoint, this view is of the full set of presentation slides in thumbnail form. Slide sorter view allows for easy reorganization, addition, and deletion of slides, as well as the review of transition and animation effects, and so on.

sort   Arranging data in a spreadsheet or database in ascending or descending order.

spell check   A feature in applications programs that searches through a file and reports any instances of text that do not match a built-in dictionary. In most cases, it offers suggestions on possible alternative spellings.

spreadsheet   A general purpose computer calculating tool. It is generally arranged in rows and columns.

Start menu   Options displayed when the Start button on the taskbar is clicked. Options generally include access to programs, help, search, and shut down procedures.

style   Text style refers to the appearance of a character without changing size or typeface (e.g., using bold or italics).

system software   The basic operating software that tells the computer how to perform its fundamental functions.

table   Data set up in a row–column format. Cells within the table can contain text and graphics. Tables are often used to organize and present information.

taskbar   A bar usually displayed at the bottom of the screen that contains the Start button, open document icons, and buttons to activate programs.

task panes   Small windows within an application program that provide easy access to commonly used commands.

text wrapping   The automatic arrangement of text from the end of one line to the beginning of the next line. Text may be wrapped within cells of a table or spreadsheet, within paragraphs on pages, and in reference to inserted graphics and objects. See also *word wrap.*

toolbar   Bars generally displayed at the top or bottom of a screen of application software that contain shortcuts to useful features and tools (e.g., shortcut to save a file, shortcut to open a document or create a new document). Use of the toolbars eliminates the need to go to the menu options.

touchpad   Input device generally found on a laptop computer that serves a similar function as a mouse. The pad allows for a finger or stylus to be used to control the position of the pointer/cursor on the screen.

trackball   Input device that serves a similar function as the mouse input device. The device is similar to an inverted mouse where the user rotates the ball with a thumb or forefinger to guide the pointer or cursor on the screen.

URL   Uniform Resource Locator. The unique address for every Internet or World Wide Web page, containing the protocol type, the domain, the directory, and the name of the site or page.

video clips   Digital video files that can be hyperlinked, accessed, and viewed within Web pages and other electronic files.

view menu   A menu option on the Main Menu of most applications programs that allows one to select various ways to view a document or file of data as well as other options such as which toolbars, rulers, task panes to reveal/hide.

watermark   Text or pictures that appear behind text in a document. For example, a picture of a mountain that is printed behind text about a trip to the mountains. Often a watermark is washed out, or lightened, so that it doesn't hinder how the main text is viewed. Watermarks are generally intended to add interest or information to printed documents.

Web-based documents   Documents that are accessed via the Internet and World Wide Web.

Web browser   See *browser.*

Web editor   Software that allows for the creation and editing of materials that can be distributed on the World Wide Web.

Web page development   The design and creation of a hypertext document appropriate for publishing on the World Wide Web. Generally this is accomplished using Web editing software or HTML.

Web site   A set of interrelated Web pages usually operated by a single entity (e.g., company, school, organization, or individual).

WebQuest   An inquiry-oriented activity in which most of the information used by learners is drawn from the World Wide Web.

"What if..."   When using a spreadsheet program, statements beginning with this phrase are used to signify how the spreadsheet may be used to make predictions and/or estimations.

Windows   A specific type of computer operating system produced and marketed by Microsoft Corporation.

window   A portion of the computer screen that displays information or a program. Multiple windows can be revealed at the same time (e.g., a window revealing an office memo in a word processing document, another revealing a spreadsheet chart, and another accessing information on the Internet. Size, number, and location of windows revealed on the computer screen can be altered by the user.

word processing   The act of creating a document through the use of word processor software.

word processor   A computer program for writing that supports the entry, editing, revising, formatting, storage, retrieval, and printing of text.

word wrap   A feature of a word processor that automatically shifts the next whole word to the next line of the document when a line of text in a computer document is filled. See also *text wrapping.*

workspace   The main screen space within an application program (e.g., word processor) where the main amount of work is completed (i.e., text, data, and graphics are inserted and edited).

workbook   A set or collection of worksheets from a spreadsheet program saved under a single file name.

worksheet   An area of rows and columns in a spreadsheet program in which text, numeric values, and formulas are entered.

WWW   World Wide Web (or the Web). An information retrieval system on the Internet that relies on a point-and-click hypertext navigation system.

INDEX